SURVEY
OF
WORLD
CULTURES

SURVEY OF WORLD CULTURES

Editor, THOMAS FITZSIMMONS

CAMBODIA

its people   its society   its culture

David J. Steinberg

IN COLLABORATION WITH

Chester A. Bain
Lloyd Burlingham
Russell G. Duff
Bernard B. Fall
Ralph Greenhouse
Lucy Kramer
Robert S. McLellan

REVISED FOR 1959 BY

Herbert H. Vreeland

HRAF PRESS *New Haven*

Already Published in this Series

1 Poland

2 Jordan

3 Iraq

4 Saudi Arabia

PREFACE

THE FOCUS OF THIS BOOK is a society as it functions. Emphasis is on the dynamics of the culture—the presence and impact of forces for change, the constants of attitude and behavior, the abiding values.

The volumes in this series are based in part on handbooks prepared for the government. Specifically designed to meet an urgent government need, these handbooks were not the product of original research but rather a collation and synthesis of the best and most authoritative contemporary materials, published and unpublished, about the societies selected. As the work progressed, engaging several hundred scholars at some twenty universities, it became evident that the resultant handbooks were for many of the countries the only available studies from current materials of an over-all character. A growing interest in the studies led us to consider their publication.

A real dilemma confronted us at this point. Following the contractor's explicit instructions, the writers had omitted the footnotes and citations customary in work of this nature, but the formidable amount of research that would be required to add this documentation was precluded by a lack of funds and the dispersal of the original scholars. There existed, however, such practical justification for a greater circulation of these studies and so insistent a demand for their publication from area specialists as well as students and nonspecialists that it was decided to proceed despite this limitation on their usefulness. An attempt has been made to cite in the acknowledgments and in the recommended reading list at the end of the volume those works that proved most vital to the writers and editor. It is sincerely hoped our readers will take a lenient attitude toward this aspect of the series.

All the books have been extensively revised: some new materials have been added and the body of the material reworked and adapted to a format uniform for the series. One important result of the process of collecting and selecting information from many, often widely scattered, sources has been to reveal new relationships, making explicit in these surveys much which had remained implicit in previous separate studies. Gaps in existing knowledge were also exposed. The series should, then, raise a number of general questions, at the same time offering certain factual answers and providing a guide for further research. That there will also result increased understanding of the seemingly endless and diverse ways in which men approach the experience of living with one another is the wish of all who have participated in making this series.

Thomas Fitzsimmons

Washington, D.C.

ACKNOWLEDGMENTS

PUBLICATION OF THIS STUDY, and of the series, is possible because many individuals gave unstintingly of time, talent, critical and creative energy. Review procedures designed to tap all the resources of the HRAF research staff as well as those of outside specialists were supervised by Dr. Herbert H. Vreeland.

The authors had the use of a monograph prepared at the University of Chicago under contract to HRAF, edited by Dr. Mitchell Zadrozny (under the direction of Professors Fred Eggan and Norton Ginsburg) and authored by Dr. Zadrozny, Albert Androsky, Naomi Noble, Martin Orans, Hong-phuc Vo, and Milton Sacks. With the exception of "Ethnic Distribution" the maps in this book have been modified from originals appearing in this monograph.

While these and many others contributed to the Cambodia study, whatever shortcomings it may have are the sole responsibility of its authors and the editor.

THE HUMAN RELATIONS AREA FILES

THE HUMAN RELATIONS AREA FILES is a nonprofit research corporation affiliated with Yale University and sponsored and supported by its sixteen member universities. HRAF was established in 1949 "to collect, organize, and distribute information of significance to the natural and social sciences and the humanities." It has concentrated upon furthering a fresh approach to the study of societies, culture, and social behavior.

The Files themselves contain carefully selected sources analyzed according to G. P. Murdock's *Outline of Cultural Materials*. Located at each of the member universities, they are a new kind of reference library in which basic information about nearly two hundred peoples can be consulted with ease and speed. Preparation of the present study was facilitated by the use of the Southeast Asia File and the Cambodia File.

MEMBER UNIVERSITIES

University of Chicago

University of Colorado

Cornell University

Harvard University

University of Hawaii

Indiana University

State University of Iowa

University of Michigan

University of North Carolina

University of Oklahoma

University of Pennsylvania

Princeton University

University of Southern California

University of Utah

University of Washington

Yale University

CONTENTS

Contents (*continued*)

LIST OF PLATES

LIST OF TABLES

CAMBODIA

THE CULTURE AND THE SOCIETY

THE KINGDOM OF CAMBODIA became an independent state in 1954 after almost one hundred years as a French protectorate. It is governed by a representative assembly and ruled by a monarch whose powers and duties are constitutionally defined. Constitutional government is new in Cambodia: the monarchy, on the other hand, is centuries old, tracing its origins back to the ancient kingdom of Kambuja. From earliest history, when the power of the king was absolute, the monarchy has been the unifying symbol of Cambodian culture—of the relation of the Khmer people to their land and religion. The monarchy continued to play a central role in preserving the nation—and the people's sense of nation—through a hundred years of colonial rule, two world wars, independence, and the current cold war. The majority of Cambodians regard their independence as the result of the efforts of one man—the former king, Norodom Sihanouk.

Clearly, then, the Cambodian throne is more than a merely decorative feature of government. During the hundred years that Cambodia was dominated by France, French policies had to be executed in the name of the Cambodian king: of all the Indochinese states Cambodia proved the most resistant to French rule. Though the formal and temporal powers of the monarchy have been brought within the confines of constitutionalism, its inherent symbolic and spiritual powers have persisted and been reinforced by the traditions of a people who, knowing little of constitutionalism, continue in times of stress to look to the throne as the source of real power and to the royal family as the source of effective political leadership. Placing their trust in monarchy and its living representatives, the people tend to expect in return that the monarchy will preserve the integrity of the Cambodian national and religious community, and to this end will exert a power that is personal, divinely inspired, and limited by tradition rather than legalism.

The indigenous people of Cambodia are the Khmer—the true Cambodians—who comprise 85 to 90 percent of the total population and speak a language unrelated to the other major languages of the area—Thai, Laotian, and Vietnamese. The ruling group, that is, the king, the royal family, the nobility, and educated commoners, are Khmer and Khmer interests and values dominate the national government and politics. The majority of the Khmer below the elite group are farmers, Buddhist monks (bonzes), and government servants; few have entered commerce or industry.

The most important minority groups are the Chinese and Vietnamese, who, although considered foreigners by the Khmer, play a role in Cambodian life out of proportion to their numbers. They dominate commerce and industry, and are the chief creditors of the Khmer peasants; in short, they control most of the economic system of the country. Poorly integrated into Cambodian society and not sharing traditional Khmer values and attitudes toward the land, the religion, and the king, they are excluded from the upper levels of government.

The Khmer religion is Theravada Buddhism, which replaced Brahmanism in Cambodia between the sixth and fifteenth centuries. Spreading from Ceylon it took root not only in Cambodia but also in Thailand, Laos, and Burma. While the Buddhist church in Cambodia is independent of the churches in these other countries, all look to Ceylon as the spiritual fountainhead.

The Buddhist church is legally separate from the state; bonzes cannot vote and are supposed to remain aloof from politics. Symbolically, however, church and state merge in the person of the king. Although not an official of the church, the king is its guardian and protector, and is looked upon as the divine leader of the nation. His actual power lies as much in the religious reverence accorded him as in any tangible means of enforcing his will. Where vestiges of ancient Indian Siva-worship still persist the king is sometimes regarded as a kind of god.

The rural people of Cambodia are devoted to their village temples, and their reaction to territorial encroachment is most intense when an old and venerated temple is threatened. It is customary for all adult males to spend some time as monks, and because the bonzes come from all walks of life, they have to some degree bridged the social gap between the rulers and the ruled.

1. The Culture and the Society

Since independence Cambodia has been caught in the cold war, and the issue of alignment versus neutrality has generated forces that again threaten the integrity of the Cambodian nation. Sihanouk, who despite his abdication as king is still the political leader of his country, has insisted that a policy of neutrality is essential if Cambodia's recent and hard-won independence is to be preserved. He also believes that independence and neutrality must be supported by economic well-being and self-sufficiency.

Economically Cambodia faces many problems. The war in Indochina wrecked the communication and transport system. Crop failures and a border dispute with South Vietnam resulted in a drop in exports and a loss of customs revenue. Revenues have been further reduced by the fact that the people, accustomed to resisting payment of taxes under the French, have continued to be delinquent under their own government. Lacking adequate credit facilities, the rural population has sunk further in debt to the Chinese moneylenders. Not only is control of what little industry and commerce exists in their country in other hands, but the Khmer lack the technical, commercial, and administrative skills required to replace foreigners in this field. There is a traditional Khmer aversion to activities involving manual or semimanual labor: the peasant works with his hands, but not the educated man.

Despite shared symbols, the social, political, and cultural distance between the ruling elite and the Khmer peasantry is wide. Government reaches down through the provincial capitals to the villages, but contact is minimal and the social and political aspirations of the governing group have little in common with those of the villagers. The villagers tend to be provincial, conservative, and profoundly religious in their outlook, while the urban elite are more secular, progressive, and internationalist.

Early in 1955 King Sihanouk, realizing that as king his activities were limited by the traditions binding the throne, abdicated in order to attain as a politician the freedom of action of a private citizen. For several months he traveled about the country, explaining his aims for the future development of Cambodia. In the fall of 1955, he was back in the government as prime minister and leader of a new political party that had swept the polls in the elections of that year.

Since that time the Cambodian government, under Sihanouk's leadership, has undertaken a large-scale program of governmental reorganization, administrative reforms, and economic, social, and educational development. An ambitious Two Year Plan was launched in 1956 which called for simultaneous attack on the various aspects of the economic question and its related social problems. But the plan, involving, as it did, new investment and credit facilities and increased imports of essential goods, could not be financed out of the national budget, or even from the economic and military aid then being received from France and the United States.

At this point Sihanouk made a decision that put Cambodia's neutrality to the test. He announced that his government would accept economic aid from any quarter as long as the sovereignty of Cambodia was respected. Cambodia, he said, would have to depend for a while on well-intentioned friends in order to achieve economic independence.

This declaration brought aid and recognition from the Chinese People's Republic and the Soviet Union. It also created difficulties within the governing elite. Political opposition, quelled for a time by the achievement of independence, again arose contesting Sihanouk's neutralist policy, claiming that it was untenable, and that Cambodia must inevitably be drawn into either the Communist or the anti-Communist camp. A new series of border incidents broke out with pro-West Vietnam and Thailand. Feeding on old jealousies and rivalries and aggravated by current pressures, discord increased among the few important families that controlled the government. A succession of cabinets toppled under the blows of political conflict and a difficult economic situation. Sihanouk himself was alternately in and out of office as premier.

As of early 1959 he was again prime minister and the monarchy remained intact—the present king, Suramarit, is his father. One of Sihanouk's greatest strengths is that for the majority of the people he still carries the aura of divinity that surrounded him as king. So far he has been the only man capable of holding the government together. How long he will retain this power is conjectural.

Although modern political and social techniques are being introduced, the theories behind them have not been fully assimilated. Influenced by technology, science, and western ideas, modernized young Cambodians are increasingly eager to have some voice in family and national decisions. These same young people, however, are regarded by many in power as a potential threat to the established order, and are not being used to great advantage. Failing to find opportunities for their talents within the government, some of them have become hostile to the party in power. Both the opposition Democratic party and the extreme leftist Pracheachon party have attracted many younger men.

New forces and ideas are penetrating society—especially through the educational system—which may have far-reaching consequences, changing the young Cambodian's conception of what his nation and society should be and where he should look for leadership. French withdrawal provided the impetus for these developments and the educational system introduced by the French has provided the intellectual ferment. The educational system remains essentially French but now that the French are no longer in control it cannot be charged that the adoption of western cultural elements strengthens foreign rule. Independence has brought new incentives and Cambodians are crowding the schools. State school enrollment has increased more than fourfold during the past eight years. In addition, students are being sent abroad by the government for training in specific fields, such as administration, economics, health, and education. To acquire as much education as possible is now considered a patriotic duty as well as an avenue for individual advancement.

The intellectual ferment has resulted even in criticism of the religious community, by some of its own members as well as westernized laymen who dislike the general conservatism of the bonzes and object to the "excessive number of unproductive men in the economy." Many bonzes are being trained as teachers in state schools where they are introduced to secular thought and methods. A small number of bonzes concerned with what appear to them certain anachronisms in Buddhism are agitating for doctrinal reforms. The highest religious school has recently adopted a curriculum which includes conferences to discuss ways of bringing Buddhism into line with twentieth-century social conditions.

In spite of these new forces which are impinging upon it, the Buddhist church in Cambodia remains a strong force for conservatism and stability. In theory remaining aloof from political activity, it implicitly supports the monarchy and is protected by it. Continuing to draw its membership from all segments of the Khmer population it imparts to all of these, whether peasant or monk, ruler or ruled, a common system of values which emphasizes individual improvement within the context of the existing social order rather than a change in that order itself.

This philosophy, explicit in Buddhist doctrine, has an implicit parallel in the secular changes now being advocated and implemented by the government under the leadership of the royal family. Such changes are directed more toward improving the standard of living and shoring up weak points in the existing order with a view to making it more viable and productive in the modern world than toward remodeling the basic social and political structure. Disagreements among the ruling elite appear to revolve around considerations of when and how such improvements should be effected rather than around any attempt by one faction to alter the system. In these matters the church and the state are in agreement and exert parallel forces for stability.

The people for whose benefit these improvements are primarily intended—the uneducated peasantry—remain themselves a largely conservative and static element. Supporting the church and the monarchy, they are responsive to the leadership of both but have little economic, social, and political initiative of their own. Apart from their continuing economic needs, they appear to have few original demands for change or for greater influence upon changes that are occurring. Whatever new awarenesses, or new goals, they have appear to have been stimulated by government rather than originated by themselves. It is here that most of the present impediments to change exist, for the people have little desire to accept the new roles and responsibilities that are necessary to implement changes designed for their own benefit.

Political factionalism and discord, intellectual ferment and change must be viewed in this context. They are having an effect which may in time alter the system within which they are working. But as yet they do not appear to have raised any serious challenge to the fundamental concepts and values of that system, or to have disturbed the relationship between the church, the monarchy, and the people. No one of these elements is alone responsible for the continuing conservatism of the society today, but rather the way in which these elements support each other. Change is certainly evident but until it is supported by a significantly large, powerful, and vocal class, possessing new economic and social values, Cambodian society will retain basically its present form.

HISTORICAL SETTING

HISTORY, FOR MOST CAMBODIANS, IS LEGEND symbolizing the subjective experiences of their ancestors rather than the more or less factual record of events usual in the West. Such legends contain facts, of course, but facts handled with great freedom. The reigning dynasty, for example, claims direct descent from the sovereigns of the Angkor Wat period, and most Cambodians not only admit the claim but take pride in it. At the same time, however, they reject any attempt to identify the Khmer with the people who built Angkor Wat, explaining them away in a legend about a people who built stone monuments, then disappeared. Similarly many Cambodians are uneasy about modern studies tending to link the Khmer with the tribesmen of Cambodia, whom they consider savages.

Cambodian legends have reinforced the cohesiveness of the people, forming a bond of common heritage and significance. One example is provided by the symbols River and Mountain—important in Cambodian thinking since the second Bronze Age. In the ancient tales, mountain men were pitted against river men. This dualism was also a feature of the social organization: tribes were divided into factions that derived their principal livelihood either from the high country or from the river. The mountain chiefs and sorcerers were considered descendants of Garuda, the divine bird, and they commanded fire and lightning. The river chiefs and sorcerers were considered descendants of Naga, the divine fish or serpent, and they ruled over the waters and rain.

The legendary origin of Indian civilization in Cambodia is linked to this theme. Chroniclers record the legend of the Hindu prince, Kaundinya (King of the Mountain), who married a female serpent, a Nagi, and founded the "lunar" dynasty which long ruled the country. A variation of the story recounts that Fu-Nan (the

Chinese name given the country) was governed by a woman. A prince of a "southern province" (India) dreamed that a spirit gave him a bow and arrows and told him to conquer the sea. He took to the sea and arrived in Fu-Nan, where the queen's troops were massed in defense. When an arrow from the magic bow struck one of the defenders the queen surrendered. Prince and queen married, and the prince taught the people to wear clothes and to make cloth. It is essentially this version of early history that is taught in Cambodian schools today, presenting in legendary form the historical fact that Indian culture was brought into Cambodia at a very early date.

Social mobility and the immediate reward of merit are illustrated in the legend of the Old Man of the Sweet Cucumbers. Once an old peasant named Ta-Chey planted sweet cucumbers in his kitchen garden. One season the cucumbers were so good that he offered some to the king. The king liked them so much that he gave Ta-Chey a lance with which to protect the garden. To test the old man's watchfulness, the king one night stole into the garden and in the dark was killed by Ta-Chey. "Whereupon all the. . . dignitaries of the realm, seeing that Ta-Chey was an upright, just, and meritorious man, called him to the throne and crowned him King of Cambodia."

There is sculpture at Banteai Srey (the Women's Citadel), an exquisite temple northeast of Angkor Wat, which illustrates a myth taken from the Indian epic, Mahabharata. The gods decided to create the beautiful Apsara Tilottama and send her to earth to distract the demons. Seeing her, each of the demons desired her for himself and in the ensuing fight killed one another. "And in this way the world was saved." This story may offer insight into Cambodian diplomatic and political maneuvering—and to the present policy of neutralism. In a recent speech about Cambodia's relation to the Big Powers struggle Sihanouk declared that, when two elephants are fighting, an ant should stand aside.

History in Cambodia was woven into folk tales, or it was lost completely. When the French naturalist Henri Mouhot came upon the ruins at Angkor Wat almost a century ago, he could find no historical awareness among Cambodians:

> If you interrogate the Cambodians as to the founders of Ongcor-Vat, you invariably receive one of these four replies: "It is the work of Pra-Eun, the king of the angels"; "It is the work of the giants"; "It was built by the leprous king"; or else, "It made itself."

The Ascent to Greatness

Cambodia's documented history begins with remains that place man in Cambodia in the Neolithic period. The people who lived there in prehistoric times probably included the proto-Malayan or Indonesian forebears of today's Chams and of the tribes known as Phnong (the Moi in Vietnam). None of the other prehistoric peoples of Cambodia have survived. The first habitations are said to have been in the delta of the Mekong, an area now part of both Cambodia and Vietnam.

Indian and Chinese influences made themselves felt early in the Indochinese peninsula: Indian to the west of a range of mountains dividing the peninsula, Chinese to the east. This division of predominant influence has a bearing today on the antagonism between the Cambodians west of the mountains and the Vietnamese to the east.

Indian culture expanded by peaceful means. Traders and religious teachers profoundly affected the thinking of the people, giving them a framework within which their own social customs could develop. Indian culture was very influential, but always the Cambodians have modified that which they borrowed and have selected those ideas or forms consistent with their own thinking.

The Fu-Nan Period

Three distinct, politically independent peoples—the Funanese, the Chams, and the Khmer—lived in the lower Mekong region in the first century A.D. Gradually these peoples were Hinduized. By the third century the Funanese had overcome the other tribes and the area became known as Fu-Nan. By the end of the fifth century Fu-Nan was at the height of its power.

According to Chinese documents, which are the only known historical accounts of the early eras, an Indian Brahman ruled over the country and in the fourth century "completely indianized the customs of Fu-Nan." He is thought to have systematized the worship of Indian deities, instituting the state worship of Siva-linga —the reigning Cambodian king, merged with the Indian deities of Siva and Vishnu. Important elements of this religion persist today in Cambodia; coalescence of religious tenets characterizes much of Cambodian history.

At the time of Indian culture infiltration, the Laws of Manu— the Indian legal code—were put into effect and the use of the central Indian alphabet was introduced. Both the legal code and the alphabet, in modified forms, are used in Cambodia today.

The chief vassal state of Fu-Nan was Chen-La, to the north on the Mekong. In the middle of the sixth century Chen-La gained control over Fu-Nan, first making it a vassal, then annexing it— a conquest which has been cited as an example of the recurrent "drive to the south" in the history of the Indochinese peninsula.

The Chen-La Period, 535-802 A.D.

During the 250 years in which Chen-La was dominant over Fu-Nan, it extended its empire to the boundaries of present-day China, was divided by civil strife, fell under Malayan rule, and became independent again. Except that it provides the background for later greatness there would be nothing particularly worthy of attention in this segment of Cambodian history, which followed the usual pattern of squabbling and change of sovereignty among petty states.

The name "Cambodia" derives from this time. Chen-La was inhabited by Khmer, and the founder of the Khmer dynasty, according to legends, was Kambu Svayambhuva. "Kambuja"—hence the French "Cambodge" and the English "Cambodia"—is traceable to his name. "Kambujadesa" or "sons of Kambuja" was a name sometimes given the country in later years, but Chinese documents of the time used the name Chen-La.

The legendary importance of the River and the Mountain is given historical substance by a series of eighth-century civil wars which split Chen-La into two parts: Land Chen-La, the upland area to the north, and Water Chen-La, the maritime area which formed the nucleus of the later Khmer empire.

The Kambuja or Angkor Period, 802-1432 A.D.

This was the time of greatness, the period modern leaders refer to when rallying their people. At its peak the empire extended from the Annam chain to the Gulf of Siam. The buildings at Angkor Wat, erected at this time, have become a national symbol, a sketch of them being a prominent feature of the national flag. The kings of this period are hailed today in political speeches. Outstanding among these kings in modern Cambodian veneration are Jayavarman II and Jayavarman VII.

Jayavarman II, who was set upon the Khmer throne as vassal to the Malays, turned away from them and asserted Khmer independence. By Brahman rite, he was installed as devaraja in 802. Folklore links him with nearly every ancient temple, although little actually remains of what he constructed. The sacred royal sword, treasured as a symbol of authority by Cambodians today, is said to be the sword of Jayavarman II. He reunited the old Chen-La empire, including the northernmost part which bordered Yunnan. All of present-day Laos and much of present-day Thailand were added to his kingdom.

Social welfare was also a concern of the kings of this period. Jayavarman VII founded over a hundred hospitals, built rest houses for travelers on the great pilgrim routes, and distributed tons of rice to the needy. Libraries and schools were established. An inscription dating from his reign was quoted in 1956 at the dedication of a new hospital in Cambodia: "The pain of their subjects, and not their own pain, is the sadness of kings."

The arts flourished. Angkor Wat and the Bayon of Angkor Thom, two of the greatest temples, were built in the twelfth and thirteenth centuries. Many of the kings themselves excelled as scholars. Sanskrit literature was raised to new heights by royal patronage. Indian scholars, artists, and religious teachers were welcomed in Kambujan courts, and many Khmer traveled extensively in India.

The Decline

Jayavarman VII achieved great things, but after his death the empire began to fall apart. The people were exhausted by huge construction projects and by wars of conquest. Mongol pressure on the Thai kingdom in the thirteenth century gave greater impetus to Thai infiltration of Cambodia. By the end of the thirteenth century independent Thai kingdoms had been created in former Khmer territory. In 1353 a Thai army captured Angkor; later the Kambujans regained it, but wars with the Thai continued for centuries. Angkor was looted a number of times, and thousands of artists and scholars were carried away to slavery in Thailand. In 1430-31 the Thai again captured Angkor, this time aided by treachery within the Khmer capital. This conquest, as nearly as any one event can, marks the end of the magnificent Khmer era. The Khmer recaptured their city but abandoned it as a capital. Significantly, the change of religion from Brahmanism to Theravada Buddhism affected this decision. The great stone temples of the old religion were too costly to maintain and no longer vital to the life of the people. The jungle was allowed in the course of centuries to overrun Angkor Wat.

Cambodia in Transition, 1432-1864

The political and artistic energy of the Khmer seems to have disappeared by this period. Ancient dances and other art forms were preserved but dynamic growth or experimentation was lacking. Politically Cambodia expended its energies in resisting the aggressions of its neighbors Thailand and Annam (present-day Vietnam) and subsequently of European nations. The emphasis was on survival, on the preservation of the status quo. This period has been called a time of independence for Cambodia—a misnomer, for Cambodia was certainly less independent than in former centuries. In reality, the period is one of transition into a French protectorate.

The basis of historical knowledge changes in this period, and this tends to magnify the impression of a great change in Cambodia. Knowledge of earlier history derives from inscriptions on buildings or accounts of Chinese travelers. From the fifteenth century on history is based on European records and narratives. Some have written that the early people appear to have mysteriously disappeared, leaving the country to lesser people. This is not so. The people who created the architectural masterpieces and the political empire did not disappear; rather, their creative spirit was subdued.

Thailand claimed suzerainty over Cambodia and for centuries tried to validate its claim by forceful means as well as through a puppet king. Cambodia sought help from Spain and Portugal; these countries took some ineffectual steps to intervene, but in 1603 Thailand was successful in seating a Cambodian king wholly under its domination.

Thailand and Annam struggled for control of Cambodia for the next 260 years, each encroaching upon Cambodian territory. Thailand won lands in the north and Annam in the south; possession of some of these lands is the basis of dispute today between Cambodia on the one hand and Thailand and Vietnam on the other (see chap. 11).

Cambodian kings sometimes tried to play Thailand and Annam off against each other but in 1846 Thailand and Annam joined together in crowning a Cambodian king, Ang Duong, founder of the present dynasty. Cambodia was subjected to a dual vassalage. Even while vassal to the two countries, Ang Duong turned to a stronger power for protection. Since British policy seemed more aggressive in Southeast Asia at the time, he turned to France. Cambodia became an ally of France, which was fighting Annam.

Ang Duong died in 1859 during the course of the war. The

coronation of his eldest son, Norodom, who had become a Thai protégé, was a point of conflict with the French. After Norodom had ceded two western provinces to Thailand as a price for its acquiescence to his acceptance of French "protection," the French protectorate was proclaimed in April 1864; two months later Norodom was crowned in his own capital by representatives of both France and Thailand.

The French Protectorate, 1864-1949

Cambodia had learned to submit to vassalage over several centuries and did not find it difficult to adjust to the exigencies of French rule. At least in the new order there was only one master; despite implied joint suzerainty, France increasingly ignored Thai claims. France exploited Cambodia commercially and profited thereby but the protectorate was never a really vital element in French affairs.

The Franco-Cambodian treaty of 1863 gave France exclusive control of Cambodian foreign affairs and the right to defend Cambodia against external and internal enemies. A French resident-general was installed in the Cambodian capital as executive officer. Widespread political, economic, and social powers were granted the French, but even more powers were demanded. With French cannon trained on his palace, Norodom signed a new treaty in 1884. An unsuccessful rebellion expressed the popular reaction. Cambodia was placed under direct French control through a parallel administration. The French resident-general was the actual ruler, the king merely the symbol of country and religion. Cambodian social and political structures were left largely intact, but sweeping reforms were instituted.

After 1887 Cambodia became part of an Indochinese Union which included Tonkin, Annam, and Cochin China (the three areas that now make up Vietnam), Laos, and Kwangchowwan, the French leasehold in South China. After initial laxness, a strong central government was set up, reducing even further the powers of local officials.

When Norodom died in 1904, after a forty-year reign, his country was peaceful, prosperous, and powerless. His brother Sisowath was king until 1927. Sisowath's son, Sisowath Monivong, reigned from 1927 to 1941. Sisowath Monivong's sons were passed over in the royal succession, and the son of his oldest daughter—Prince Norodom Sihanouk, great-grandson of Norodom through the paternal line—became king.

World War II

The first abrupt change affecting the French protectorate over Cambodia occurred with the beginning of World War II. In August 1940, Thai forces, encouraged by the Japanese and by France's defeat in Europe, sought to make up for their territorial losses of 1904 and 1907—the latter to Laos—and attacked the French in Indochina. After several weeks of inconclusive fighting the Japanese intervened diplomatically in favor of Thailand and compelled the French authorities to agree to a peace treaty with Thailand on May 9, 1941; the treaty again stripped Cambodia of the border provinces regained in 1904.

Until the spring of 1945, although the Japanese in the course of war had stationed garrisons throughout the country, French Indochina remained nominally under French control. In order to be able to deal effectively with any problem arising on the spot, however, the Japanese had compelled the French government to give the governor-general in Indochina diplomatic powers which enabled him, if need be, to sign agreements in the name of France. This in turn allowed the Japanese to appoint their representative with the rank of ambassador to the French governor-general.

The whole French colonial administration was removed by a Japanese coup on March 9, 1945. The Japanese representative, in the name of his government, immediately authorized the states of Cambodia, Laos, and Vietnam to declare their independence within the Greater East Asian Sphere of Co-Prosperity, with the Japanese representative in Saigon becoming simultaneously ambassador to Cambodia and Laos. The Japanese appointed the nationalist rebel leader, Son Ngoc Thanh, prime minister of Cambodia, and King Sihanouk, on his advice, declared the independence of Cambodia on March 12, 1945.

Return of French Control

With the collapse of Japanese power after V-J Day, Cambodia was faced with a reappraisal of its international and domestic situation. French troops landed in Saigon in September 1945, and later in the month a French paratroop unit reoccupied Pnompenh and arrested Son Ngoc Thanh for collaboration with the Japanese.

At the same time, Admiral Thierry d'Argenlieu, the new French high commissioner in Indochina (the title, though not the essential functions, of governor-general had been abolished), requested that Cambodia send a delegation to meet him to negotiate a new set of rules to govern France's relations with Cambodia. Sihanouk agreed to send delegates provided they would be considered "delegates from an independent country" and that such negotiations would not "infringe upon the independence of our Fatherland." The achievement of full political independence from the French had become a primary Cambodian goal.

In the ensuing negotiations the French made some concessions to the Cambodian desire for independence, particularly in recognizing Cambodia as "an autonomous kingdom within the French Union" in a modus vivendi signed on January 7, 1946. The title and functions of the former resident-general for Cambodia were abolished, and a French Commissioner of the Republic was appointed to Pnompenh. But to many Cambodians the modus vivendi was exactly what the term meant—a temporary measure that permitted "coexistence" with the French pending further negotiations.

The Struggle for Independence

As France applied itself to the prosecution of the Indochina war, which was fought mainly on Vietnamese soil, the Cambodian government began a long struggle to obtain a constantly wider range of power. France was reluctant; nevertheless, on November 9, 1949 a treaty finally was signed between Cambodia and France that gave Cambodia the first prerogatives of internal sovereignty.

The 1949 agreements were far from satisfactory to the Cambodians. In the words of a Cambodian representative to the French Union Assembly during Assembly debates of January 19, 1950:

> We were entitled to hope that a contract of association would be concluded which would give equal satisfaction to the two partners concerned. . . . Instead of the expected [favorable] effect, the announcement of the treaties has aroused no enthusiasm whatever in Cambodia. Even the official circles which approved of them singularly lacked conviction. How was such a contradictory result attained? First of all, it seems that the [French] officials entrusted with the negotiations with the Cambodian representatives were more accustomed to command than to negotiate.

Particularly irksome to the Cambodians was the fact that non-Cambodians residing in the country were still outside Cambodian jurisdiction, as in the time of the protectorate. There were other obvious limitations upon Cambodian sovereignty in the fields of defense and economic policy.

Transfer of Government

An immediate problem requiring negotiation between Cambodia and France concerned the orderly transfer of government departments and services hitherto controlled by the French.

At Pau (France) representatives of Cambodia, France, Laos, and Vietnam negotiated the so-called Pau Agreements, providing for the joint administration by the three Indochina states and France of such economic services as customs and telecommunications. Originally scheduled to last only a few weeks, these negotiations were carried out in a marathon conference from June to November 1950.

South Vietnam loomed unexpectedly large as a Cambodian problem, for until the Cambodian deepwater port of Sihanoukville could be built, most of Cambodia's foreign trade had to go through the transit port of Saigon.

Undaunted by French and Vietnamese pressures, the Cambodian delegation stood firm on its major point of internationalization of river traffic on the Mekong and of one section of the port of Saigon; the delegation's closing statement, after a deadlock on those issues had been reached, was merely that "the era of negotiations is not yet closed, this effort must be pursued in further detail."

The transfer of services began but still the operations were too slow for the taste of the Cambodians. King Sihanouk, afraid that he and his government would lose their popularity to extremist elements, both nationalist and Communist, that had begun to accuse the royal government of being "soft" with the French, sought a more direct solution. He left Cambodia in March 1953 on what he asserted to be a pleasure trip to Europe, Canada, and the United States, making as he traveled a series of declarations highly critical of the French refusal to grant full independence to his country.

Upon his return to Cambodia in June, he went suddenly to Bangkok, swearing to return only in exchange for French assurances that Cambodia would be given all the prerogatives of full independence.

The King did not remain for long in exile in Bangkok but returned to the frontier province of Battambang, later moving to Siemreap, a sector controlled by Khmer armed forces. He still vowed that he would not return to his capital until the French had given him full satisfaction. At the same time, Sihanouk, Prime Minister Penn Nouth, General Nhiek Tioulong, and Defense Minis-

ter Sirik Matak elaborated a secret plan which provided for several eventualities—including armed resistance against the French—should the French not show themselves ready to negotiate on Cambodian terms.

The embattled French were ready to negotiate, for they were already faced with a difficult military situation in Vietnam and Laos. Vietminh Communist forces had made deep inroads early in 1953, reaching the Thailand border in Laos a mere hundred miles north of Cambodia, and there were dispersed Communist groups holding large stretches of land within Cambodia. In a solemn declaration on July 4, 1953, the French government declared itself ready to "perfect the independence" granted the three Associated States. Later in July the Cambodians came forward with their own specific terms: sovereignty over their defense establishment, their tribunals, and their currency.

The French yielded. On September 1, 1953 all of Cambodia was placed under Cambodian military command; a few days later a separate Khmer Army High Command was activated. By virtue of a separate agreement of October 1953, the French army retained only operational control in Cambodia east of the Mekong and tactical command of three Khmer battalions operating in the area. Both the police and the judiciary had been transferred to Cambodian control at the end of August.

Sihanouk, now a hero in the eyes of his people, returned to Pnompenh.

Last Transfers of Sovereignty

Essentially, the French still retained extensive powers in the economic field. But here again, and unlike its neighbor Vietnam, which sought a solution to its independence struggle with France in a single treaty, Cambodia successfully applied a "whittling down" policy, which was the more effective since it was inconspicuous. Without fanfare, by a mere "exchange of letters," Cambodia obtained in February 1954 the transfer of all residual economic and technical services still in French hands. Ahead of both Vietnam and Laos, Cambodia had become a truly independent nation.

By the middle of 1954 the international conference that had met at Geneva to negotiate the situation in Asia had arrived at an agreement. The basic convention, signed by the French and Vietminh representatives on July 20, 1954, called for a cessation of hostilities in Indochina and stipulated that all Vietminh forces be withdrawn below the 17th parallel. In a separate agreement signed by the Cambodian representative, Brigadier General Nhiek Tioulong of the Royal Khmer Army and now minister of defense, both the French and the Vietminh agreed to withdraw all forces from Cambodia by October 20, 1954.

There remained but one additional shackle upon Cambodia's total independence: the system of four-power boards and services (Bank of Issue, customs, communications, etc.) to which it was party under the Pau Agreements of 1950.

The four-power ties were severed in negotiations which began in Paris in August 1954 and ended on December 29, 1954; the quadripartite system was dissolved, and each of the three Associated States was given full sovereignty over services that had previously been subject to joint administration. Since that time Cambodia has elected to remain within the French Union as a sovereign and independent state.

The Growth of Representative Government

Concurrent with the drive for independence, the leaders of Cambodia had sought to establish the machinery of popular representative government. In spite of the difficulties in achieving full sovereignty, the modus vivendi of January 1946, which recognized Cambodia as an autonomous kingdom, permitted the Cambodians to proceed with internal governmental organization. A constituent assembly was elected in September of the same year, and a constitution was promulgated on May 6, 1947. The lower and upper houses of the Cambodian legislature were convened in January and February 1948 and parliamentary government began.

Political factionalism emerged almost immediately, however, and threatened the government that had up to now been dominated by King Sihanouk and the members of his family. In the first full representative elections, in December 1947, opposition to French rule was a basic issue. Many Cambodians were adamantly opposed to any sort of collaboration with France. They either organized themselves as dissident groups, which were collectively called Khmer Issarak (Free Cambodia), or joined the Communist Vietminh who had crossed the border from Vietnam. At the time of the elections there emerged a party, known as the Democratic party, under the leadership of Son Ngoc Thanh, the former nationalist rebel leader. This party opposed the government of King Sihanouk and was also the legal cover for the Khmer Issarak (see chap. 8).

2. *The Growth of Representative Government*

This party won an overwhelming majority in the National Assembly and began systematically to block all legislation sponsored by the King or his followers.

Many personal feuds broke out within the National Assembly and soon one administration was being quickly followed by another—reflecting elements of parliamentary instability found in the French system of that time. To forestall compete chaos, King Sihanouk dissolved the National Assembly in September 1949 and ruled for nearly two years without it, aided by prime ministers and cabinet members of his own choosing.

New elections were held in September 1951, and a new National Assembly was seated in October. The Democratic party, again the winner, failed to come up with a firm program, however, and ran the government on a "spoils system" basis. Many able civil servants were eliminated and replaced by the party faithful.

In June 1952 the King announced in a speech to the Council of the Kingdom and a message to the National Assembly that he was taking full powers until he could restore order in the national administration and order and security throughout the country. Known as the Royal Mandate, this measure was not based upon any constitutional provision giving the king the right to assume such powers in an emergency; it was an autocratic measure fully outside the Constitution. Under these plenary powers the King on his own initiative dissolved the two houses of the National Assembly in January 1953.

The Royal Mandate

The Royal Mandate lasted from June 1952 to February 1955. During this period the King ruled directly; he created a temporary Advisory Council to serve in the place of the national legislature.

The Mandate succeeded in establishing a semblance of order throughout the kingdom. The number of government crises (for cabinets were still free to resign, although they had been hand-picked by the King) was considerably reduced, and Sihanouk was able, in behalf of full independence, to devote his energies to obtaining major concessions from the French.

On February 7, 1955 a nation-wide referendum was held to decide by a "yes" or "no" vote whether the King had fulfilled his three-year mandate of attaining independence and security for his country. Soldiers and bonzes were allowed to vote. King Sihanouk obtained more than 925,000 of the approximately 927,000 votes cast, or a majority of 99.8 percent. Soon thereafter he resigned from the throne in favor of his father in order to be able to enter politics (see chap. 21). In his own words:

> It is my aim to insure that these powers [of political organiza-
> tion] will be exercised by the people themselves and to give
> them the means of removing the injustices, corruption, and ex-
> ploitation for which they have suffered for so long. It is my
> belief that such a task cannot be properly fulfilled by a reigning
> sovereign. . . . By renouncing the throne I desire, therefore, to
> serve my people in order to achieve these aims.

The Sangkum Party

After his abdication Sihanouk began building the People's Socialist Community, Sangkum Reastr Niyum (SRN), the most efficient political machine Cambodia has ever known. Though no longer king he was still a prince of the royal family and he had further-more gained considerable prestige during the years leading up to full independence. He had applied himself to the dual task of suppressing armed rebels and achieving freedom from the French. Doubt as to his patriotism, a key point in some Cambodians' justi-fication of their seeming disloyalty to him, had been removed. Many rebel chiefs, convinced that he was sincerely working for Cambodian independence, had come over to his side and been commissioned in the Royal Cambodian Army. Even Son Ngoc Thanh, leader of the Democratic party and his strongest opponent, had declared in a radio broadcast at that time: "I was mistaken about the King in thinking him a tool of the French. He is a patriot."

On the basis of this prestige Sihanouk began a vigorous per-sonal campaign throughout the country, seeking the support of the people for his new party. New national elections were held on September 11, 1955 and the Sangkum won all of the seats of the ninety-one-member National Assembly. Since that time until the present, the Sangkum has been the dominant party, never losing its control of the government. Aware that its opposition, as re-flected in the membership of the Democratic party, stemmed mainly from the frustrated and discontented younger generation, the Sangkum has in recent years made special efforts to secure their active support and participation through a youth auxiliary called the Socialist Youth of the Khmer Kingdom, Jeunesse Socialiste du Royaume Khmer. Sihanouk himself continues to be one of the most vigorous propagandists for his movement and has written long articles explaining its activities and goals.

Though still firmly in the saddle, the Sangkum has been plagued with continual internal dissensions, due in part to the growing pains of a new nation and in part to the host of economic and social problems which beset the country in its attempts at postwar reconstruction and development.

Current Problems

The problems with which the Cambodian government has had to cope since independence have been many and varied. At the outset the new nation was faced with a huge economic task of repairing war damages to the communications system, raising the standard of living of the rural population, installing essential schools and industrial plants, all while striving for an economic independence commensurate with political sovereignty. In an effort to deal with this task in a rational manner, a two-year development plan was inaugurated early in 1956 and later extended to June 1958. The financing and implementation of this plan has been a major concern, as well as a stumbling block, of each successive Sangkum administration. Even though the plan is now officially terminated, the projects which it started are still under way and it has left in its wake a number of national agencies, and national and international commitments, which will remain a part of the economic picture for some time to come.

Foremost among the international commitments are economic and military aid agreements with the United States, which were in effect prior to 1954, and commercial and economic aid agreements with the Chinese People's Republic, the USSR, and other Soviet bloc countries, signed in 1956. These have made it possible for Cambodia to maintain a rising scale of imports, now far ahead of its exports trade, but they have also placed Cambodia squarely in the middle of the struggle between the United States and its allies and the Communist countries. In recent years Sihanouk has clung fervently to his policy of "neutralism" and "coexistence," continuing to draw aid from both sides yet hoping to steer a middle course and retain full sovereignty while on the road to economic independence. In public he has expressed quick resentment at assumed efforts of the United States to draw Cambodia into an alliance with avowedly anti-Communist powers. Privately, however, he has shown alarm at the growing Communist influence in his country (see chap. 11).

Within this larger issue, other issues older and more local, have persisted and taken on new meaning. Since the breakup of the Associated States of Indochina, border troubles with South Vietnam and Thailand have never been fully resolved and today relations with both of these countries are subject to supervision and mediation by the United Nations. These troubles stem originally from territorial claims that antedate the present situation, claims which the French did not settle when they left Indochina. But today military actions along the borders are discussed increasingly in terms of Communist infiltration from Cambodia and of underhanded attempts by Cambodia's neighbors to force it out of its neutralist position and into the anti-Communist camp.

In the midst of these difficulties, Cambodia has been faced internally with some fundamental social problems which have impaired its ability to cope with the tasks it assumed and the tensions thrust upon it from outside. The essence of this problem is that the numerically and politically dominant element in Cambodia—the Khmer—do not yet fill all of the occupations or possess all of the skills necessary to manage a Khmer state. The leaders of the country are Khmer and the people for whom they seek a better life are Khmer. The nation they visualize is a Khmer nation identified with Buddhism and with the ancient grandeur of the Khmer kingdoms, and able eventually to take its place as a modern state among the other nation-states of the world. Yet the Khmer have been for centuries, and still are today, either rulers, priests or peasants. Few of them have been trained in commerce, banking or other economic activities; few of them have been trained in the technical and administrative skills needed to create and run an industrialized economy. By and large the economic life of the country has fallen by default to the Chinese and the Vietnamese communities in Cambodia. Well aware of this situation, and anxious to free itself internally as well as externally from dependence on foreigners, the Khmer government has made serious efforts to train cadres of Khmer technicians and administrators, to establish Khmer-controlled institutions, to educate the people in commercial and financial activities, and to encourage Khmer-controlled industrial and commercial enterprises.

While this problem is being solved, another and in some ways more deep-seated condition is impeding the machinery which must eventually produce the solutions—the tradition of a small ruling elite with inherent right to rule and the lack of any tradition or knowledge of ruling on the part of the mass of the people. Today this elite, as well as the country as a whole, is led by Sihanouk, a man who has never lost the aura of inherited and divine kingship even though his actions have been challenged and in spite of his abdication. On those occasions when he has resigned from the premiership, no one except his opponents have felt fully confident in taking over and, inevitably, he has been recalled by popular demand or royal request. As of January 1959 he was again premier of Cambodia, but as he frequently says, his party cannot be permanently dependent on his presence to maintain its cohesion and to control the operations of the government. Under his guidance Cambodia has and is borrowing ideas, materials, and methods from the rest of the world, but it still is far from achieving its goal of becoming a modern, politically and economically independent national state.

GEOGRAPHY AND POPULATION

CAMBODIA—A SMALL, BROAD COUNTRY about the size of the state of Washington—is one of the most productive areas of Southeast Asia. Together with Burma and Thailand it has helped feed Malaya, Indonesia, India, and Ceylon. Among its neighbors Cambodia is unique in being relatively underpopulated; not more than a quarter of its arable land is under cultivation. There is a Chinese phrase, "wealthy as Cambodia," but whether the less than five million Cambodians are capable of fully exploiting, or even defending, the land they hold is a question.

The dominant topographical feature of Cambodia is the Mekong River, which rises some 800 miles to the northwest in South China's Szechwan (four rivers) Province, the watershed of Southeast Asia. From the "Four Rivers" Province the Brahmaputra River runs down into India and Pakistan, the Irrawaddy into Burma, the Yangtze east through China, the Mekong into Cambodia and South Vietnam. The Mekong is one of the longest rivers in the world—2,700 miles. At its source, and as it courses through China, Thailand, and Laos, it is narrow and swift, full of rapids, and largely unnavigable. Reaching the Cambodian plains it becomes broad and quiet; two hundred miles from the sea it is three miles wide and deep enough to accommodate ocean steamers.

For Cambodia, the Mekong and its tributaries have been the source of both prosperity and affliction. Down the flooding river has come rich alluvial soil carried through Thailand and Laos by turbulent rapids and deposited at the rate of millions of tons each year over the Cambodia flat and the delta of the Mekong. But Cambodia's fish-stocked rivers and its broad plains have been a continuous invitation to covetous neighbors and invaders—be they the Thai, Chinese, or Vietnamese (see chap. 2)—who have found the river an easy route.

Geography

Cambodia is bounded to the northeast by Laos, to the east and south by Vietnam, to the southwest by the Gulf of Siam, to the west and north by Thailand. Of its approximately 69,800 square miles (181,000 sq. km.) half is forest and about one-tenth water, leaving approximately 40 percent arable. Only some 25 percent of the arable land—a tenth of the whole—is under cultivation.

There are almost 900 miles of navigable rivers and lakes and these are the focal points of population settlement. They provide some of the more important means of communication. The easy accessibility of the inland waterways together with the mountains and forests that form a barrier along the Gulf coast has made of the Cambodians an inland-oriented people, and despite direct access to the sea there has until recently been little development of port facilities on the Gulf of Siam.

The climate of Cambodia is mild, the temperature averaging about 82° F. and varying from about 75° to 90°. The coldest month is January; the warmest April. The rainy season—the southwest monsoon—lasts from May through October; the dry season—the northeast monsoon—from November through April. The mountain chains to the south give Cambodia a drier, clearer climate than that of most lands at the same latitude.

The central part of the country, bordering the Mekong and the Tonle Sap (literally "great lake") is a level plain, a basin that stretches over three fourths of Cambodia; little of it is more than 10 feet above sea level. The plain is ringed to the south and west by a high plateau, including the Elephant Range ("the mountains round which the clouds turn") that runs down to the Gulf of Siam. In the west the granite Cardamom Mountains rise to 5,000 feet, their steep slopes densely forested. To the north is the Dangrek Range, sandstone terraces that fall abruptly to the Cambodian plain. To the east the hills of what is usually called the Moi Plateaus reach in some places to 3,000 feet; this is the home of the primitive hill peoples (see chap. 4).

Because of the flat alluvial plain, inundated part of the year, and the wet tropical climate, rice cultivation is comparatively easy, even with the crudest implements, and despite the fact that the soils of Cambodia generally are low in inherent fertility; poor in humus, potash, and lime, they are, however, extremely rich in phosphate. There is a Cambodian saying, "If it grows, why plant it?" In the province of Battambang, rice seed is sown broadcast and there is no need to transplant.

The Mekong River, its river tributaries, and its natural reservoir, the Tonle Sap dominate Cambodian life and economy. Once an arm of the sea, the Tonle Sap has become an inland lake. Silting in the Mekong delta gradually has prevented the movement of tidal waters back into the lake, and it causes the river's flood waters to back up into the Tonle Sap instead of escaping to the sea during the rainy months. By June each year the Mekong has risen 40 or 45 feet, causing the Tonle Sap to spread over an area of 770 square miles, inundating the marshes, forests, and cultivated fields. During the dry season the lake shrinks to 100 square miles with a maximum depth of 5 feet. It leaves behind rich alluvial soil and shallow receding waters teeming with fish.

The Tonle Sap is the center of some of the most extensive fishing in the entire region. It supports a fishing population of about 30,000 and accounts for half of Cambodia's annual production of 130,000 tons of fresh-water fish. The fish, taken as the water recedes, sometimes by hand, are either dried, salted, smoked, or fermented for the production of *nuoc-mam* sauce or *prahoc* paste—staples of the Cambodian diet.

Cambodians accept the capriciousness of the Mekong since from its tremendous deposits of alluvial soil each year comes their own food as well as much of the food of the rest of Southeast Asia. Each year at the end of the rainy season, when the Tonle Sap reverses its course, one of the most important celebrations in Cambodia takes place—the Festival of the Waters. Both secular and religious features characterize this festival celebrating the good harvest and the return to their communities of the bonzes, or Buddhist monks, from their annual retreat, the Vassa (see chap. 5; chap. 21). Rejoicing because the evil spirits have been driven out is mingled with thanksgiving for the fertility of the soil and a general clowning amid a carnival atmosphere.

Dense virgin forest covering more than half the country, another important factor in the Cambodian economy, provides fuel as well as building materials for houses and boats, and is a potential source of wealth in foreign exchange. About half the timber is hardwood. It is cut during the dry season and floated across the Tonle Sap at flood tide.

The forest and mountains together, however, pose a formidable obstacle to transportation, settlement, and trade. Alluvial plain, marsh, bush, forest, and mountain—all support a wide variety of plant and animal life. Palm, rubber, and coconut trees, kapok and mango trees, banana and orange trees, the high sharp grass of the savannas, cultivated corn, peppers, tobacco, cotton, sugar, mulberries, indigo, vegetables, and the betel nut vine, paddy and lotus grain are found in profusion. Birds—herons, cranes, grouse, pheasants, wild ducks, marabous, pelicans, cormorants, egrets— swarm everywhere, even around Pnompenh. Elephants, rhinoceroses, wild oxen and buffaloes, tigers, panthers, leopards, bears, reptiles, and small game are found in every province. The Cambodian government describes the country as a sportman's paradise, and hunting may well become one of its chief attractions. The National Tourist Office offers to furnish experienced guides for foreign sportsmen, and trophies of the chase may be exported tax-free. Some of the more dangerous animals may be shot the year round.

There has been no extensive or adequate geological survey of Cambodia's mineral resources. Deposits of iron ore, jet, limestone, and phosphate are known to exist, but are not being exploited. At present there is some commercial production of jade, rubies, sapphires, garnets, corundum, and zircons. The central province of Kompong Thom is said to present interesting mining possibilities; cursory studies have shown traces of minerals including copper, manganese, and gold.

To assist in building the new port of Sihanoukville in the heavily wooded Kep-Kampot region of southern Cambodia, some geological surveying has been undertaken in a search for quarries and adequate water. Although the final results are not yet known, preliminary reports indicate that the chances for success may be high.

Transportation between settlements is for the most part by road, by water, occasionally by air, and less frequently by rail. Roads in Cambodia are concentrated in the settled areas along the rivers and lakes. Large areas of bush, marsh, forest, and mountain are roadless. In 1953 there were about 2,500 miles of hard-surface two-lane roads, connecting all the major cities. Many minor roads are inundated during the rainy season.

Good roads connect Pnompenh with Saigon, Bangkok, and Vientiane. Rail connections exist between Pnompenh and Bangkok, and there are air connections between Thailand, Laos, and Vietnam. War needs in the early 1950's resulted in the establishment of many small airfields and some of these are still in use. Buses, mostly owned by Chinese but, until recently, driven by Vietnamese, leave the capital every half hour during the day for Saigon, and buses connect Pnompenh with all the provincial capitals and intermediary cities and villages.

Current government development projects, begun under the Two Year Plan (1956-1957), include improvement of basic communication services. A new port on the Gulf of Siam, formerly Kompong Som but renamed Sihanoukville has been under construction with French aid since May 1956 and is scheduled for completion during the first half of 1959. First-class roads linking the port with Pnompenh and Ream have been under construction with United States aid since October 1956; the Pnompenh road is scheduled for completion by the end of June 1959. Other road and bridge construction has been undertaken with economic assistance from the Chinese People's Republic. At Pnompenh a large new airport (Pochentong) is being built, with some foreign aid, to serve both internal and external transportation.

The enlarged port of Pnompenh on the Mekong can receive medium ships of 8,000 tons in the rainy season and ships of 3,000 tons in the dry season. It connects directly with the outside world by way of the Mekong through South Vietnam.

Population

No accurate census of population has ever been taken in Cambodia. Official population estimates by province and by ethnic group made in 1950 are given in Tables 1 and 2.

These figures are based not on a head count but on statements of native authorities, centralized and checked in the chief town of each of the fourteen provinces. An error of at least 10 percent has been regarded by various authorities as probable. Absolute numbers, even when issued by official government and United Nations sources must be taken merely as estimates or projections.

Estimates of total population for 1955 varied from approximately 4,800,000 (by the United States Department of Commerce), to 5,125,000 (a projection of Canada's Department of Mines and Technical Surveys figures, based on a sharp increase since 1946 of approximately 2.5 percent per year). The official Cambodian government figure of 4,740,000 for 1958 is used in this book.

Cambodia is unique in Southeast Asia in having a real problem of underpopulation. The population densities of Burma, Thailand, and Vietnam also are low, but only one-fourth of Burma's land, one-fifth of Vietnam's and, at most two-thirds of Thailand's is

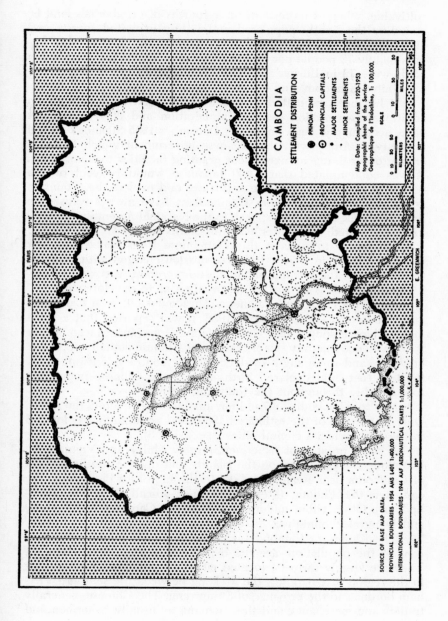

CAMBODIA

SETTLEMENT DISTRIBUTION

● PHNOM PENH
◉ PROVINCIAL CAPITALS
• MAJOR SETTLEMENTS
· MINOR SETTLEMENTS

Map Data: Compiled from 1920-1953
topographic sheets of the Service
Géographique de l'Indochine, 1: 100,000.

SCALE

SOURCE OF BASE MAP DATA:
PROVINCIAL BOUNDARIES · 1954 AMS L401 1:400,000
INTERNATIONAL BOUNDARIES · 1944 AAF AERONAUTICAL CHARTS 1:1,000,000

cultivable, whereas more than three-fourths of Cambodia's land is, including the lightly populated and lightly exploited forests and high plateaus. In 1955 Cambodia's population density was approximately 78 people per square mile; 1952 figures for comparable lands were 72 in Burma and 97 in Thailand, 289 in India, 535 in the United Kingdom, and 601 in Japan.

It has been estimated that Cambodia could easily absorb an additional two million people. Immigration and citizenship laws have, accordingly, been liberal. In December 1955 Sihanouk signed a Treaty of Amity with the Japanese government which included among other things an agreement granting facilities to immigrants. It was contemplated that 2,000 Japanese would be sent over a period of five years to settle, cultivate, and exploit the mountain areas and wastelands where Cambodians have always refused to live. Sihanouk, in a policy speech to the National Assembly on April 21, 1956, stated: "We later want to settle people in the frontier zones in order to prevent the Vietnamese from penetrating our territory." Early in 1956 a Japanese mission charged with studying conditions for the settling of Japanese immigrants arrived in Cambodia, but there is no further information as to developments.

After the Trade and Payments Agreement between Cambodia and Communist China in April 1956, it was reported that a great many Chinese sought exit visas to Hong Kong and Macao. There is no evidence that any sizable exodus of Chinese actually occurred, however, and some slight evidence to the contrary is supplied by the fact that total declared births among the Chinese population rose steadily throughout the following year.

Most of Cambodia's 4.7 million inhabitants live along the rivers. Only 11 percent of the estimated 1950 total population was located in the 14 provincial capital cities (see Table 3).

A small number of fishermen, largely Malay and Vietnamese, live along the coast and on the islands that dot the southern coast of Cambodia near Ream and Kep. In the high Moi Plateaus to the east live the Phnong (literally, savages—so-called by the Cambodians). Other tribal minorities live in the Cardamom, Elephant, and Dangrek mountains.

The Khmer, or Cambodians proper, representing 85 to 90 percent of the population, are the major ethnic group (see chap. 4). They are largely farmers, located either in southern Cambodia or in the region that parallels the Mekong between the southern Vietnam border and the province of Stungtreng. The Chinese, generally traders and merchants, and the Vietnamese, usually fishermen and rubber plantation workers but also artisans and merchants, live in the major cities—chiefly Pnompenh and Battambang—or in the larger villages. Each represents about 5 percent of the population. The other 2 or 3 percent of the population, scattered over the country, include Thai, Laotians, Cham-Malays, Europeans, Indians, Pakistani, Japanese, Filipinos, and the tribal hill peoples. The hill people live by hunting and some crude rice agriculture based on on the *ray*, the slash-and-burn method. They usually establish only temporary settlements and move as local resources become depleted.

In recent years Chinese and Vietnamese have migrated in substantial numbers to Cambodia and have intermarried with the Khmer to some extent. Legal Vietnamese migration, however, has been at a virtual standstill since 1940; since 1949 the Chinese have no longer come directly from China—though they continued to migrate by way of Vietnam until 1951, and from Hong Kong. Illegal entries have occurred constantly.

Between 1952 and 1954, as a security measure against the Communists, about 10 percent of the population were removed from areas close to the fighting zones in the south to new homes along roads or in urban areas. This unsettling of hundreds of thousands of people, many of them Khmer as well as Vietnamese, and the change in their settlement patterns from inland groupings to settlements dotted along the roads resulted in a drift to the large cities and has tended to swell the urban population, changing its character and ethnic ratios. The drastic failure of the rice crop in 1954 also tended to crowd rural peoples into urban areas. This over-all trend has continued. The population of Pnompenh, for example, has rapidly increased since World War II. Some contributing factors have been: natural increase in 1952 as much as 20 percent, in 1953, 35 percent; a lower death rate reflecting improved health conditions; immigration from outside Cambodia; and resettlement from rural areas, particularly as a result of dislocations caused by the Indochina hostilities.

In late 1958, the Ministry of Planning published the results of a preliminary demographic survey carried out by one of its agencies, the office of the Director of Statistics and Economic Surveys. This survey showed, for the first time, a breakdown of the over-all population census by sex and by age in five-year intervals, but not, however, by ethnic group. Working within the limits of this survey data, the average birth rate was estimated at 45 live births per 1,000 per year, and the average fertility rate at 117 children (5 years of age and over) per 100 females (20-44 years). The figures also indicate that Cambodia has one of the youngest populations in the world, along with a high mortality rate and a short life expectancy. Direct statistics of birth and death were not collected, in part at least because of inadequacies in the registration procedures, but the same agency is now engaged in a more detailed and thorough census which is expected to produce more precise results.

ETHNIC GROUPS AND LANGUAGES

APPROXIMATELY 85 TO 90 PERCENT of Cambodia's population of 4,740,000 people are Cambodians (or Khmer); about 5 percent are Vietnamese, another 5 percent Chinese, and the remaining 2 or 3 percent consist of Cham-Malays, Europeans, Japanese, Indians and Pakistani, Thai, Laotians, Filipinos, and tribal hill peoples (see Map, Ethnic Distribution).

The majority the Khmer enjoy in numbers and in political strength lends a large measure of homogeneity to the ethnic composition of the country. The minority groups, however, though small numerically, play an important role in Cambodian economic life. The Vietnamese in Cambodia from time to time become a critical political problem; the Chinese an economic one. The Cham-Malays are an example of Moslem religious autonomy in an overwhelmingly Buddhist atmosphere. How the rights and aspirations of the smaller ethnic units are to be reconciled with the Khmer demands for a higher loyalty poses a serious problem. As long as the sharp separation of power along ethnic lines continues—the Chinese and Vietnamese in the economic sphere, the Khmer in the political sphere—potential friction will remain a deterrent to rapid realization of Cambodian (Khmer) nationalism (see chap. 6; chap. 23; chap. 24).

Cambodian is the dominant language of daily social intercourse. Vietnamese and, to a lesser extent, Chinese are the lingua franca of the market place. Cambodians hold their own language aloof from such unsavory and boisterous demonstrations as bargaining, using Vietnamese when haggling over quoted prices with the Vietnamese and Chinese merchants. French is still the accepted language in government, intellectual, and professional circles, though a determined effort is being made to replace it—a symbol

ETHNIC DISTRIBUTION

ETHNIC CAMBODIANS (KHMER)

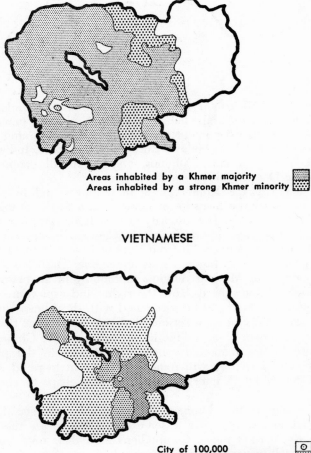

Areas inhabited by a Khmer majority
Areas inhabited by a strong Khmer minority

VIETNAMESE

City of 100,000
Area with 30,000 to 50,000
Areas with 15,000 to 30,000
Areas with less than 15,000

ETHNIC DISTRIBUTION

CHINESE AND CHAM-MALAYS

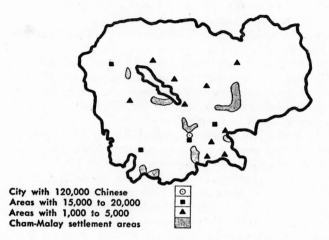

City with 120,000 Chinese
Areas with 15,000 to 20,000
Areas with 1,000 to 5,000
Cham-Malay settlement areas

THAI AND LAO MINORITIES AND HILL TRIBES

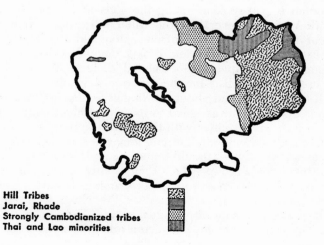

Hill Tribes
Jarai, Rhade
Strongly Cambodianized tribes
Thai and Lao minorities

of colonial rule—by the native Cambodian language. It has been estimated that approximately 10 percent of the population is bilingual in French and Cambodian. Cambodians do not pay particular attention to dialects in their language. There are, however, as in all languages, some dialect regions that are more distinct than others; the northwest provinces of Cambodia, for example, have easily identified dialects.

Pali and Sanskrit are both confined to the Buddhist community. Pali is the sacred language of Theravada Buddhism and appears in religious texts and incantations. Some Cambodians understand Pali, but only those permanently in the bonzehood are able to write it. Sanskrit is reserved almost exclusively for religious scholarship. Pali and Sanskrit serve as sources for the formation of technical and scientific terms in Cambodian.

The Cambodian language, called Khmer by its speakers, was once distributed over a far-flung territory that encompassed the entire Mekong valley, the present-day states of Thailand, Laos, and Cambodia, and a portion of South Vietnam (formerly Cochin China). The boundaries of this territory have receded since the thirteenth century under the impact of Thai cultural invasions and as a result of the annexation of Cochin China by the Vietnamese.

Today the Cambodian language extends beyond the national frontiers of Cambodia a short way into Laos; there are also Cambodian speakers to the north in southern Thailand. To the east, Cambodian is still spoken among the 450,000 Cambodians settled in South Vietnam. Several of the tribal hill groups—among them the Pear and Kuoy in the Pursat region and the Stieng in the upper basins of the Song Pe and Prek Chlong—have been identified by ethnologists as speakers of related dialects, the term Khmer being used by specialists for the group as a whole.

All that can be said about the linguistic classification of Cambodian is that it can be assigned to the Mon-Khmer language stock, which in turn has affinities with the Munda languages of India.

Members of Cambodia's ethnic minorities are bilingual and in some cases multilingual. In addition to being fluent in the language of their own ethnic group—which they usually reserve for use within the family circle—most can speak Cambodian and some, especially the educated Vietnamese, speak French as well.

The principal minority languages are Vietnamese, Chinese, Cham, Thai, and the languages of the hill tribe minorities: Rhade, Jarai, Kuoy, Stieng, Samre, Saoch, Pear.

Information in Cambodia is still diffused largely by word of mouth, but this emphasis on the unwritten word has not weakened literacy standards. Absolute illiteracy is rare among the male segment of the population, even among the more isolated peasants. Most Cambodian boys learn at the pagoda school to read and, more or less awkwardly, to write the Cambodian letters. Girls, however, are not admitted to the pagoda school and must rely on tutoring in the household to attain literacy. Lower-class women can rarely afford this luxury.

The Khmer

The Khmer once dominated the entire Mekong delta, but these holdings have been narrowed by Vietnamese conquest in the east and Thai occupation in the west. Although they form close to 90 percent of the total population, the Khmer today constitute only a third of the population of Pnompenh and are eager to regain their capital from "foreign hands"—meaning the Chinese, Vietnamese, and French.

The modern Khmer are the end-product of countless centuries of intricate cultural and racial blending. The origin of the ancient Khmer is obscure, the archeology of Southeast Asia being imperfectly known. Archeological research shows only that Indochina was inhabited in the Neolithic period by at least three racial types —Negrito, proto-Melanesian, and Indonesian (proto-Malay). The proto-Melanesian and Indonesian types are still in evidence among the tribal hill groups in Cambodia.

The Khmer were already racially complex before arriving in Southeast Asia, having moved down from a northwest direction into the corridors of Cambodia prior to 2000 B.C., displacing the Chams in the fertile Mekong delta. At the beginning of the Christian era the Khmer came into more direct contact with the indigenous peoples of Indonesian stock already living in what is now Cambodia and drove them into the less favorable mountain zones.

Cambodia was Hinduized by successive waves of migrations from India starting in the third century B.C. This process, with its concomitant racial mixture, reached its climax in the ninth and tenth centuries A.D. In the eighth century Cambodia underwent an Indo-Malay invasion from Java. From the tenth to the fifteenth centuries occurred the great Thai migrations into Cambodia which resulted in the depopulation of Angkor. In more recent history the physical make-up of Cambodians has been affected by the movement of Vietnamese and Chinese into Cambodia from Vietnam. A new type, the Eurasian, has been added since the late nineteenth century.

As a result of this varied racial admixture to the Khmer stock, today's Khmer show wide variations in physical traits. For example, though normal skin color is bronze, pigmentation may vary from light brown to deep tan. Racial mixture is more evident in the cities, where Chinese ancestry is especially noticeable, than in the rural areas.

Compared to the Vietnamese, the Khmer are darker, slightly taller (average, 5'4"), and more robust; and their noses are flatter. The typical Khmer has oval eyes and wavy hair, which both sexes wear close-cropped, sometimes making it difficult to distinguish males and females from a distance.

Two body types based on traditional Hindu classification—the "ox" and the "deer"—are distinguished by the Khmer. The "ox" type can be identified as somewhat tall, with muscular build, a sensual face, full shoulders, and thick ankles. These traits are usually associated with peasants, especially peasant women who have a tendency to grow stout through the years. The "deer" type is more slender in build and nervous in temperament and is supposed to be a product of the urban environment. "Deer" women are long-necked, small-breasted, thin, and above all supple; they retain, even in advanced age, extraordinarily elegant figures. The extremes of the "ox" and "deer" types can be seen in the brawny farmer and the frail, delicate royal dancing girls in Pnompenh.

The ideal physical type for the female is "deer"—for the male, "ox." In reverse: "deer" features in men and "ox" features in women are considered repulsive. The taller and more muscular the male Khmer is, the handsomer he is considered; the more petite and graceful the Khmer woman, the more alluring. Wide-open eyes are considered an indication of intelligence and power; any semblance of the Mongolian fold is aesthetically unappealing. Daily Khmer garb consists of any odd assortment that happens to be handy. Both men and women prefer the *sampot*, a loose-fitting garment wrapped around the waist and tucked through the legs. Khmer women sometimes wear a sarong-type skirt which is suspended from the breasts. The more elegant *sampots* are made of silk; those for work are usually patchworks of cotton rags.

Yellow and ocher are sacred colors—especially used for the robes of the Buddhist monk. Native silks are rich in texture and color; silvery-blue and golden-green *sampots*, crimson bodices, red-gilt and orange sashes are seen. Khmer cotton cloth is usually hand woven and may be dyed black, prune, olive, or oxblood red. Tailored vests, short trousers, and long-sleeved tunics are popular among the rural folk. Bright-colored ornaments and glittering jewelry are prized by little girls and women.

Loose-draped, turban-like headgear is used by both sexes as protection against an uncompromising sun. The men seem to be also partial to the felt hats sold by Chinese peddlers—hats that are soon misshaped by the effects of the sun and rain and are then cut into bonnets.

In remote rural sections the women prefer to work in the fields naked from the waist up. The plump Khmer boys scamper around nude but Buddhist religion requires some coverage for the girls.

The semiautonomous, self-sufficient settlements of between 200 and 300 people in which the Khmer generally live are found in all accessible parts of lowland Cambodia—along the rivers or wherever water supply and drainage conditions favorable to rice cultivation exist. Their thatched (sometimes tin-roofed) dwellings are similar to those of the Chinese and Vietnamese but stand 3 to 6 feet above the earth on piling.

Most Khmer live on and work their own land, often combining agriculture and fishing. Those who engage in fishing as an exclusive occupation nevertheless do so only to the extent of meeting the subsistence requirements of their own families. Among their French, Chinese, and Vietnamese neighbors, the Khmer are regarded as indifferent farmers, poor traders, uninspired fishermen, and unreliable laborers.

Even the larger Khmer landholders cannot match the prosperity of the Chinese and Sino-Cambodians. The Khmer are not attached as Chinese and Japanese peasants are to a particular tract of land, and resettlement programs in recent years have presented no serious morale difficulties for the Cambodian government. The Chinese and Vietnamese have labeled the Khmer inferior cultivators and chronic vagrants. Khmer internal migrations, however, have on occasion been the result of the dislocating effects of invasion.

When the Cambodian government recently began resettling war-displaced rural populations in urban areas a sizable number of Khmer successfully switched to new occupations. Rice mills and distilleries were formerly operated exclusively by the Chinese; an increasing number are now under Khmer ownership. The Khmer are beginning to play a more active role in trade and transportation, furthering the nationalist objective of wresting economic control from the Chinese and Vietnamese. Movement to the cities has also made the Khmer increasingly available for industrial employment.

In the political sphere the Khmer retain their decidedly upper hand. Besides monopolizing succession to the throne, they occupy nearly all of the important positions of government administration.

The Vietnamese

Nowhere in Cambodia do the Vietnamese form a clear-cut provincial majority. In the areas of heaviest concentration there is little hint that numbers alone pose a potentially explosive situation. Yet the presence of Vietnamese in the southern Cambodian provinces, as well as the Cambodians in South Vietnam, have been and can again be exploited politically.

The earliest Vietnamese colony in Cambodia dates from the late seventeenth century when the Empire of Viet-Nam occupied large tracts of the country. Since then the Vietnamese have earned a reputation as poachers on Cambodian soil. Under constant military pressure from the north, they have in the course of history shifted progressively southward, spilling over into South Vietnam (formerly Cochin China) and the southern Cambodian provinces.

In the last quarter of the nineteenth century they migrated into Cambodia in a steady stream and came to dominate the more fertile agricultural sites along the river banks from Pnompenh to Stungtreng and from Battambang to Chaudoc, incurring the resentment, usually passive, of Khmer peasants. By establishing a protectorate over Cambodia in 1864, the French halted Vietnamese military aggrandizement but provided protective legal cover and economic incentive for large-scale Vietnamese movements into Cambodia. This policy was designed to fill the ranks of a newly created French colonial civil service and to secure a reliable labor force for French owned and operated rubber plantations. It is not surprising that the Vietnamese population has doubled since the turn of the century and is today estimated at about 300,000.

Displacement rather than social assimilation and integration has been the standard ethnic pattern of Vietnamese settlement in Cambodia, particularly in the rural districts. More often than not, the Khmer peasants have abandoned their traditional settlements in the face of Vietnamese encroachments. Where the Vietnamese have moved in, the Khmer have moved out.

The Vietnamese are smaller in body structure and typically

Mongoloid in hair color and facial features—jet black hair, Mongolian eye fold, broad heads, high cheek bones. They average 61-62 inches in height and 110-130 pounds in weight. Body hair is sparse.

Vietnamese dress is distinctive. Both sexes wear wide, loose trousers reaching to the ankles and a robe, split at the sides, which in the case of city dress hangs down over the trousers to the knee for the men and to the ankle for the women. In the fields a Vietnamese farmer wears a short jacket instead of the robe.

The Vietnamese are bilingual in the agricultural areas (Vietnamese and Cambodian) and often trilingual (adding French) in urban professional circles. They are, however, rarely fluent in Cambodian. In the urban centers, especially Pnompenh where they constitute 30 percent of the population, the Vietnamese earn their livelihood as skilled artisans, petty merchants, and professionals (doctors and dentists); in the countryside, as rice farmers and plantation laborers.

Vietnamese are also industrious fishermen. Their fishing villages stretch along the banks of the Mekong and several floating colonies dot the shores of the Tonle Sap, the dwellings supported by pontoons or sampans. The Vietnamese living in these colonies migrate seasonally but even under such mobile conditions maintain the established order of their daily community life. Of the 20,000 Vietnamese who subsist on the rich resources of the Tonle Sap, many are at the mercy of the Chinese lessees who hold fishing rights and of ever-present Chinese moneylenders (see chap. 14).

In the larger cities Vietnamese administrative clerks and domestic servants in favored contact with westernized officials tend to snub their peasant countrymen. Generally, the Vietnamese in Cambodia are commercially ambitious and push themselves forward in a way that irks most Khmer. Chinese in Cambodia, too, disrespect the Vietnamese, who always look to them for leftover scraps of business. The Vietnamese manage also to squeeze into the empty occupational cracks of Cambodian society as clerks, small shopkeepers, and factotums.

While the Khmer have more or less accepted commercial exploitation by the Chinese—apparently feeling that it is somewhat natural—they find the same treatment by the Vietnamese highly objectionable. The Khmer describe the Vietnamese as "vagrants and sellers of anything." Temperamentally Vietnamese are viewed as malcontent, insolent without justification, hysterical, and—even more obnoxious to Cambodians—boisterous. Khmer are quick to

believe that Vietnam rids itself of undesirables by sending them
to Cambodia and generally look upon the Vietnamese in Cambodia
as fringe members of society.

Recently the high birth rate of the Vietnamese has loomed
as a new barrier to smooth ethnic relations. The Khmer are now
fearful of internal population expansion from the Vietnamese at
the same time that they cast an anxious eye toward Vietnam's
hunger for Cambodian territory as a relief of the pressures brought
about by refugees from north of the 17th parallel.

In the past, ethnic discord has been exploited as a matter of
military and political expediency. During World War II, for
instance, the Japanese backed Vietnamese minority claims in
pursuance of a divide-and-rule policy.

The Vietnamese are also suspected of political activity in
Cambodia: though conclusive proof is lacking, they were said to
have supported Son Ngoc Thanh (of Vietnamese-Khmer parentage)
in his 1946 bid for power. Vietnamese are also alleged to have encouraged Vietminh thrusts into Cambodian territory (see chap. 8).

In summary, friction between the Vietnamese and Khmer in
Cambodia is tied to a long history of political contention and
accentuated by periodic reports of discriminations against the
respective ethnic minorities on both sides of the border. The wedge
that has been driven between the two peoples has inhibited cultural exchange and ethnic assimilation. With the Khmer once
again in political control of their country it is possible that grievances and distrust will be translated into discriminatory action.

The Chinese

There is one fundamental difficulty connected with any census of
Cambodia's resident Chinese. The ethnic category "Chinese" is
indistinct; it can be inclusive or exclusive of the Sino-Cambodians,
the products of Khmer-Chinese intermarriage. Nonetheless, the
number of pure Chinese was conservatively estimated at 275,000
in 1955. The distribution pattern shows that the majority live in
urban districts. Approximately 130,000 Chinese (30 percent of the
city's population) are located in Pnompenh, itself a mosaic of ethnic
groups. Elsewhere the Chinese live principally in the cities of
Oudong, Kampot, Battambang, and Kompong Chhnang. The remainder, itinerant merchants or "general store" proprietors, are
scattered throughout rural Cambodia. Nowhere are they forcibly
segregated. Because Chinese customarily form the nucleus of trade,

the number of Chinese shops and the volume of their trade serve as reliable indicators of community growth. In recent years there has been a steady flow of Chinese into the urban centers from the outlying regions to escape Vietminh and Issarak intimidation and extortion practices.

Chinese colonization in Cambodia has been going on for a long time. Waves of Chinese migrations originated mainly in the southern China provinces of Kwangtung, Fukien, and Hainan, the immigrants embarking at the ports of Canton, Amoy, and Hoihow. The influx into Cambodia between 1949 and 1953 of Chinese who had planned to settle in Vietnam—can be traced to political unrest in Vietnam. The largest number have entered Cambodia via the Vietnamese port of Cholon as traders on temporary visas. During the colonial period incoming Chinese were screened by French authorities and the infiltration of Communist Chinese was minimized.

The Chinese in Cambodia follow their well-known inclination toward clannishness and are organized in associations (*bang*) according to home province and dialect affiliation; these dialects are mutually unintelligible.

Linguistically, the Chinese are bilingual. Many speak Cambodian as a second language, especially in commercial intercourse, reserving Chinese for the family circle. Private Chinese schools are required by law to teach the Cambodian language.

The Tiechieu dialect group predominates (60 percent—165,000), followed in numerical order by the Cantonese (20 percent—55,000), the Hokkienese (7 percent—19,000), and the Hakka and Hailam (4 percent each—22,000). These dialect groups mark not only lines of occupational specialization but also lines of intragroup competition and tension. The diversity of dialects prevents the development of a Chinese in-group and produces different rates of assimilation which tend to split the Chinese community.

Occupationally, the Chinese excel as bankers, moneylenders, speculators, entrepreneurs, contractors, retail merchants, and transporters. Found wherever there is merchandise to be sold and a few riels to be made, they prosper in Cambodia as in many other parts of Southeast Asia. Even the lean and penniless immigrant Hainan coolies soon flourish. If Cambodia can be said to have a newly rich or genuine middle class, it is the Chinese. By and large they have a firm grip on Cambodia's retail trade and, as rice brokers, on the wholesale markets; by default, virtual monopoly over coastal fishing has gone to the Chinese. Except for those who are pepper planters near Hatien in the province of Kampot, proportionately few have turned to the cultivation of staple crops as the primary means of subsistence. This is not to say that the Chinese do not retain and lease agricultural land. The Khmer peasant frequently finds himself in debt to a Chinese moneylender. At this level Khmer-Chinese antagonisms become most severe.

Occupational guilds, coinciding for the most part with the dialect groups, have been established as mutual benefit societies and as a means of tightening cooperation in the face of trade restrictions imposed by the French and Cambodians. The head of each guild is elected by popular vote and functions as an intermediary between the Cambodian government and the members of his *bang*. Control within the *bang* is maintained in conformity with Chinese customary law; this is actually a minor form of extraterritoriality. As noncitizens the Chinese are exempt from military draft.

The fragmentation of the Chinese population into the *bang* has weakened the Chinese position in Cambodia and has tended to play up internal discord within their ranks. It also has prevented any Chinese political ascendancy.

Attitudes toward Chinese

Cambodians harbor ambivalent attitudes toward the Chinese. They are admired and envied for their economic talents and personal wealth, but all the more resented as the Cambodians grow increasingly conscious of their own economic impotence. Yet, because of their reputation for industry and financial shrewdness, Chinese are eagerly sought as marriage partners. In Khmer eyes, the Chinese male is a superb breadwinner and many Cambodian fathers dream of a Chinese son-in-law. The Cambodian preference for light skin pigmentation (Cambodian complexion is normally darker than Chinese) has also worked as a factor favoring intermarriage among the two groups, as has the belief that such intermarriage tends to strengthen the Cambodian ethnic stock.

The Chinese in Cambodia are law-abiding and careful to stem any adverse criticism, but are otherwise apathetic to events in the surrounding Khmer community. They have adapted imperceptibly and inoffensively to local conditions and customs, always respectful of the religion, superstitions, and biases of the Khmer among whom they live.

In some ways the Khmer and Chinese are direct opposites. Chinese tend to be thrifty, persevering, self-controlled, and realistic; Khmer, lackadaisical, free-willed, and easily taken with fantasy.

The Khmer view the Chinese as quick-witted and intelligent if not always wise and stable.

Cambodia is reputed to be a paradise for swindlers, and to many Cambodians the Chinese seem the stereotype of the crafty and greedy merchant. But Cambodians seem favorably inclined toward the Chinese ethnic group as a whole.

Cambodia is faced with the classic Southeast Asian problem of Chinese economic power under the roof of native political control. The Cambodian government has openly refused equal civil rights for the Chinese. They remain second-class residents. So far the twofold pressure, economic and political, on the Chinese community has not been strong enough to produce fanaticism, extreme intolerance, or overt disturbances. Since independence, however, the Cambodian government has actively encouraged native businessmen to replace the Chinese—part of the attempt to win back commercial initiative. A policy of infringement on basic Chinese interests could lead to the consolidation of the *bang* and guild units and to the creation of a united ethnic front by Cambodia's Chinese population. Feelings on both sides could become heated, producing acts of outright discrimination.

But in spite of majority attitudes toward the Chinese and deterrent domestic policies, it is conceivable that the process of cultural assimilation will move steadily forward and that the ultimate solutions to minority problems will be found in assimilation.

The Cham-Malays

The Cham-Malays rank fourth in numerical size among Cambodia's ethnic groups. In 1955 the combined estimate of Chams and Malays was about 73,000, or one percent of the total population.

The Chams were militarily expelled from the ancient kingdom of Champa in the fifteenth century, and many of the vanquished preferred exile in Cambodia to servitude and humiliation under the Vietnamese. They were later brought to a rigorous Moslem orthodoxy by the invading Malays, who penetrated Kampot and interior regions. This early contact marked the formation of joint Cham-Malay communities. Today, the two groups are almost completely assimilated, with the one exception of language, but both belong to the Malayo-Polynesian linguistic family.

Though the Cham-Malays have lived side by side with the Khmer for centuries, long adherence to the Koranic law prohibiting marriage outside the Moslem community has resulted in the evolution of a noticeably different physical type. Cham-Malays typically have coarse skin varying in color from a dark to a reddish brown. Their hair is auburn or black and they have more facial and body hair than the Khmer. Of all Asian groups, the Cham-Malays have the most nearly occidental facial profile. Only in height are Cham-Malays and Khmer the same: both average 5'4".

Cham-Malays are fairly fluent speakers of Cambodian but their use of the language often has a "pidgin" quality. Malay is used in all religious contexts. The Chams still retain the ancestral Cham language, but mainly as an oral tradition. The Arabic alphabet, learned at the Koran school, is used in writing the language. Cambodian is the second language for purposes of trade and commerce.

By all indications—the care of their mosques, the exactitude of their prayers, their fidelity to Koranic precepts, their direct links with the Islamic world—Cham-Malays seem to be Moslem zealots. About 7 percent of them have completed the coveted pilgrimage to Mecca and are allowed to wear the fez or turban as a sign of this accomplishment. The others are haunted by desire for the pilgrimage and direct their lives and fortunes to this end. In recent years air transport, though expensive, has facilitated the pilgrimages.

The *batik* (Malay sarong similar to the *sampot*) knotted at the center is the main item of Cham-Malay clothing. The women continue to wear the ancestral black or dark green tunic open at the throat and closely fitted, with tight sleeves. The men's costume includes a shirt and an elongated robe extending to the ankles. Flamboyant colors are popular—for instance, red and green striping on white background.

Most Cham-Malays live in compact villages north and east of Pnompenh, mainly those in Kompong Cham province. They are also located in cities where they enter into trade and industry. In rural areas they are oriented toward fishing, agriculture, commerce, water transportation, and cattle breeding. Chrui Changvra, located in the vicinity of Pnompenh, is a typical settlement and enjoys some reputation among Cambodia's Cham-Malays as a spiritual center in view of the presence there of certain high Moslem personages. Among these dignitaries is the Supreme Chief of the Chams, who is appointed by the king and is considered equal in rank to members of the Royal Court. For historical reasons the Cham-Malays are accustomed to a certain amount of royal favor: a solicitous attitude is implicit in the government guarantees of their right to worship as they please and to adhere to their traditional customs. Privately, however, most Khmer consider Cham-Malays cultural and religious inferiors.

Through relatively favorable contact with the Khmer, the Cham-Malays have been brought into the circuit of modern life. Their children are gradually entering Franco-Cambodian schools and the adults are beginning to take their place in public life as nurses, midwives, interpreters, and secretaries.

Almost all Cham-Malays have adopted many aspects of Khmer culture. Even the Moslem mosques have taken on the architectural design of the Buddhist pagoda. Their adherence to the Moslem faith has not detracted from participation in Cambodian cultural life; assured of religious tolerance, the Cham-Malays have turned openly toward their protectors.

Sino-Cambodians and Eurasians

As noted, intermarriage of Khmer and Chinese is a frequent occurrence in Cambodia and has done much to strengthen relations between the two groups. Marriage with a Chinese man affords financial security and higher socioeconomic status for the Khmer family involved. In status and prestige, the Sino-Cambodians—products of Chinese fathers and Khmer mothers—rank above the Eurasians (French-Cambodians). A widely held belief among the Khmer is that the offspring of a Khmer-Chinese union combine the most vigorous qualities of both groups. The general attitude is that non-Chinese genetic strains upset the purity of original Khmer attributes. Many Cambodians boast of being "pure" Sino-Cambodians.

In 1921 there were approximately 68,000 Sino-Cambodians. Up-to-date statistics are unavailable because the government assumes that after two or three generations Sino-Cambodians either blend into the Khmer population or consider themselves Chinese. The Chinese population in Cambodia has been preponderantly male, but even with the recent introduction of Chinese women the Chinese husband often takes at least one Khmer woman as a concubine.

In the past twenty years intermarriage of "pure" Chinese and "pure" Khmer has been steadily decreasing. The newly arrived Chinese and the younger generation prefer to marry only Sino-Cambodians or pure Chinese. Consequently the Sino-Cambodians are being absorbed, largely by the Khmer population but also, to a certain extent, by wealthy Chinese families.

The size of the Eurasian population in Cambodia is uncertain.

The earliest Eurasians were probably descendants of Portuguese and Filipino mixtures driven out of Malacca in the seventeenth century. They have since lost all trace of European physiognomy but retain Portuguese and Spanish family names—e.g., Men de Diez, Col de Monteiro, Norodom Fernandez. They play an influential role in Cambodian administration.

Eurasians of the present day are almost exclusively the offspring of French or French-African fathers and Cambodian mothers (Eurasian is somewhat of a misnomer for those with African fathers). True Eurasians are exclusively city dwellers and are most often employed in white-collar occupations.

Not all have been successful in surmounting the color bar. In the past Eurasians have pressed for equality with and acceptance by the French, who do not always regard them as compatriots. On the other hand Eurasians tend to reject identification with Cambodians. Thus, Eurasians in Cambodia, as in other parts of Southeast Asia, are marginal beings and move in a social vacuum. Only the Catholic missions have consistently and unconditionally received them at orphanages and educational institutions. Intermarriage with Eurasians is looked upon as thinning racial vigor.

Other Minorities

The European and minor Asian populations, numbering about 4,500 in 1950, include besides the French small numbers of Italians, Germans, Filipinos, Japanese, Thai, Laotians, and Burmese. There has been a decrease in the number of Europeans in Cambodia since 1936. The majority of Europeans and Asiatic foreigners are located in the urban centers.

Cambodia's approximately 1,500 European French constitute an impermanent population of military personnel, government officials, commercial executives, and plantation administrators. The French influence on Cambodian society, through French-sponsored education and French government planning, has been profound—particularly in intellectual and professional circles, where admiration for French culture was long the rule. Being further removed from French cultural activity, Cambodia's peasants and nobility were much less affected. The educated classes have become increasingly critical of the French in recent years, however, charging for example that French emphasis on the revitalization of traditional Cambodian culture has been at the expense of progress toward other objectives. There is growing realization that the cause of nationalism must be identified with Cambodian, not French, values.

Pailin, ten miles from the Thailand frontier, and Bokeo, in Stungtreng province, are two exclusively Burmese settlements. Here the Burmese are prospectors, jewel cutters, and gem merchants. They have a reputation for being shiftless wasters and are always under suspicion as agents of violent crimes. They retain Burmese citizenship and receive no special concessions from the Cambodian government.

About 20,000 Thai and Laotians live peacefully as cultivators in the northern provinces of Siemreap and Battambang. They rarely live in the same communities as the Khmer.

Indians in Cambodia (2,500) have met with an unpopularity that can be attributed to their being identified by the Cambodians with French colonial policy and to their tendency to shady commercial dealings. Originating in French colonies on the Indian subcontinent, they migrated to Cambodia on the heels of the French as French citizens, and have taken advantage of their eligibility for favored positions in government and business. Cambodians have been especially incensed by the tactics of the *chettyar*, the moneylenders from southern India.

Tribal Groups

The forested highland plateaus and intermountain valleys of Cambodia are sparsely inhabited by an array of primitive tribal groups (54,000). They are collectively called Phnong (savages) by the Cambodians. None of the tribes, however, accepts this degrading term.

Although there is a similar folk tradition, Cambodians refuse to acknowledge any common origin or cultural affinity, no matter how remote, with the tribal groups. They prefer to consider themselves descendants of Hindu princes and are humiliated by any less dramatic interpretation of their heritage. Ethnological studies, on the other hand, reveal that Cambodians are perhaps little more than Hinduized Phnongs.

The tribal peoples are socially, politically, and economically outside the main stream of Cambodian life and culture. Their social organization is based essentially on kinship and they depend on slash-and-burn agriculture, hunting, and the gathering of forest products for subsistence.

The highland tribesmen are not entirely isolated from Cambodian society. Rather, they are restricted to subordinate roles, but as laborers and craftsmen have traditionally played an important part in the Cambodian economy and under French leadership served in the military forces with notable success. Because of cultural barriers, intermarriage with Cambodians has been relatively rare, although—upon questioning—a few Cambodians will admit to tribal ancestry.

The conditions of tribal life vary from region to region, depending on the available natural resources and the political arrangements of the local group, but the fabric of tribal society is surprisingly uniform. Each principal tribe is broken down into multiple clans based on kinship bonds. Intratribal clans are frequently bitter enemies involved in blood feuds that preclude any political hegemony on a tribal scale.

The highlanders range in body structure in some rough accordance with location of the tribe. The lower altitudinal plateaus are inhabited by a shorter, squattier type; the higher summit reaches by a taller, lankier type. Regardless of build, they are all vigorous and capable of great endurance. Many can be classed as genuine athletes. Skin color is normally reddish-brown; the nose straight or arched; hair, a glittering black, sometimes floating on the shoulders, sometimes gathered in a chignon. Members of the more bellicose tribes sport in their chignon locks of hair of fallen enemies.

The main article of dress for the men is the *longhouti,* a long narrow band of red or blue cloth wrapped several times around the waist and passed through the legs, hanging to the ground like a queue. In the more advanced tribes, the Rhade and Jarai, the men wear tunic jackets and small turbans. Women are more scantily covered than in the lowlands—usually wearing only a brief skirt and, on occasion, a sleeveless bodice. These rudimentary clothes are made of a coarse grass fiber and are ornamented with a border of simple geometric design.

A highlander never wanders far without his trusted weapons: a krislike sword with an extended, curved handle, and a lance of durable rattan. The bamboo crossbow with considerable projectory range is another familiar weapon. Arrow tips are rarely poisoned, though the preparation of venomous saps such as curare is known.

The highlander is primarily an agriculturalist and hunter. By no means can he be accurately called nomadic, in spite of the periodic shifting of hamlet and cultivation sites. With the depletion of the soil, the village usually fragments into hamlets which relocate as settlement blocks in a new locale approved beforehand by the sorcerer. Slash-and-burn agriculture involves a slow migration rhythm, and the rotation circuit frequently ends at the point of origin. Some large villages have not been uprooted in generations.

At any crisis period—such as the founding of a new settlement, embarking on a war venture, an epidemic, or the death of a village notable or courageous warrior—animal sacrifices are offered and the spirits courted. Sacrifices never occur without the consumption of large quantities of beer. These revels, in which men, women, and children participate, are accompanied by sonorous gong concerts.

Gongs are one of the few items eagerly sought from the lowlands and constitute the sole claim to personal wealth. Weapons are the only other private property. All other material goods are communally owned.

The highlander does not recognize any authority beyond his immediate village chief, the sorcerer, and celebrated warriors—personalities who stand out clearly for ingenuity, intelligence, and physical bravery and have come to command a personal prestige over the clan or village. These figures of authority should not be confused with native district chiefs appointed by the Cambodian government to act as agents for diffusing information from the lowlands and executing certain policies.

Some tribes follow a patrilineal kinship system, inheritance and kin relations being reckoned principally through the male line; others a matrilineal system.

Highlanders are very superstitious and are fervent animists. In constant apprehension of supernatural powers, they place their safety and destiny in the hands of the village sorcerer. At the slightest pretext a sorcerer can declare an entire village in quarantine, thereby prohibiting the intrusion of any outsider under penalty of death. Even European administrators have had to bend to such dire proclamations, realizing that it would be gross political folly to force an entrance into the community.

Dwellings, usually constructed on piles, can be either for individual family units or, in communities that support the longhouse institution, for the communal group. In the latter case, each family has its own partitioned section in the long house. Some of these communal dwellings exceed 300 feet in length. At the center is an interior plaza where bachelors and other unattached males are lodged and where communal ceremonies are conducted.

Rice granaries are constructed in the surrounding village area

and left unguarded except against marauding animals. Even on the
threshold of famine, highlanders never resort to pillaging food
supplies from adjacent communities. Such rules, however, are
canceled during periods of warfare.

Epidemics, especially smallpox, take a heavy toll of the native
population, decimating whole villages. Moreover, intermittent famine and complete lack of modern sanitation have induced pulmonic
and intestinal diseases among infants.

Specific Tribes

French physical anthropologists have divided the tribal population
into two broad racial types: an Indonesian type characterized by
comparatively light skin, long head, absence of the Mongolian
eye fold, and wavy to straight hair; and a Negroid type characterized by much darker skin, woolly to peppercorn hair, and somewhat shorter stature than the Indonesian type.

The Stieng, Samre, Saoch, and Pear tribal units have been
tentatively designated as Negroid and the Rhade and Jarai as
Indonesian, although this classification is by no means definitive.
The Rhade and Jarai speak Cham dialects, while the other tribes
speak dialects more directly related to Cambodian.

It is important to stress that the highlanders have little sense
of unity or loyalty beyond the village or clan. Most often it is the
village community that marks the limits of sociopolitical cohesion.

According to recent accounts, there are thirteen distinct tribal
groups in Cambodia. Brief notation of five of these is presented
here. Only fragmentary information is available on the remaining
eight tribes.

RHADE. The bulk of the Rhade are in the province of Banme-
thuot in the Darlac sector of Vietnam, but settlement overlaps into
Stungtreng province of Cambodia. The Rhade language is a dialect
of Cham. The Rhade have been depicted as longheaded, having
prominent cheekbones and a straight and low forehead; hair is
black and wavy; height varies from 5 feet 4 inches to 5 feet 7 inches;
bronze skin color is prevalent; eyes are brown and the Mongolian
eye fold is rare.

The Rhade are socially organized according to the matrilineal
extended family, property and inheritance rights being transmitted
through the female line. The typical residence group consists of a
mother, her female relatives, and their respective families grouped
in a long-house dwelling.

The village is the standard political unit—composed of a number of kin groups united by common purpose or fear of a powerful chief. Like all the Phnong groups, the Rhade cultivate dry rice by the slash-and-burn method.

J A R A I . The Jarai closely parallel the Rhade in physical appearance, language, and basic culture. That part of Jarai territory which lies in Cambodia is in the eastern section of Stungtreng province and extends as far north as the Cambodian-Laotian frontier. The Jarai must vary somewhat from the Rhade in height since the French traditionally recruited only Jarai taller than 5 feet 7 inches as foot soldiers and horsemen.

S T I E N G . The Stieng inhabit the forested sector south of Kratie. They speak a Mon-Khmer language and, according to a tenuous nineteenth century account, are of medium height, are quite dark in skin color, and sometimes have frizzy hair.

Stieng villages are governed by a council of notables or senior lineage heads and not by solitary chieftains. The Stieng are reputed to be capable elephant hunters and trainers. The Cambodian government has experimented with a reservation program (educational and economic) in Stieng territory, but the outcome of this program is still uncertain.

K U O Y . The Kuoy are widely distributed in northeastern Cambodia and are interspersed with Khmer settlements. No information is available on their physical characteristics.

They have been more influenced by Cambodian culture than any other tribal group and considerable intermarriage with Cambodians has taken place. They are industrious and have carved a niche for themselves in Khmer villages as iron forgers.

P E A R . Pear settlements stretch along the northern slopes of the Cardamom Mountains but Pear are also spottily found in the Kompong Thom area intermingled with the Kuoy tribesmen of the Dangrek chain and with lowland Khmer. Slavery has reduced them to a miserable economic state and they are rapidly disappearing as an identifiable ethnic group. With bulging foreheads, woolly hair, dark skin, and short stature, the Pear display Negroid features.

The Cambodian Language

Very little is known about the structure of Cambodian. In contrast with Vietnamese and Thai, Cambodian is a nontonal language—

that is, variations in pitch are not part of the basic sound structure of words. Cambodian has a monotone but staccato quality, with a rising inflection at the end of each sentence.

Most Cambodian words are short—usually one syllable, sometimes two—though Sanskrit and other foreign loanwords are often longer. There is said to be a "clipped" quality to Cambodian speech, possibly due to distinct breaks between the short words. Patterns of speech are often rhythmically stylized; Cambodians are extremely conscious of rhythmic phrasing and a very thin literary line separates an excellent piece of rhythmic prose from poetic verse. Restraint is not overly stressed in normal speech.

Writing

Cambodian is written in a system of characters that originated in southern India around the sixth century A.D. and was introduced into Cambodia with other aspects of Indian culture.

Efforts have been made to romanize the Cambodian language, but no uniform system has been agreed upon. The French made several attempts in this direction but met with stiff resistance from various religious quarters. Many bonzes felt that romanization would eventually crush traditional sacred teachings and consequently would infringe on Buddhist control over the people. As a result, the proposed plans for romanization were never implemented. What little romanization the French were able to accomplish is unsystematic, and the mechanics of transcription (diacritical marking, phonetic spelling, etc.) are not uniformly applied or generally understood.

The orthography of Cambodia is historical and does not accurately or consistently represent the language as spoken. An exact transliteration would therefore be misleading, and the romanizations used in this book are approximations of the pronunciation rather than reflections of the original Cambodian spelling.

Two printing styles of the Cambodian alphabet prevail today: *chrieng*, which may be roughly described as cuneiform (wedge-shaped) and is the ordinary style for formal announcements, administrative texts, books, and journals; and *mul*, which is cursive (with rounded strokes) and was once restricted to the transcription of Pali texts. The utilization of *mul*, however, has been extended more and more, and now includes both the capital letters of a title page and the "italicized" words in a *chrieng* text. It is also used for inscriptions on public buildings.

4. *The Cambodian Language*

The ordinary Cambodian peasant has great respect for writing, both for its sacred origin and for its magical potency: the spirits are supposed to be restrained or manipulated by talismanic inscriptions or tattooed formulas (see chap. 5). The Cambodian script has a decorative and artistic appeal, and the unsophisticated person derives pleasure from the orderliness of well-drawn letters. Even in the poorest huts, little pieces of yellow paper with nothing more than a simple greeting are pinned near the statue of Buddha.

Usage

It is not considered shameful to display emotions outwardly and they are on occasion mirrored in facial gesture and intonation. On the other hand, any hint of exaggeration or melodrama is considered capricious. Anger can be detected, as in English, by increased tempo of speech and a raised voice. Sorrow and sympathy are expressed by a low grumbling sound.

Witticisms and humorous retorts are considered conversational gems. In spite of a gentle temperament the Cambodian tends to have a sharp tongue, or at least his tongue in his cheek. Any talent for improvisation or impromptu versification is greatly admired and socially rewarding.

Cambodian lends itself to oratorical flourishes. Allegorical references occur profusely in conversation. It is advisable, however, for nonnatives to avoid these allegorical entanglements; the true implication of the allegory may be obscure. Cambodian has been called an ambiguous language in the sense that it contains innumerable "hidden" meanings. The Cambodians themselves, of course, respond to any number of linguistic cues so that the meaning is no longer "hidden." The inability of outsiders to decipher these sometimes elaborate linguistic cues accurately is one of the main obstacles to an understanding of Cambodian behavior.

In the Cambodian salutation, the hands are placed together and balanced at lip level while a half bow is executed. The higher the hands are postured, the greater the expression of deference. A child in the presence of a parent or an adult before his superior will repeat this gesture innumerable times. Repetitious bowing has been interpreted by some observers as a manifestation of nervousness.

Falling to one's knees or even knee-walking is not an uncommon sight at the pagoda or at the Royal Court. Knee-walking is performed ritually in royal dances.

The Chinese, Vietnamese, and Europeans tend to view such submissive and refined poses as evidence of inferiority and seldom conform to the prescribed conduct.

Certain greeting techniques are completely foreign to Cambodians and are forbidden. The friendly stroking of a child's head, for example, is generally considered not only impolite but downright injurious. Even parents have some apprehension about accidentally fingering a child's head. Cambodians believe that the "life-essence" or "soul stuff" of the individual is planted in the head and can be impaired by mere touching.

The most natural opening topic for conversation among Cambodians is the family, particularly the latest news on pregnancies. The correct formal position for conversation is to be seated, with legs bent to the left. Use of the hands to gesticulate is limited, and body contact of any sort—a slap on the back, for example—is considered crude.

When a woman converses with a man or when a man converses with someone of higher rank, courtesy calls for downcast eyes. The eyes of intimate friends and relatives, however, can and do exchange glances. In accord with Buddhist principles, a woman must never attract the gaze of a bonze or attempt to engage a bonze in conversation. Even as a bonze pauses in front of a doorway with his alms bowl extended, the Cambodian housewife makes her contribution in an atmosphere of complete restraint—her eyes downcast and her voice stilled.

In the course of conversation, anyone may interrupt a speaker without incurring social stigma, but disagreement with or sudden criticism of what has been said creates a certain amount of suspicion toward the challenger.

The mention of an individual's given name is avoided in ordinary speech for fear of drawing the attention of evil spirits and thereby inviting misfortune.

Status relationships are underscored by obligatory speech patterns. Royalty, holy men, and persons of other high station are accorded an honorific language reserved for them alone. An infraction of this ethical code is invariably interpreted as an insult and can incur sanctions of public shaming or can bring on the "freeze"—total lack of response, or the refusal of an interview—on the part of the offended individual.

Both within the family circle and in Cambodian society at large, age and sex distinctions are also observed. Children use respectful language in addressing their parents; parents resort to a curt, familiar language in conversation with children. The prefix *a* is generally directed at preadolescent children but takes on a scornful meaning in reference to an adult; it can be applied in giving orders to a criminal or prisoner, or in brusque censure of an adult for misbehavior. The same prefix becomes benevolent again when a master uses it paternally toward a servant, indicating that the servant is accepted on a par with the children of the household.

The prefix *neay* is most appropriate for minor officials. Titled and high-ranking individuals are addressed as *neak* or *luk* (lord); all Buddhist monks as *luk*. For members of the Royal Court, proper deference terms vary according to priority in the line of succession to the throne.

Young girls are *me* and women of humble birth are *neang*. Old people are categorically called *ta* (for males) and *yeay* (for females). In the event that the person to whom one is speaking is of lower social rank but in a higher respect-bracket due to age, it is considered mannerly to use the generalized terms *bong* (older brother) or *phaon* (older sister). As a general rule, younger people show respect for older people regardless of rank.

Certain liberties in speech are permitted within each peer group, but only between members of the same sex. Here stratification patterns are almost completely relaxed and individuals move through life in devoted friendship.

Politeness formulas and the language peculiar to each social class—"the language of the people," "the royal language," "the language of the bonzes," etc.—are instilled in the Cambodian child from an early age by his guru (see chap. 5).

Trends

Once Cambodia obtained its independence French became the symbol of the colonial era and the problem arose of how to translate French materials—administrative documents, texts, technical books—into Cambodian, a language rich in an everyday concrete vocabulary but poor in technical and metaphysical terms. Pali words are being used to form the new terms.

The majority of educated bonzes and the scholars at the Buddhist Institute—those responsible for this task—read the scientific, medical, agricultural, and literary journals issued from Bangkok. Relatively few bonzes can handle French adequately but many are familiar with Thai. The technical and scholarly vocabulary of the Thai journals also is almost exclusively based on Pali or Sanskrit.

By this wholesale borrowing from common sources, Cambodian and Thai tend to merge at the technical and abstract levels despite the fact that they belong to two basically different language families.

The Laotians, linguistically close to the Thai, also have drawn closer to the Cambodians for similar reasons, and the entire process of borrowing from Pali and Sanskrit has reinforced a consciousness of communality among these three Hinduized societies. A language community of this nature can facilitate cultural interchange and perhaps promote a degree of political cordiality.

As a symbol of political power, wealth, and social status, French continues to rank highest among foreign languages used in Cambodia, but, since 1950, there have been signs that English may in time replace it. Government workers and some bonzes have taken the initiative in learning it. Those who already had a grasp of French find English relatively easy. The majority of bonzes, who have never devoted themselves to the study of French, are faced with the initial jump from a Southeast Asian language to a western language but find English more useful for communication with coreligionists in, say, Japan.

RELIGION

THERAVADA BUDDHISM IS THE DOMINANT RELIGION in Cambodia, adhered to by nearly 90 percent of the population.

The second largest church is the Roman Catholic. According to the 1953 official Vatican statistics, Roman Catholics number 120,000 (Khmer and Vietnamese, mainly the latter) and are found principally in the southern provinces and the urban centers. There are 40,000 to 50,000 Catholics in Pnompenh and a Catholic cathedral was recently erected there. Catholic missions are located in Battambang, Banghi, Chlong, Kasthom, Kompong Cham, Kompong Chhnang, Kratie, Krauchmar, Prekpring, Preyveng, Pursat, Thomh Mau, Soairieng, and Takeo.

An American Unitarian mission that maintains a teacher-training school is established in Pnompenh. Baptist missions have been reported in Battambang and Siemreap provinces. Other than this, information about Protestant missions is lacking.

First-generation Chinese are generally Mahayana Buddhists and several Mahayana pagodas are maintained in Pnompenh. Their practices and beliefs are, however, barely distinguishable from those of the Theravada (or Hinayana) Buddhists and most Sino-Cambodians become Theravada Buddhists.

The Cham-Malay population, estimated at about 73,000 is Moslem and supports its own mosques, including three in Pnompenh.

Buddhism

Cambodia is part of the Theravada Buddhist orbit, which also includes Laos, Thailand, Burma, and Ceylon. Theravada Buddhism, a form of Hinayana Buddhism, reached Cambodia by way of

Thailand, following the earlier introduction by way of Vietnam of the Mahayana Buddhism of China. Great numbers of Cambodians embraced Theravada Buddhism and eventually it became the state religion.

Doctrine

For its devotees in Cambodia, Theravada Buddhism is a rational religion possessing a coherent philosophy; it is unquestionably conservative, neither inciting violence nor exciting passion. The sacred edicts that expound the Buddhist morality (written almost three centuries before the birth of Christ) stress charity and humility.

Theravada theology is contained in the Pali Canon. Pali, one of the literary languages of India, has become through the course of doctrinal evolution the sacred language of the Theravada Buddhists.

The fundamentals of the Buddhist doctrine are embodied in the Four Noble Truths (*Mahavagga*):

1.   Existence inevitably leads to unhappiness (*dukha*), which follows from the impermanence and disintegration of all living elements.

2.   Unhappiness is caused by desire (*tanha*); inherent in human nature, *tanha* causes man to become attached to the impermanent.

3.   Unhappiness can be avoided by the crushing of desire.

4.   Desire can be crushed by strict adherence to a prescribed moral path.

The First Noble Truth expresses very simply the equation of existence and sorrow.

> Birth is sorrow, senility is sorrow, sickness is sorrow, death is sorrow, union with that which one doesn't love is sorrow, separation from that which one loves is sorrow, not to achieve one's objectives is sorrow. . .

The Second and Third Noble Truths contain the heart of the whole doctrinal structure.

> It is the thirst for existence that leads the way from rebirth to rebirth, joined by pleasure which finds its satisfaction here and there—the thirst for existence, for pleasure, for impermanence.

> The extinction of this thirst by the complete annihilation of desire, in banishing desire, in renouncing it, in delivering oneself of it.

The Fourth Noble Truth charts the eightfold moral path that leads to an end of the thirst for existence: right understanding (of the sources of *dukha*); right motivation (the intent to eliminate the thirst for existence); right speech; right conduct; right vocation; right diligence; right alertness; and right concentration. Speech, conduct, and vocation are the backbone of Buddhist ethical and moral stature. Diligence, alertness, and concentration are the attributes necessary to achieve the Buddhist goal—nirvana: the ultimate reality, eternal serenity.

The constant preoccupation with *dukha* (unhappiness) absorbs the religious thoughts of Buddhists and is the underlying theme that gives Hinayana Buddhism, as practiced in Cambodia, its charactertisic stamp. The *dukha* motif should not be confused with fatalism. Spiritually, at least, death is not deliverance as much as the announcement of a new round of *dukha*. *Dukha,* however, is matched by the countervailing force—merit.

Man controls his own destiny by sheer will power, without the moral assistance of providence or predestination. Through proper behavior the Theravada Buddhist feels assured of an enriched reincarnation; the conditions of the next life hinge on his behavior in this one. A series of virtuous efforts pursued through a series of reincarnations contributes to nirvana—a state of sublime selflessness and the final deliverance from all earthly suffering. The Theravada Buddhist realizes that he can count only on his own endeavor. Thus "merit-making" can be viewed as a strong stimulant capable of motivating "meritorious" individual behavior. Within the framework of "meritorious" behavior other areas of behavior can be more readily understood.

The doctrinal formula of Theravada Buddhism can be restated as follows: that which a man is, is the fruit of what he has been. Each malicious deed or intent—or, for that matter, the failure to gain adequate merit in this life—carries a seed which germinates into misfortune in a later existence. Similarly, each adversity or misfortune encountered in the present life can be traced to some misdeed committed in an earlier one.

Numerous interpretations of nirvana have been proposed, but the Buddhist scriptures, in the absence of a precise declaration from Buddha, throw little light on the subject. One point alone is certain—nirvana is the end of reincarnation. When the Buddhist has fully embraced the truth concerning *dukha,* he casts off not only all desire to live, but also all desire not to live. Thus the circuit of rebirths is severed.

> I do not have an urge to live, I do not desire to die. I await
> the appointed time like a mercenary who has finished his task.
> (The disciple, Cariputra.)

Buddha himself offers but an elusive imagery of nirvana:

> It is as if oil is not poured on the wick of a lamp that is burning
> low. The old fuel exhausts itself and since new fuel is not added,
> the lamp is extinguished, lacking nourishment.

While Buddha's disciples have probed into nirvana with a
number of provocative and as yet unresolved questions, for the
Khmer peasant nivana is a "never-never land." Not only is it
eternity, it is a goal he will never reach. Nirvana is reserved for
the select holy men who adhere scrupulously to Buddha's teachings. The ordinary Cambodian admits to and stoically accepts his
worldly imperfections; knowing that he only approximates ideal
conduct, he aims at the lesser goal of a better life in the next
reincarnation.

Merit and Cambodian Character

"Merit-making" is for Cambodians the most important vehicle for
the character improvement that will contribute to the slow process
of deliverance from imperfection. The concept of merit places a
man's destiny squarely on his own shoulders. It depends on offering, not receiving, on achievement, not inheritance. It is a concept
that liberates the individual from anxiety by placing stress on the
performance of virtuous deeds. Merit-making is not intended to
chart new paths, in the western sense of progress, but to steady
a traditional course. Within Buddhism, the Cambodian is able to
develop personal strength by increasing the potency of his character.
If he has a staunch character he can ward off the evil forces of the
spirit world; the surest way to strengthen character is to accumulate merit.

The individual must follow the dictates of Buddhist principles
or lose merit. A Buddhist monk—called bonze in Cambodia—is
expected to follow scrupulously all ten of the following commandments; a layman, only the first five: (1) do not suppress life in
any form; (2) do not steal; (3) do not be unchaste; (4) do not lie;
(5) do not consume intoxicants; (6) do not eat after the sanctioned
hour; (7) do not participate in any activity that excites the senses
(dancing, singing, music); (8) do not use adornments, cosmetics,

or perfumes; (9) do not recline on a raised bed; (10) do not handle money or gold.

Certain of the commandments are not taken too literally by the laity. Cambodians have a less than strict concept of private property: petty theft is often excused, sometimes on the basis of need, sometimes simply because an object is too tempting to resist. And very few Cambodian men abstain from wine: weddings and festivals of any kind are not considered worthwhile unless large quantities of wine are served. Drinking, however, rarely results in brawls, and drunkenness is definitely not a social problem.

It can be said that Buddhism punctuates life with positive behavior—acts of merit that fortify individual character and move the Cambodian through the series of enriched reincarnations. Demerits may also be accumulated, and these subject the individual to attacks from the spirit world. Spirits lurk everywhere—always touchy, easily offended—and must be placated. Failure to quell these spirits can be a source of demerit and a man's undoing.

Although merit-making is motivated primarily by the hope of reward in the next reincarnation, it is also held to be an ethical principle for the good life here and now. The immediate rewards of merit-making may come in the form of approval from one's fellow villagers or neighbors, and thus one may enjoy harmony and calmness in his relations with his fellow men. Too, merit-making opens the door to pleasurable pastimes—for example, festivities at the pagoda.

For the average Cambodian, then, the essential doctrine by which conduct can be gauged is merit: a man's character and all that happens to him are weighed on the merit-demerit scale. His good deeds and bad deeds are irrevocable and become sculptured into his character. The simple axiom of his behavior is that a man reaps what he sows, whether he be born a king, a commoner, or, through unfortunate reincarnation, a dog. Cambodians do not doubt that he who does good receives good and he who does evil receives evil.

Devout Buddhists feel no compulsion to improve life. Life is good if it is accepted. Those whose lot is bad are frequently butts for Cambodian jokes but they laugh at themselves as much as they are laughed at. Life in the present incarnation cannot be changed, but the measure of man's emotional development is his reaction to his circumstances.

In the present national drive for economic progress and independence, the government is making efforts to convince the people that greater happiness can be found on earth in the present life just as it can be found in a future incarnation. Religious leaders to some extent are cooperating in these efforts. Actually there is no deep conflict between traditional Theravada doctrine and the new steps toward economic and technological advancement. For instance, in the dialogues of Buddha the virtues of diligence and thrift are highly praised as avenues leading to the accumulation of material wealth; this "philosophy of success" made early Buddhism the religion of the rising merchant class.

It is difficult to predict what effect the present acceleration of economic development will eventually have on the religious values of Cambodians. But Theravada Buddhism appears to be firmly imbedded in the minds and customs of the majority of Cambodians, despite recent criticism of some of its practices. No serious decline in the prestige of the traditional faith appears probable in the foreseeable future.

The Bonze

The bonze in Cambodia is seen everywhere—plodding along the roads, meditating in the cool of the forests, silently proffering his alms bowl in the villages. He is inseparable from his parasol, which under the uncompromising Cambodian sun is not a luxury but a necessity.

The ratio of bonzes to total population is striking. Approximately 100,000 bonzes (of whom about 40,000 are novices) minister to the spiritual needs of a population of about 5 million. They are omnipresent in Cambodian life. They perpetuate the moral laws, give instruction in the sacred texts, console the sick and unfortunate, and perform medical services that range from magic to genuine scientific therapy.

The assortment of backgrounds is wide since almost every Cambodian male takes on monastic attire at some time in his life. A bonze may have been a prince or a high official; he may have been a peasant, a coolie, or a servant. Some hold European baccalaureates, others can barely read the words of Buddha. Some, especially those of wealthy birth, have been characterized as "gentle dreamers who twiddle their thumbs and wait to be fed"; yet the bonzehood is frequently the only refuge for landless and destitute peasants in a country where tenant farming is not customary. The urban unemployed also find the bonzehood a refuge. Fed, lodged, exempt from taxation, the urban outcast waits at the pagoda for a job opportunity; when one develops he doffs his religious robes and re-enters the secular world.

There are, then, permanent bonzes and temporary bonzes, bonzes by choice and bonzes by necessity. Some are highly estimable, some are not; some act from motives of pure spiritual devotion, others from motives of material opportunism. Some desire only to be loyal Cambodians or to conform to the traditions of their ancestors or to "pay their debt of recognition" to their parents. Others are motivated by a desire for education.

Whatever his motivation, the bonze in the eyes of most Cambodians is above reproach. Anticlericalism was until very recently completely unknown in Cambodia, and it is unlikely that the present criticism, which stems mainly from the western-educated, will receive wide popular support.

The Pagoda Community

Nearly every Cambodian male over 16 years of age serves a term as a bonze. The term can last for several months or several years; it can also become the permanent profession of an entire lifetime. The majority of those who do not intend to make the bonzehood a life career take the religious vows for from six months to one year. Such vows are the mark of full adult status for the male and the most readily available means of accumulating merit.

To enter the inner sanctum of the pagoda and the permanent religious community, the novice must be at least 20 years old and must secure the consent of his parents or, if married, his wife. A non-Buddhist may become a bonze; pronouncing the initiation vows implies that the individual has renounced his former religion.

The ordination ceremony, recapitulating the circumstances under which Buddha withdrew from the world, is colorful and ritualistic. It is held only during the Cambodian months of Pisakh, Ches, and Assath (April 15 to July 15). This is Vassa, the rainy season, considered the most sacred period of the year. During Vassa, the bonzes' movements are restricted to the pagoda area.

Life at the pagoda is regulated and routinized. In theory the bonzes are submissive to the severe ritualistic prescriptions of the ancient texts, although laxity is by no means unknown.

On entering the pagoda community, a novice or bonze prays for indigence and purity. All food and clothing is supplied by laity of the village or city in which the pagoda is situated; these donors earn merit by their charity. The outfit of the bonze consists of three pieces of cloth, either silk or cotton, usually tinted a bright yellow: a *sbang*, a type of sarong; a *sanghati*, a length of cloth wrapped around the body in sari fashion; and a *chipo*, a large mantle which resembles a Roman toga.

Daily activities of the community are in principle determined by the ten commandments. For instance, a bonze cannot labor in the rice paddies because of the first commandment: in turning the soil he would obliterate countless insects and worms. While walking, a bonze will pray for the insects being crushed under foot; before drinking water, he will filter it through linen to save the lives of the innocent aquatic amoebae. Poisonous insects, scorpions, and reptiles also are spared.

The daily routine is taxing. The community arises between 4:00 and 5:00 A.M. and spends the first waking hours in meditation and prayer before Buddha. Each bonze then leaves the pagoda to seek charity. In anticipation of the early morning visit a housewife usually prepares an extra portion of the family meal to present to the bonze. There is often some sort of reciprocal relationship whereby a bonze will regularly request alms of the same persons, those who feel a special attachment to him and especially wish his spiritual services.

The bonzes reassemble at the pagoda before noon with filled alms bowls. The meal is communal and the only one of the day. It must be finished before high noon; thereafter bonzes must abstain from all food, though they may drink water.

Twice a month—the day of the new moon and the day of the full moon—the community meets together for public confession. On each eighth day, the "day of precept," the bonzes promise to obey the ten commandments. On precept days the laity engage in festivities at the pagoda, which contrast strangely with the solemn atmosphere of the bonze reaffirmations.

Status and Conduct of the Bonze

A code of conduct regulates the relations of the laity to the bonzes. A bonze must never be made to feel that he is an average mortal: his person, especially his shaved head, is considered sacred. Cambodians use a special obligatory vocabulary in conversation with their bonzes.

The bonze is outside the scope of legal and civic action and is exempt from all public duties. He is not permitted to vote and in principle he avoids all political intrigue (for actual practice, see below, and chap. 8). A bonze can neither witness a legal document nor give legal testimony; he cannot lodge a formal complaint if injured, assaulted, or robbed. His suspension or expulsion from the pagoda can be decided by the pagoda head but only on authority of the sect superior.

A bonze clearly guilty of a common-law offense can be brought before a civic tribunal but only after first being defrocked. Generally, the sect superior decides the defrocking of a bonze after prolonged deliberation with the religious assembly (*therac-saphea*). Occasionally, however, when a quick decision is necessary, the provincial Buddhist leader, upon the request of the provincial governor, may summarily declare the bonze defrocked, thus permitting the civil trial to proceed.

There are times when the holy commandments are stretched to the near-breaking point. It is no secret, for instance, that the contents of alms bowls are sometimes thrown to the dogs that swarm in every pagoda while the bonzes sit down to good food prepared especially for them by the novices.

A bonze is never supposed to touch money but with the growing popularity of the western handshake, it is not uncommon for a bonze who has thus greeted a wealthy parishioner to draw his hand away well filled. By rule, a bonze must not wander out alone at night nor entertain any attitude other than decent modesty but bonzes can be seen strolling on the streets of Pnompenh at dusk, their thoughts quite apparently not focused on spiritual perfection but on the objects for sale and the events of the busy area.

The sacred vow of chastity, however, is almost never broken. The folk tales that lampoon the greediness and other laxities of bonzes make no mention of sexual excesses. Even the impostor bonzes who are reputed to swindle the villagers seem to respect the vow.

The criticism of the bonzehood which has recently been increasing among young and western-educated Cambodian liberals is based not so much on violations of vows as on the fact that the system allows large groups of men to play unproductive roles in the Cambodian economy. But faith in Buddhism as a religion seems to persist even among the critics. A recent bulletin of a Pnompenh youth organization carried on its cover a significant illustration: a menacing finger of Buddha points at a bonze, the caption reading, "The past accuses the present."

Role of the Guru

From early childhood, the Cambodian is encouraged to confide in the bonze. Even before a child comes under the tutelage of the bonze-master (guru) at the pagoda school, he has been considerably influenced by the clergy.

When the child first enters the pagoda school his father traditionally remarks to the bonze: "Do what you will. Treat him as you see fit, provided that you return his eyes and bones." The father thus declares his complete trust in the judgment of the bonze; family obligations are in part transferred to the religious institution from then on. In effect the bonze becomes the child's master, supplanting paternal authority during a crucial phase of development.

The role of the guru is obviously important in Cambodian personality formation and in the development of attitudes that will be manifest in adulthood. The association with the guru continues long after the child has finished his studies in the pagoda school. The guru, his role as disciplinarian ended, becomes father-confessor and adviser. A "good" Cambodian respects his guru and listens to his wise counsel; devotion to the Sacred Laws is symbolically expressed in this loyalty to the guru.

Organization of Cambodian Buddhism

Cambodian Buddhism has no formal administrative ties with religious bodies in other countries and its clergy are entirely independent of the cross-nurturing that obtains among other Theravada Buddhist countries. The Cambodian Buddhist hierarchy is firmly centralized on a national basis: each village pagoda is directed by a head bonze who is responsible to the provincial leader; in turn the provincial leader accedes to the authority of the national sect leaders in Pnompenh. The national leaders are responsible in theory to the king, who is at the apex of the structure; actually, the king's role is that of religious symbol rather than functioning administrative head (see chap. 7). He does appoint certain bonze officials—notably the superiors (Sangneayuk) of the two bonze sects, Thommayut and Mohanikay—but he can never tamper with doctrine.

Ecclesiastic Rank

The Buddhist dignitaries are organized by rank into two main groups, the Reachea Khanac (the highest official rank, divided into four nominal subranks) and the Thanah Ouckram. Promotion to the rank of Reachea Khanac is at the personal discretion of the king on the recommendation of both the sect leader concerned and the Ministry of Religion. To be eligible for nomination to Reachea Khanac a bonze must have served twenty years at a pagoda. Promotion to the rank of Thanah Ouckram is by approval of the superior of the sect in agreement with the Ministry of Religion.

Each province in Cambodia has a diocese (*kon*), at the head of which is a *me-kon* of Reachea Khanac rank. The *me-kon* is responsible to both spiritual and secular authority—his sect superior and the Ministry of Religion. He is assisted in his duties by an executive assembly (*salakon*) composed of four members, the *me-kon* serving as chairman.

The district subdivisions (*srok*) of the province are staffed by *anouckon*, of Tanah Ouckram rank, who come under the direct jurisdiction of the *me-kon*. The work of the *anouckon* is facilitated by a lower assembly (*sala-anouckon*) composed of three members. (It should be noted that this subprovincial structure pertains largely to the Mohanikay sect, which sustains the majority of clergy and pagodas in the hinterland; the Thommayut sect functions only in the cities.) The capital city of Pnompenh constitutes a diocese for both sects, but does not have an *anouckon* or a *sala-anouckon*.

A pagoda is headed by a *chau-athikar*, who is seconded by a *krousot*, sometimes called *chau-athikar-rong*. A layman who functions as a temporal intermediary (*achar*) is attached to each pagoda; he represents the bonzes, novices, and lay supporters of the pagoda in dealings with government officials. The *chau-athikar* supervises the bonzes, novices, and also the students at the pagoda school, seeing to it that all conform to lay as well as religious behavior standards. The *achar* and the *chau-athikar* together are responsible for all pagoda real estate. It is the *chau-athikar's* obligation also to take full initiative in encouraging the intellectual and moral development of his subordinates.

All pagodas are periodically visited by inspectors dispatched from sect headquarters at Pnompenh. The functions of the inspectors are to secure the over-all welfare of the pagoda, to draw the pagoda activities into the main stream of Cambodian cultural life, to disseminate medical and hygienic information, to safeguard the pagoda property from damage or misappropriation.

The inspectors can issue warnings to bonzes whose conduct is not up to par. In a case of manifest abuse or grave negligence of sect codes, the inspectors are qualified to bring the offense to the attention of the local sect authorities; disagreements over interpretation of canonic texts must be referred to the sect superior.

The Sects

The two groups of Cambodian bonzes, the Thommayut and the Mohanikay, are referred to as sects but are more like different orders or monastic brotherhoods within Roman Catholicism than like sects in a denominational sense. Both groups use the Pali Canon's deposition of doctrine, but make different interpretations of some aspects, chiefly in regard to the rules governing monastic life.

In external appearance there is little to distinguish members of the Mohanikay from those of the Thommayut. Their garments are practically identical in color—a brilliant saffron yellow—and in style. A Mohanikay bonze, however, carries his alms bowl suspended from his shoulder by a cord or sling while a Thommayut carries it in his hand.

By far the larger of the two, the Mohanikay brotherhood ministers almost exclusively to the masses and is completely unchallenged in the rural areas. Of the total number of permanent bonzes in the entire kingdom, over 90 percent belong to the Mohanikay sect, which also maintains more than 2,500 of Cambodia's 2,650 pagodas.

The members of the Thommayut are estimated as fewer than 1,600, but the Thommayut's role in the Cambodian religious community is of great magnitude. It is highly influential in Pnompenh and is identified with the king, the extended royal family, and other upper-class groups. The Thommayut pagodas are without exception located in either Pnompenh (where the Royal Court finances them) or the capital cities of the provinces.

The Thommayut order was introduced into Cambodia in 1864 by Prah Laukoun, a zealous bonze who spent most of his life in seclusion at a Bangkok pagoda, and it has been characterized by its admiration for Thai cultural elements. The Thommayut zealousness was directed toward a re-evaluation of the sacred texts (as in Thailand); the reformers were also strongly critical of the Mohanikay bonzes for their less strict teaching of dogma and their mechanical recitation of the scriptures. From time to time the Thommayut has supported revival movements in the Mohanikay.

Within the Mohanikay is a faction, the Thommakay, which might be called an orthodox wing. The Thommakay occupies a somewhat anomalous position: it shares the orthodox objectives of the Thommayut but remains part of the more liberal tradition of the Mohanikay. It is possible, however, that the Thommakay serves as an unofficial intermediate force to aid the orthodox revivals that the Thommayut instigates for the Mohanikay.

Through hard work, shrewdness, and tenacity the Thommakay faction has gained a considerable degree of control in the Mohanikay hierarchy. A first-rank Thommakay leader was recently appointed supreme head of the Mohanikay sect, a development which appears to play into the hands of the Thommayut in its efforts to consolidate its influence over Cambodian Buddhism and to stimulate a renaissance of orthodox Buddhism in Cambodia.

Within the Mohanikay sect, the introduction of certain bonzes to western scientific and intellectual knowledge and especially to the writings of European scholars on the subject of Buddhism has stirred a critical spirit and led to a re-examination of the Buddhist scriptures. These bonze scholars, loosely called Modernists, stand in opposition to the Traditionalists, who prefer a reversion to orthodoxy rather than an adjustment of doctrine to the dictates of modern life and thought.

Under constant pressure from fundamentalist forces, the internal discipline of the Mohanikay community has been gradually weakened. Factions have risen not only within the sect as a whole but also within pagoda units. Not infrequently the pagoda officers must deal with orthodox-traditionalist or heterodox-modernist cliques, and the pagoda discord appears at times to be fed and aggravated by personal ambitions. It has not been uncommon for the head of the pagoda to capitalize on the confusion: soliciting his immediate superior for clarification of the doctrine, he may also have an eye on replacing the superior. Anarchy sometimes reigns in pagodas where the higher officers have gained excessive control to the detriment of the *chau-athikar's* authority.

It must be remembered that Buddhism in Cambodia has had a strong oral tradition which, over the centuries, has resulted in a wide range of interpretations of the scriptures as well as the acceptance of some changes in their essential meaning. The various aspects of the oral tradition—impromptu orations, prayers, and supplications—have always been open to critical attack. Formalism becomes most uncompromising during revival periods, especially if some bonzes are suspected of heterodoxy.

Dissension in the Buddhist hierarchy has created conditions making political infiltration possible. For example, the directors of the Higher School of Pali and the Buddhist Institute work closely with lay organizations (such as the Association of Friends of the Pali Schools); these organizations supposedly exist to assist in religious instruction, but under the religious veneer they occupy themselves above all with political matters.

Certain members of the Thommakay, in permitting themselves to be concerned with political affairs, have provoked within the Buddhist community a primary fissure that stands every chance of deepening and widening. The immediate result has been a weakening of the Buddhist hierarchy and consequently a fomenting of disorder and, on occasion, rebellion reaching as far down as the heart of the Buddhist community, the village pagoda. The orthodox revival movement has, in part, been carried on under the pretext of upholding Buddhist tenets; but this motivation, when carefully examined, seems to be little more than a purely formal exercise that does not concern essential Buddhist thought.

But Buddhism as a faith is not in any imminent danger. For the people, the teachings of Buddha, his life and doctrines, are his flesh, his blood, his soul; there is no more secure depository for Buddhism than the pious Cambodian people themselves.

The Clergy in Politics

In the past Cambodian monks had been strictly apolitical, but during the Japanese occupation both bonzes and intellectuals were stirred to political consciousness for perhaps the first time. In 1942 bonzes demonstrated before the quarters of the French Resident Superior at Pnompenh, thereby setting a precedent for the entrance of the clergy into the political arena (see chap. 8).

Officially the forces of the government and of religion are in accord; in reality they are not, because their objectives differ essentially. To the extent that the clergy enters into the dynamics of nationalism with its many ramifications, it will be subjected to civic impositions that can only undermine the secular immunity that is vital to its other-worldly position in the eyes of the Cambodian people.

There are, however, few religious points of contention in the Buddhist community that do not have political or social overtones. Most issues suggest also the eventual examination of all current social and political problems, and are thrashed out in an atmosphere of bitter and calculated criticism. To understand this progression from a narrow doctrinal base to a broad sociopolitical plane is obviously important if one wishes also to understand emerging leadership patterns and channels of problem solution. The techniques of the progression, however, are not altogether clear.

Among the social and political overtones one finds undertones of "independence" and "liberation." There have been reports of monks who have actively encouraged the Issarak and Vietminh movements as well as domestic and scattered terrorist groups (see chap. 8) under the pretext of working for independence. The bonzes involved insist on a rebaptism of "real liberty" and "true independence"—in the same soundtrack that has cut across the ideologies of all Asia.

Disintegration of Buddhist discipline is reflected in this participation of Cambodian bonzes in such movements. The King and his ministers have manifested grave concern over this departure of the clergy from strict adherence to religious duties; since the holy men have such influence with the masses, bonze activities in the political arena could pose a threat to the present government leadership. The King has voiced his disapproval in public messages and, as protector of the national religion, advocated such measures as reinforcing the authority of the pagoda heads and strengthening the superstructure of the Buddhist hierarchy.

Brahmanism

Brahmanism, with its associated Indian philosophy and deities, is the oldest formal religious element of Khmer culture. Although it has now lost much of its ideological base, its influence is still evident in ceremonies, especially those conducted at the Royal Palace by the ancient Brahman priesthood, the Baku. Vestiges of the golden age of Brahman sculpture, art, drama, and literature are found everywhere in Cambodia, still closely associated with the aesthetic tastes of the people.

The penetration of Brahmanism and its sacred language, Sanskrit, from India into Cambodia probably dates from the first century of the Christian era; it maintained its ascendancy until the twelfth century. The Brahmans, usually priests and scholars, received many royal favors and donations.

Brahmanism and Buddhism have not only existed side by side for a long period in Cambodia but have, to a certain extent, blended in ritual and belief. As noted, Theravada Buddhism in no way sought to evict the Brahman gods; instead, in its great tolerance, it preserved them, incorporating them into the sacred texts. Brahma, Vishnu, Siva, Indra, and Yama were made figures of worship and defenders of Buddhist law. Brahma (Prah Prohm) occupies a major place in Cambodian art; representations of him are frequently confused with Buddha.

Siva and Vishnu share with Brahma the three forces of the universe: creation, preservation, and destruction. Indra reigns over heaven and Yama over hell.

Vestiges of Siva-worship persist, and the sacred status of Cambodian kings derives from an ancient merging of the kingship with Siva and Vishnu. Siva (Prah Eysor), who destroys to create, is well represented at Angkor Wat, sometimes seated on a throne in royal attire, sometimes almost nude except for a Brahman cordon indicating rank. The face is almost always that of an ascetic. Siva has never been portrayed in Khmer art as ferocious or with the necklace of human skulls that he wears in Hindu iconography.

Vishnu (Prah Noreay), the god of preservation, is the valiant defender of humanity, and devotes himself entirely to this cause. He takes many forms and has recourse to many ruses in saving the world. In folklore, giants and demons harass and menace him and seek his downfall. His famous ten incarnations (*avatars*) correspond to the acts of devotion by which the world and humanity are retrieved; two of them—in the persons of Rama and Krishna—remain to this day sources of inspiration for Cambodians.

Indra (Prah Eynt), who issues the thunder and governs the universe, is perhaps the Brahman god most popular with Cambodians. Indra once occupied an important position in the ancient Vedic religion; in Cambodian folklore, however, he has lost much of his divine character in favor of diverse roles that enable him to intervene on the side of mortals. He is considered guardian of the fortunate and blessed.

Yama has also remained a divinity of wide appeal. He judges the dead and decides their fate: the just, after judgment day, soar up to heaven, the evil descend to hell.

The celestial creatures (*tevodas*) of Brahmanism are, for Cambodians, no longer deities but fortunate people who exhaust in the heaven of Indra the merits previously acquired in the course of earlier existence. Certain *tevodas* live not in paradise but in the forests, where they watch humans, noting their faults and good deeds. For many rural Cambodians the *tevodas* merge into the world of *neak ta* (guardian spirits). In popular stories and in the drama *tevodas* play important parts.

Spirit Worship and Magic

Primitive religious elements—primitive in the sense of lacking dogma and a priesthood—preceded both Brahmanism and Buddhism in Cambodia. As previously noted, Buddhism did not impose itself obliteratingly on either Brahmanism or the primitive cults but existed with them in a profitable union. This union provides the key to an understanding of Cambodian religious behavior.

The cult of tutelary spirits (*neak ta*) is complementary to the teachings of Theravada Buddhism. Buddhist doctrine teaches that death, disease, and personal misfortune are inevitable, but the mass of Cambodians still look for some immediate means of coping with unhappiness. When Buddhism does not seem to satisfy the full spiritual appetite, comfort and explanation are sought in the supernatural. This withdrawal into inner religious resources has permitted Cambodians to withstand the shock of numerous ordeals: in the midst of disorder, calmness is preserved that has amazed many westerners.

The supernatural tradition has deep historical roots in Cambodia. It combines animism, sorcery, naturalism, and magical rites of propitiation and immunization in an attempt to manipulate the spirit world and tap its hidden powers. Cambodian folk religion is characterized by an array of tutelary spirits and magical practices. The Cambodian peasant attends the pagoda, but he also erects here and there, sometimes even in an obscure corner of the pagoda, small rustic altars (*taub*) in recognition of the spirits, then prudently makes offerings of rice and incense sticks.

The *neak ta* are primarily guardian spirits, but they are also said to possess an instinct for malevolence and vengeance. There seems to be a great variation among the spirits. Some are compliant, others act mercilessly against those who fail to show proper respect. When a Cambodian passing an altar is wearing some sort of head covering, he must remove the covering and beg the spirit's protection. If he is bareheaded, he addresses the spirit by holding clasped hands at the level of his forehead, a sign of humility. Should he omit either of these required gestures, dreadful consequences may befall.

The cult of the *neak ta* seems to harbor three main categories of spirits: (1) local spirits that inhabit mountains (*neak ta phnom*), rivers (*neak ta tuk*), trees (*neak ta dam*), rice paddies (*neak ta sre*), swamps (*neak ta beng*), and forests (*neak ta prey*); (2) ancestral spirits, probably demonstrating the last traces of an ancestral cult, the nature and origin of which are vague, although historical events can be reconstructed and cultural heroes can be recognized through associated legends; (3) spirits that are an intermingling of Brahman gods and mythical heroes. Sacred Buddha figurines carved from ivory, iron pyrites, or wild boar tusk are prized as *katha*. The tooth of a parent is also considered especially potent. Size and shape have no bearing on the efficacy of the *katha*; its magical power depends on its innate ability to harness external magical forces.

Katha are worn variously—about the neck, around the waist, or over the genitals. A good-fortune belt consisting of seven to twelve *katha* is the occupational badge of soldiers, police, and outlaws—those who risk their lives professionally. Military personnel usually secure a single *katha* in their hair; in combat, a talisman is carried in the mouth. Anyone who carries a *katha* on the person must avoid contamination; it is considered dangerous to pass under a pile dwelling or in front of a house of prostitution. If the individual goes to a W.C., he must leave his *katha* at the entrance. *Katha* are never stolen as stealing a talisman involves serious risk of spirit reprisal.

The sorcerer (*kru*—"he who knows") confers power on a *katha* by drawing on the formulas of his secret repertoire. Once a *katha* is impregnated with the desired magical properties and ownership is ritually established, the owner takes exclusive possession, guarding and honoring his link with the supernatural world. (*Kru* are in a position to acquire considerable local political power, and the government in Pnompenh has learned that it is well to keep a watchful eye on them.)

Certain drugs are reputed to confer invulnerability to various evils. One potion—*tuk thnam kong*—is believed to make the skin resist the penetration of a spear or a bullet. The ingredients of this potion are oily liana, pieces of dried python, excrements from the nest of a red vulture, and water. After an impressive ritual performed by the *kru*, the liquid is consumed. At the end of the seventh day, the skin is subjected to a penetration test; if a wound results, another drink of the potion is given.

Sorcery involves rules of procedure that were devised in early tribal periods, conserved by oral tradition, and altered under the influence of infiltrating formal religions. The significant fact is that many of the present-day rules of sorcery bear a striking resemblance to Buddhist doctrine.

FAMILY

IN CAMBODIA THE IDEAL HOUSEHOLD consists of a married couple and their unmarried children, and this pattern is general in the urban districts. Parents usually live apart from their married children, although a widowed parent may live with a son or daughter. In rural areas, because of economic factors, households sometimes include married children and their families, but this is not the preferred arrangement.

Plural marriage is sanctioned, but monogamy is the rule for the majority of Cambodians. The average Cambodian does not have the means to support more than one wife; only upper-class persons, high civil servants, and wealthy Chinese can maintain a polygamous household. Western hostility to polygamy also has influenced Cambodian thinking on the subject.

A family of five children is considered ideal. Unlike the Chinese or Vietnamese, the Cambodian does not want unlimited offspring, although he accepts with genuine pleasure those that come. Since sterility may lead to criticism of the wife, a childless couple may try to adopt an orphan or the child of a poor family. Children are never abandoned; orphans (even if they are Eurasian) usually are taken into some family.

Cambodians refer to children born out of wedlock as "children of the wilderness." No legal distinction, however, is made between them and others, nor are they shamed by public opinion.

In contrast to the Vietnamese and Chinese, Cambodians do not attach special importance to tracing descendants through the male line. The Cambodian kinship system is markedly bilateral—relations among kin members, marriage ties, inheritance patterns are all regulated without maternal or paternal bias. No distinctions are made between the way a Cambodian child refers to or behaves toward his paternal relatives and the way he behaves toward his maternal relatives. Sons and daughters both can inherit and the inheritance may come from both parents. Of family property, sons usually receive the land and daughters the movable goods.

While formal respect is paid to both paternal or maternal ancestors at weddings and funerals, ancestor worship is not a major family function as in China. Filial piety is a less compulsive moral obligation than in either China or Vietnam, but respect for one's elders is expected of everyone.

Today's emphasis on education, with its western influences, is widening the gap between younger and older generations and some educated Cambodians feel that poorly educated parents should not have power over their children. Buddhist teaching, however, still stresses deference to the wishes of an elder and is still the dominant influence on a young Cambodian's behavior.

Until 1910 there were no family surnames in Cambodia. In that year a royal ordinance decreed that the name of the head of the family should become the family name and precede an individual's given or first name. This led to some confusion at first but is now standard.

Family Life

Ordinarily, each small family group occupies a separate house, owns its rice paddy and vegetable garden, plans and operates as an independent unit. Major domestic, social, and religious activities, as well as the minor shared activities of daily life are handled by the members of the immediate family.

A Cambodian peasant's house is raised on mangrove piles, sometimes as much as 10 feet. There may be several rooms, separated by partitions of dried palms, but poorer homes often have but a single room. Behind the house and joined to it by a ramp is a kitchen shed, also on stilts. Looms, carts, and livestock are kept beneath the house. Crowding is general and privacy at a premium; since there is also little protection from outside curiosity, everybody in the community knows a good deal about everyone else.

The houses of wealthier families, especially in urban centers, are capacious villas, affording privacy. Such a house may contain three or four rooms and have a large veranda.

Should a rural family move to an urban area, rice fields and any other real property it may own are managed by remaining relatives. Even though a family leaves its native village it maintains close ties with relatives and friends and makes every effort to return at the first opportunity. It will seldom, unless compelled by dire circumstances, sell all rights to rural property.

In the rural Cambodian family the husband does the more arduous agricultural work, such as hoeing and preparing the fields for seeding. Husbands and wives work together when it is time to transplant the rice. In general, however, women are fully occupied with household chores and the children and spend less time in the fields than do women in many other peasant societies.

The Cambodian woman occupies a key position in the household, and in many ways the prosperity, well-being and development of the family as a unit revolve around her. Her ethical influence over the younger minds is very important. As a carrier of the basic social and moral values of Cambodian culture, she is highly regarded by the men in her own family and by Cambodian society at large. In the round of family activities the wife stands on an equal footing with her husband—in some matters she surpasses him in initiative. Generally it is the wife who is the family treasurer, controlling the purse strings and budgeting the family assets.

In polygamous families a first-rank wife is ushered into a central position in the household by an elaborate wedding ceremony studded with expensive gifts. Her primacy in the household is thus materially guaranteed. A second-rank wife can be taken into the household before a first-rank wife but is specifically tagged as second-rank. Publicly she is spoken of as the "middle wife." Although solicited for marriage she foregoes the full nuptial ceremony accorded to a first-rank wife, and the symbolic betel and areca nut exchange. In rare instances there may be a third-rank wife, the "little wife," who, though in a subservient role in the household hierarchy, still outranks a concubine. In the past the third-rank wife was often purchased. Parents will offer a daughter as a second- or third-rank wife only to a wealthy man.

Widows in Cambodia are accorded considerable respect, and women who carry out the legal duties of a widow are extremely powerful. Upon the death of the husband, the wife becomes head of the household; she is legally endowed with paternal authority and directs all family matters, but she has only the power of executrix over joint property and may not dispose of it. After three years in retreat she can remarry.

Cambodian children are treated affectionately but not fussed over and are encouraged to take care of themselves from an early age. They are at the same time allowed to be "children" and are not constantly goaded into adopting adult attitudes or behavior. Once the child begins to assert his own personality, however, parental attentiveness diminishes.

Preadolescent children have few chores in the household; real responsibilities do not begin until the child is 12 or 13. A girl learns household duties from her mother—cooking, sewing, tending to the younger children. She also joins the mother in trips to the market and picks up fine points in the art of bargaining: Cambodian women take pride in using fast and shrewish talk to beat down the established price of any item. A boy learns the techniques of agriculture from his father and older brothers.

In principle, the authority of the Cambodian parent is sacred and unqualified, but parents actually prefer to teach approved behavior by means of examples set by adults and older children. Sharp reprimand and physical punishment are avoided as much as possible, and parents are seldom viewed as objects of fear.

On the few occasions when rebellion or opposition of a child builds up and an open break appears imminent, the parents usually back down rather than sacrifice the child's happiness and security to an abstract principle of filial piety.

Boys are somewhat more exempt from discipline than girls. From the time the Cambodian boy enters the pagoda school, however, he is under the scrutiny of the guru (bonze master), who functions almost as a second father. The boy receives as much social indoctrination at the pagoda as he does in the family. Supervision is stricter for girls, who must always be above reproach if a favorable marriage is later to be arranged. Parental domination falls doubly hard on the daughter, and her life is mapped out along the lines of family advantage and interest.

The primary duty of parents toward a son is to prepare him for the period he will spend at the pagoda in his young adulthood studying Buddhist precepts when he becomes, in effect, a bonze. The period symbolizes a breaking away from family supervision and activity. When the son joins the procession with the other monks —his eyes cast down and his alms bowl before him—his mother makes obeisance to him for the first time, not as her son but as a holy man. This is a moment of rich reward, of repayment for the mother's "milk" and childhood care, of spiritual plenitude in a mother's life. Later, the son may elect to join the religious order permanently, or he may return to society.

Another important duty of parents is to settle a son or daughter in a profitable marriage. Advantages gained through marriage benefit the whole family.

The family functions as a social-security organization for its immediate members only. Financial assistance to immediate relatives is a part of the Cambodian family system; aid to an intimate relative—father, mother, brother, or sister—is regarded not as the sort of favor that warrants a debt of gratitude but as part of the natural order of things. Aid to distant relatives may be offered, but it is considered a distasteful burden; there is a conscious effort to restrict interdependence to the immediate family and to avoid intricate patterns of reciprocity with remote relatives.

Individual Life Cycle

The birth of a son or daughter is an occasion for rejoicing. Cambodians believe, however, that confinement and childbirth expose the household to very real dangers from the spirit world and every precaution is taken to prevent the wandering phantoms and evil spirits from gaining the upper hand during this period of contamination. Literally translated the Cambodian expression for giving birth is to "cross the Tonle Sap." It is believed that a woman who dies in childbirth becomes a sinister ghost and that her wickedness is augmented by the anger of the fetus, furious at not being born.

A midwife and various kinswomen are on hand for the delivery. Normal childbirth hardly disrupts the daily routine; a few days after delivery a Cambodian woman resumes her household chores. When the mother's strength is partially restored a celebration is held and she ceremoniously begs forgiveness for the contamination she has brought on the household.

The child is breast fed until two or three years old, sometimes even four, depending on when the next brother or sister arrives. From the first months large amounts of mashed bananas and masticated rice also are fed.

Children are nicknamed after astrological numerals or grotesque animals to frighten off the evil spirits. If a child becomes sick his name is changed to confuse the spirit responsible. The child's head generally is considered sacred; even an amiable pluck of the cheek is considered extremely poor manners.

Affection for a child is shown by the Cambodian kiss—pressing of the nose close to the cheek and strongly inhaling. A Cambodian child is not "kissed" as much as an American child but is probably cuddled and fondled more.

Cutting the top tuft of hair (*kor sak*) of both boys and girls 11 or 12 years old is the puberty rite symbolizing passage from childhood to adolescence—and in part to adulthood, though full adult status is not attained until the religious and marriage vows have been taken by the man and the first child has been born to the woman.

The onset of menstruation is ritually marked by the practice known as "entering the shade." (The custom is now disappearing in urban society but is still generally found in the villages.) At the first sign of menstruation the girl is isolated from her family and from the community. The seclusion may last from several days to six months, depending on the socioeconomic rank of the family: the higher the rank, the longer the isolation. A girl's qualifications for marriage are considered enhanced by a long isolation. During the cloistered period the girl is protected from all "desire"—including the glances of any man, whether kin or stranger. Foods that do not have a rice, fruit, or vegetal origin are taboo.

After leaving the "shade" there is a ceremony; thereafter, the girl no longer is referred to by the prefix "*me*," and she is eligible for marriage.

Young children are not permitted much knowledge of sex. The feeling among parents is that too much knowledge can lead to desire and eventual trouble. Bits and pieces of information on sex are picked up from peers in the play group, but parents discourage curiosity and usually give inaccurate or fragmentary answers to direct questions. A girl receives little information until the last night of a wedding feast, when the bride's parents and the *achar* (pagoda wise man) take the bride aside and explain the basic facts of sex.

Adults avoid discussing sex but there is considerable allusion to it as a symbol in certain competitive games and in chants used at festivals. One game involves a scarf rolled into a ball that is rapidly passed (with sexual invitation) around a group of young boys and girls. In alternating chants with rhymed responses, the boys make urgent pleas and the girls answer coquettishly; the lyrics to one of the chants used during the Water Festival are:

It has rained much this year
The river has overflown
There will be much joy and rice
All the women will be with child either by their husbands or by
  their lovers, it doesn't matter much which.

Cambodians love all night, Vietnamese all day long
People say that French women are only in love during the
  evening.

Girls! Take off your sampots so that I may see which one of
  you I like the best.
Women! You are cunning, but I am in love!
You are cunning but you will grow large with child and you
  will give suck to my children.

Such verbal license in games and chants may bring a high pitch
of excitement, but premarital consummation is condemned. Most
Cambodian women seem not to experience premarital sexual relations; more men do, especially in the cities, where Chinese and
Vietnamese prostitutes are found. In the rural areas virginity in
a bride is almost mandatory; in the cities attitudes about this are
less rigid. In either country or city a bride who is pregnant by her
betrothed may come to the altar without exciting comment, a
betrothed couple being considered practically married.

The western concept of romantic love has caught the imagina-
tion of westernized Cambodians but is still a purely urban phenomenon. In Pnompenh there is some "dating" among college
students.

Rural and urban patterns of courtship differ but a young man
in either place might begin a flirtation by remarking about the
captivating beauty of the sky or of a banyan tree. To speak directly
of a girl's beauty—her figure or her face—or even about her dress
is considered blatant. The more sophisticated young man may
turn next to writing love letters. Finally, if his intentions are serious,
he will visit the girl's home and initiate formal procedures.

Aside from the monk, who is a figure of reverence, the unattached man is severely reproved by public opinion. Unattached
women are also disapproved of. If the individual is mentally and
physically normal only two patterns are acceptable—the family or
bonzehood.

A man generally marries between the ages of 20 and 25, a
girl between 16 and 22. Marriage within the circle of blood rela-

tives is strictly forbidden; first cousin marriage, however, is not included in the prohibition and occurs frequently. Standards may differ for royalty: in Cambodia (as in Thailand) it was once common for the king to marry a close relative such as an aunt or a half-sister. A widower may marry his former wife's sister if he can secure legal authorization.

The selection of a suitable mate from a reputable family calls for caution and prudence. All outward appearances suggest that Cambodian parents select the mates for their children, but the children can and do have considerable influence on the outcome.

A marriage project ripens slowly in the course of gossip and conversations with neighbors, relatives, and friends. Festivals, funerals, initiation ceremonies are all considered appropriate occasions on which to bring up the subject and to move the project forward. Cambodians are inveterate matchmakers and, although the final decision is that of the families involved, neighbors and friends participate from the sidelines.

During the first phase the families "feel each other out," as the Cambodians say. The two potential mothers-in-law carefully search out good and bad points concerning character and the relative social status of the two families. Then come impromptu visits to the girl's mother, during which only insignificant matters are discussed. The issue is never pressed but clues are given and clearly understood. If the girl's mother casually mentions that the girl is too young for marriage, this is interpreted as disapproval and the project is abandoned. If the girl's mother seems favorably disposed, the proposition is brought to a head. Throughout, there are exchanges of gifts, until, finally, the girl accepts a box of betel nut: a symbolic act that seals the engagement.

An *achar* thoroughly familiar with the Khmer calendar is consulted to examine and compare the birth dates of the young people, the concurrence of astrological patterns, lucky and unlucky days. Eventually, after minute calculations, the wedding date is set.

In the period before the wedding there are occasional gift exchanges of betel nut, sampots, and scarves. The scarves are primarily of symbolic value: "to fix the words and tie the hearts" of the engaged couple.

The engagement ceremony confers privileges and responsibilities similar to those conferred by the actual nuptials. The young husband-to-be takes a vow of servitude (*thvo bamro*) to his future in-laws and embarks on a courtship that puts his qualities as a husband to the test. (This procedure is now more frequent in rural communities than in the cities.) For a period of anywhere from one month to two years he assists in daily agricultural and household tasks. If he displays poor character, voices disrespect, or complains, he may be dismissed and the engagement dissolved. A good deal of hostility may build up in the young man during this period and sometimes he is unable to stomach the indignities of his trial. Infidelity during the trial period is punished as adultery.

The wedding is a lavish and elaborate affair. At one point during the ceremony the bridegroom presents a final gift to the bride's mother as prescribed by tradition—the so-called "milk price" or repayment for the mother's early care.

In rural areas remote from urban influences the traditional customs persist unchanged, but in the cities marriage patterns have been greatly modified by Chinese, Vietnamese, and French influences. Rites which were once marked by archaic simplicity have been complicated and formalized. The Ford sedan has replaced the palanquin and the bridegroom takes special pride in his polished shoes.

Divorce is infrequent whatever the social class. It can be obtained under specified circumstances: (1) prolonged absence of the husband, (2) abandonment by either husband or wife, (3) incompatability, (4) introduction of secondary wives into the household without the consent of the first wife, (5) refusal of the husband to provide for his wife and children, (6) adultery.

A divorce is legalized by a letter endorsed by a magistrate and is granted without elaborate red tape. Property settlement is clearly defined: the wife's dowry is returned but items accumulated during the marriage are divided, two parts going to the husband and one part to the wife. A divorced man or woman may remarry.

Whatever the family's personal emotions, a Cambodian funeral is not an occasion for demonstrating grief; death may lead to a higher reincarnation. Like birth, death exposes the household to invasions by evil spirits and calls for various precautions. Cambodians do not have a cult of the dead, but they are superstitious and attribute bad fortune to the influence of ghosts and spirits. A corpse is to be feared.

Unless burial is requested the body is cremated. If the fire does its work quickly it is taken as a sign that the departed leaves this world without sorrow, possessing everything that he needs. But if the fire is slow to consume the pyre, something is wrong— there has been some omission, some lack of respect, improper behavior by some member of the family—and misfortune may result.

SOCIAL ORGANIZATION

CAMBODIAN SOCIETY CONTAINS THREE main occupational segments—
the government bureaucracy, the clergy, and the peasantry. While
integrated, each has its separate function, both socially and, to a
large extent, politically. The society as a whole centers on these
three segments and the way in which they relate to each other.
Other occupational segments—commercial and professional—are also
present but are relatively peripheral.

Another important distinction made in the society is that
between royalty-nobility and commoners. The royal family and
the nobility form the core of the government and for the most part
confine their occupational activities to government service, although some of their members join the clergy or the military forces.

The nobility, the government bureaucracy, and the clergy
have distinct internal ranking systems, with different levels clearly
defined and titled. A basic distinction within the clergy is made
between the permanent professional clergy and the temporary
clergy (see chap. 5). Within government there is a clear distinction between the decision-making power level at the top and the
large mass of administrative officials and lesser civil servants.

Certain ranks in the religious hierarchy are equated with certain ranks in government or the nobility, and any given religious
official may be of superior or inferior rank to a particular government official or noble. These ranking systems are important to Cambodians, and relative rank is continually manifested in the use of
titles and in rather highly formalized patterns of respect and deference.

Prescribed patterns of address, speech, and manner obtain
among members of the three occupational groups and between
nobles and commoners. As would be expected, religious and govern-

mental officials have greater prestige than the peasants and nobles greater prestige than commoners; the peasants are also deferential to their fellow commoners in the clergy and the government. Age and reputation for righteous conduct have a special prestige of their own. Difference in age is an especially important factor in social relationships; greater age can offset the respect normally due a person of superior rank.

Although Buddhism does not support the ultimate validity of such status differences and the individual Cambodian is encouraged to believe that through the achievement of merit any man can become a Buddha, the fact of superior and inferior social rank is accepted by the Cambodians as one of the primary reference points for social relationships. High status is rationalized mainly as a reflection of merit in a previous life, and it is thus generally assumed that the higher a man's rank, the greater his accumulation of merit through successive reincarnations (see chap. 5).

Although present information does not permit a precise or detailed description of the class structure of Cambodia, certain kinds of distinctions, such as that between royalty-nobility and commoners, are readily apparent. Male members of the nobility occasionally have married commoners, but only recently have women of the nobility been known to do so. The French fostered class consciousness to some extent by distinguishing the rural peasantry from the people of the cities and, further, the urban civil servants from people less educated and less sophisticated in western ways. The leveling influence of Theravada Buddhism acts against all distinctions, however, as does the fact that social mobility is possible through advancement in the governmental or religious ranking systems, through favorable marriage, and, increasingly today, through education and betterment of economic status.

Power in Cambodian Society

The king occupies the top position in both the political and the religious hierarchies. Formerly, the people's lives were unconditionally in a king's hands: the control of the nation was centralized in his absolute power. Today, though his powers have been delimited by a constitution, he is still the symbol of the highest power.

While both the religious and governmental systems culminate in the capital city of Pnompenh and are unified at the top in the person of the king, each has its separate sphere of authority. This separation of authority and activity holds from the highest to the lowest administrative levels. In the village, for example, the *me-khum*, or village headman, is an entirely secular official, concerned only with such things as tax collection and the police, while the *chau-athikar*, or director of the village pagoda, is an entirely religious official concerned only with management of the pagoda and the conduct of religious ceremonies and instruction.

The religious system draws many more of its personnel from the peasantry than government does. Service as either a temporary or a professional bonze is a socially commendable career open to any young Cambodian male, and with proper conduct and advanced training it is possible to rise through the religious hierarchy to a high-ranking position. The requirements for entrance into government service are initially more highly selective in that they involve a partial conversion to secular values and a certain education and sophistication in an urban-western context.

The Political Hierarchy

Below the king in the political hierarchy come the members of the Crown Council, the appointed members of the Council of Ministers, the partially elective members of the Council of the Kingdom, and the popularly elected members of the National Assembly (see chap. 9). These executive and legislative bodies control the decision-making functions of the government. The posts are filled by members of the royal family and the lesser nobility and by commoners of high social status.

The government of Cambodia is organized on a national and provincial basis, but administrative power is predominantly centered in the cities. The villages are semiautonomous, their powers confined to matters of local interest. Administration rests on the shoulders of a limited, French-educated staff of professional civil servants, who have a special prestige as "white-collar" government workers and who feel a loss of face in transferring to a job in the country, no matter how lucrative.

The motivations and values of the members of the governing group show certain conformities and certain disparities. In general the occupation itself and its accompanying title are far more important than economic status, although it is true enough that many members of this group use their political status for private gain. The essential pride of government officials lies in possession of a title; today many of the higher civil servants insist on being addressed by their titles (in the same way that members of the nobility are addressed by their designations of rank) and feel insulted if the title is omitted. Behavior in office varies: some officials are extremely well-educated, intelligent, and alert and are sensitive to the interest of the people and the nation as a whole; others, content with any formula that satisfies their pride and ensures prestige, take the responsibility of high posts lightly.

Besides being the core of the governing group, the nobility occupies a powerful position in general. The royal family ranks the rest of the nobility. One of its special prerogatives is having in attendance a few hundred families belonging to a hereditary caste of Baku Brahmans, the only known caste in Cambodia. The Baku wear a special headdress, are guardians of the sacred symbols of court and nation (such as the royal sword), and officiate at ceremonies of the Court. Their special privileges include tax exemption.

Most members of the Cambodian nobility are related to the royal family but no noble family has a permanent claim to a particular rank and title, owing to a traditional principle of successive downgrading in rank whereby one degree of rank is lost in each succeeding generation. Sons of princes, for instance, are demoted one rank, their grandsons two ranks, and so on. The descendant of a once royal prince may become an untitled and unprivileged commoner in about four or five generations.

Since the king reserves the privilege of promoting or demoting anyone of rank, quick upranking and downranking are possible. Commoners may move up into the ranks of the nobility either by royal fiat (in which education is usually a prime factor) or through marriage into noble families or even the royal family itself.

The Buddhist Hierarchy

The king is at the apex of the Buddhist clerical structure but since his role is that of the sanctified protector of the national religion, he is more a religious symbol than a religious executive.

Cambodian Buddhism consists of two distinct orders—the Thommayut and Mohanikay—each of which has its own organization and personnel (see chap. 5). The Thommayut order ("those who are attached to the doctrine") consists of some 1,600 bonzes and confines its duties mostly to the cities, particularly to Pnompenh. Of the two orders, the Thommayut is the most influential in Court circles—hence its members regard themselves as among the Cambodian "elite." The Mohanikay ("great congregation") has an infinitely larger number of followers and clergy and finds its greatest strength in the villages. In its adherence to orthodox Singhalese practices it is much less strict than the rigid Thommayut order.

The king is the official head of both orders, although he takes no part in matters of religious dogma. It is his prerogative to select the chief of each order (*sangneayuk*), who must be chosen from among the members of the first ranks of bonzes.

The orders are subdivided regionally, and heads of dioceses are in charge at the provincial level. In the Mohanikay organization the provinces are divided into districts, the heads of which are responsible to the chief of the diocese and responsible for the various village pagodas in their district. Each pagoda has its prescribed permanent staff and director, as well as a complement of temporary and novice bonzes. The Thommayut have no district or village levels.

It is not an easy matter to achieve membership in the high levels of the permanent religious organization. No bonze is eligible until he has been in the religious community for at least twenty years. The size of membership of the top level of each order is fixed; the dignitaries assume different titles but are all of equal rank and are set apart in the country's social structure.

Class Structure

Although the over-all class structure of Cambodia is not clearly defined, it can be blocked out in terms of major groupings and their approximate relationship to each other. Further, the society of the villages is in general distinct from that of the urban centers. Many urban families, however, are recently derived from the villages and maintain close relationships with their rural relatives and friends.

Urban Society

Cambodia's "elite" class centers around the king, the royal family, and the Royal Court. In addition to the nobility it includes families whose members, though commoners, hold high-ranking positions in the church, in government, and in the armed forces. Although a distinction between noble and commoner is made within the civil service, at this upper level there is a display of considerable social equality. While individuals of high political position, including the nobility, may be removed from office or downgraded by royal authority and while tenure of office is often insecure, high class status once obtained tends to be self-perpetuating as a result of the opportunity it provides for displaying merit and for obtaining education, wealth, and power.

The white-collar workers who fill the ranks of the government administrative services make up the largest segment of the urban middle class. They are generally Cambodian (Khmer), occasionally European and Eurasian.

The second largest group is the lower echelon of the clergy of both the Mohanikay and Thommayut orders. Clerics are celibate and their way of life is oriented economically, socially, and politically toward the pagoda.

The third group is essentially commercial and professional—businessmen, shopkeepers, lawyers, and doctors—most of whom are Chinese and Vietnamese. Until very recently Cambodians have shown no interest in professional training or in following business careers. Economically, the role of the Chinese is distinct, but they tend to blend into the Cambodian social and cultural life more than the Vietnamese do. There has been considerable intermarriage of Chinese men and Cambodian women, and Sino-Cambodian off-spring are much desired by the Cambodians; but social mixture of Vietnamese with Cambodians is rare (see chap. 4).

Village Society

In the Cambodian villages the absence of landlord-tenant distinctions and the importance placed on family and communal interdependence suggest that class distinctions are minimal and less clearly defined than in the urban centers. Only a small percentage of the rural population has significantly large landholdings, and in terms of income and material assets the range from the wealthiest household to the poorest is narrow when compared to the range in the cities.

Groupings based on relative economic and political standing in the community can be discerned, however, and special power interests are partially reflected in the economic and political decisions reached by the village leaders, who select and later influence the village headman. At the same time, any internal friction seems usually to be mitigated by a very strong desire on the part of the peasants for village solidarity.

Ownership of land and material wealth do not alone assure prestige and respect to the individual. A poor man may earn prestige and respect by means of righteous conduct and faithful service to the pagoda; conversely, a well-to-do farmer who has willfully dodged religious responsibilities may have less prestige than the poorest man in the community.

There is little class consciousness at the pagoda, the common social, religious, and even political meeting ground for Cambodians from all walks of life. It is possible that higher rank and finery of dress might secure for an individual a seat closer to the bonze rostrum, but this is about the extent of preferential treatment. An illiterate peasant will not hesitate to rub elbows socially with a more educated villager, although he may perhaps consider it "profitable" and more respectful to remain silent when present at a discussion.

Status and Mobility

Social status in Cambodia is thus defined both by birth and by attained or inherited position within the religious or governmental hierarchies. More prestige and power result from religious or governmental rank than from either economic or professional status. Among lay occupations a position in the government eclipses all others in prestige; officials and civil servants at even the lower levels of government are accorded special respect.

The religious hierarchy has traditionally provided the major opportunities for individuals to rise in Cambodian society. The son of a poor farmer can hope, on entering the pagoda as a novice, to build an illustrious career through successive promotions; it is not impossible for him to become a high sect official at Pnompenh, or a *samdech*, a position equated with nobility or Court rank. Status in the religious hierarchy can also be utilized as a steppingstone or "bridge of merit" to the political hierarchy. Even if the highest rank is not reached, recognition for service to the community and respect from his fellow villagers can be achieved by any Cambodian through service at the local pagoda, either as an outstanding spiritual guide or in some administrative role.

A comparatively recent avenue for social advancement is education. Through a series of competitive hurdles a Cambodian with ability can progress through the school system. The pagoda school and government elementary schools are open to all. At the *lycée* and college levels government and alumni scholarships are available to those who can qualify in competitive examinations. About one thousand Cambodians are said to be studying in Paris, many at the expense of the government. The government expects that some of these students will make use of their higher learning by joining the educational system.

Educational achievement has in the past led mainly to the highly coveted civil service; today, two other fields—commerce and teaching—are attracting attention. Westernized education has been partly responsible for this new interest, since it emphasizes the idea of education and economic achievement as mutually reinforcing goals.

The new educational ideas are also raising the status of students and teachers, thus attracting men to the teaching profession, which formerly was not considered as desirable as the civil service and was far less well paid. Today, urban Cambodians with a good education are honored and respected, and both students and teachers have gained in prestige. The professors at the Institute of Legal and Economic Studies in Pnompenh are the most highly regarded of all. Pay has been raised to make the profession more attractive, and the government is emphasizing improvement of the educational system (see chap. 19).

Status upgrading can also be achieved through wealth. Though economic status carries little prestige in itself, wealth can be used to advantage. It makes possible, for instance, a favorable marriage into an influential family. It is also important in providing the means for a better education, which in turn can lead to rising status in the political and religious structures.

In present-day Cambodian society both education and wealth, as ends and as means to ends, are assuming greater importance. As a result, the social gaps between the educated and uneducated and between the urban dweller and the villager are increasing.

While any ambitious Cambodian male can chart his career along culturally approved lines as outlined above, the fact remains that most Cambodians are not preoccupied with reaching the top of the various scales of individual and class status and are content to return to the soil after a short stint at the pagoda or after finishing elementary school. It is true that many are imbued now with special initiative and ambition, but few have caught the virus of "keeping up with the Joneses." Competition for status involves values of an order completely foreign to most Cambodians, who dislike scheming or stepping on others to gain prestige. They are quick to rationalize their failures in the secular world by means of their Buddhist ideology: the sum total of merit accumulated in the previous existence obviously did not warrant any better status in the present existence; perhaps success will come in the next existence.

Cambodians do not think in Marxian terms—of an "elite," a bourgeoisie, and a proletariat which are in any way antagonistic to or in basic competition with each other. The various segments and classes of the society are viewed as facts of life, the "given quantities" which are to be accepted, and there is little concern with changing the social structure. The Cambodian is more concerned with self-improvement in the religious sense of advancing status, either in this life or the next, through personal merit and individual achievement.

DYNAMICS OF POLITICAL BEHAVIOR

THROUGHOUT THE EIGHTY-FIVE YEARS of the French protectorate, Cambodian political attitudes and behavior were centered almost exclusively on the problem of independence from France. On this issue Cambodians generally were united but their resistance to French rule remained on the whole passive. The Buddhist religion provided a symbolic assurance of eventual liberation from France, and nationalism was kept alive in the shadow of the pagoda and in the pagoda schools.

World War II ended colonial rule in Southeast Asia, revealing in Cambodia political forces that were militant but disunited—though at first only the militant aspect was apparent. In 1940, with the weakening of French control in Indochina, a more vocal nationalism emerged in the Cambodian press; in 1941 there was a demonstration of Buddhist monks against the French, precipitated by the arrest of one of their more nationalistic number. Later, the end of the war and the return of French control revealed the disunity that had developed among Cambodian leaders during the five years of hostilities.

Between 1945 and 1955 the Cambodian government, under the leadership of King Sihanouk and the royal family, engaged in a concerted struggle to free the country once and for all. This struggle was waged openly, by legal and diplomatic means. The government was opposed, however, by a new and more militantly nationalist movement whose leaders were impatient with what they viewed as the insincere and compromising approach of the government. This militant element had one head but two bodies—a legitimate political grouping known as the Pracheathipatey, or Democratic party, and a rebel force, known as Khmer Issarak, or Free Cambodia. Both looked to Son Ngoc Thanh for at least nominal leadership. From the government standpoint, the activities of both became increasingly subversive.

The militant movement was temporarily neutralized by the achievement of full independence in 1955. The Democratic party, which had won the first elections in 1947 and had since systematically blocked the government in the National Assembly, was roundly beaten at the polls later in 1955 by Sihanouk's new Sangkum Reastr Niyum, or People's Socialist Community party; and the Khmer Issarak, its main argument and most of its popular support lost, found many of its staunchest leaders surrendering to the government.

The government had reason to believe that its position was secure. Vietminh Communist forces that had operated on Cambodian territory after hostilities broke out with the French in 1946, had been withdrawn under the Geneva cease-fire agreement of 1954, and the Cambodian Communists whom they had sponsored, lacking popular support in Cambodia, either were evacuated to North Vietnam or withdrew to the Cambodian countryside. By mid-1956 it seemed that the opposition, both legal and subversive, had been silenced, and that Communist activity was stopped.

In recent years, Cambodia's involvement in the cold war has provided the government's opponents with a new issue—Cambodian neutrality. The opposition has rejected Sihanouk's policy of neutrality on the grounds that it actually fosters the growth of Communist influence in Cambodia and that Sihanouk himself is no longer capable of controlling that influence. With the Democratic party out of power opposition is now centered in the Khmer Issarak movement, and the recent resurgence of antigovernment guerrilla activity in Siemreap province has been ascribed by Sihanouk to the Khmer Issarak.

Early in January 1959 the Cambodian government revealed that it had discovered a conspiracy to overthrow the government. Sam Sary, former ambassador to the United Kingdom and onetime secretary-general of Sihanouk's own party, was accused of plotting in collusion with Son Ngoc Thanh. The conspiracy, said to have been hatched in Bangkok by Son Ngoc Thanh, is known in Cambodia today as the "Bangkok Plot." Following its exposure, Sam Sary fled to Bangkok but several of his supporters in the Cambodian government were ousted and other agents reportedly were arrested in Pnompenh.

While denying charges that he is permitting Cambodia to serve as a base for Communist infiltration into Thailand and South Vietnam, Sihanouk nevertheless admits and decries increased Communist activity and propaganda among the Cambodian population.

From the standpoint of Sihanouk's government, then, Cambodia today faces two subversive threats: one from Son Ngoc Thanh and the Khmer Issarak, who oppose the government policy of neutralism and its refusal to align with SEATO, and in general take a pro-West stand; the other from the Communists, who while claiming to respect Cambodian neutrality are working toward the ultimate goal of creating a Communist state in the country.

At this writing, Sihanouk's Sangkum party is in control, but its electoral victory of September 1955 may have been too complete in the sense that it left little room for expression to an ever-growing group of discontent youths who are being educated in Cambodian schools and French and American higher institutions. There assertedly are many teachers who disapprove of government policy. Personal loyalties between teachers and students are strong in Cambodia. Pnompenh (the scene of repeated student riots since 1942) experienced serious student strikes in 1955 and 1956. Some students threatened to follow their professors in rebellion against the government.

Frustration among the younger generation was carefully exploited by the opposition parties during the 1955 elections. Out of a total of 108 candidates in the twenty-five to thirty-five age group 62 were presented by the Democratic party and a smaller, leftist party, the Pracheachon, or People's party, categorized by Sihanouk as pro-Communist. They were soundly beaten by their generally older rivals and thus eliminated from formal participation in the political life of the country—but it is precisely there that danger may lay. Having been beaten, the young candidates did not lose their taste for politics; yet for a long time the only parties that showed a willingness to give them a chance were those of the opposition.

On the other hand, many among the youthful segment of the population have continued to look toward Sihanouk himself for a change in the system. Realizing that it had much to gain or lose by its attitude toward Cambodia's youth, the Sangkum undertook in 1957 to organize an auxiliary corps known as the Jeunesse Socialiste du Royaume Khmèr (JSRK) or Socialist Youth of the Khmer Kingdom. The first cadres of JSRK were graduated in April 1958 and labor battalions formed of JSRK personnel have been used by the government in reconstruction work. During recent internal disturbances, Sihanouk proposed to arm and train them.

Sihanouk has attached great importance to the role of the JSRK. In an article in April 1958 he said: "The JSRK is our hope. It is its spirit and ideal of patriotism, sacrifice, work, and integrity which must prevail in parliament, in the administration, and in other vital sectors of the country."

Today, the Sangkum stands almost unchallenged in its control of the government. The Democratic party did not present any candidates in the elections of March 1958, and the People's party presented only five. A new opposition party organized by Sam Sary dissolved upon exposure of the "Bangkok Plot" and Sam Sary's subsequent flight from the country. Other smaller parties that appeared in the 1955 elections are no longer in evidence. The government's main concern now is not legal opposition at the polls but subversive activity, internally and along the borders with Thailand and South Vietnam.

Despite its domination of the legislature the Sangkum has not been able to avoid government crises caused by personality clashes: from September 1955 to the end of 1958 six cabinets were overthrown; a seventh cabinet, purified of the supporters of Sam Sary, now rules the country. But given continued pressures revolving around the issue of neutrality, further crises may be expected.

The Strong Men and Their Parties

In Cambodia, as in France, the supreme executive is theoretically "above politics"; the position of the king is not affected when a cabinet falls. At the cabinet level portfolios rotate among a small group of professional politicians; a man who yesterday was prime minister may well be defense minister today and minister of public health tomorrow. Most of the articulate leaders among the Cambodians, recognizing that this is bound to be detrimental to their country, clamor for a "strong man." National existence without one seems to them as impossible in reality as it is in their legends.

Since the government controls all media of mass communication (see chap. 10) it is clear that the small power group at the top has the best chance of guaranteeing that a strong man will come from its ranks. Of this group, one person by virtue of his family background as well as personal successes stands out as the most important: Prince Norodom Sihanouk, son of the present King and Queen of Cambodia, and formerly (1941-55) King of Cambodia. Dominant among his rivals is Son Ngoc Thanh, leader of the Khmer Issarak and the Democratic party.

8. *The Strong Men and Their Parties*

Sihanouk

Having fought for independence for nearly ten years and having gained it almost singlehandedly, Sihanouk for a time stood at the apex of Cambodian society—not only was he king, he was popular.

Almost simultaneously with the end of the struggle against the French there developed civil strife and general insecurity in the country. The young king faced problems whose solution could not be attained through negotiations or quick action. Social and economic reforms required both a long-term effort from the small power elite at the top and large-scale popular participation at the base. In this area the average Cambodian politician proved all but powerless; the problem—even with American and French help—is of overwhelming proportions and of an intricate technical nature comprehensible even within the government to an infinitesimal minority.

Sihanouk felt that as a monarch "above political struggles" he could not fully identify himself with controversial measures, no matter how pressing these might be, without endangering the throne itself by making it unpopular. Any measure he might take or advocate would no doubt be accepted without murmur by his own following—but could immediately be exploited by the opposition as "dictatorial." He decided the only way he could assume an effective political role in the circumstance was to abdicate, surrendering the ceremonial and symbolic powers ascribed to him as a king. Having abdicated, he was free from the constitutional as well as the cultural restrictions placed upon him by his royal rank, yet he retained the aura that in Cambodia attaches to everything royal.

Sihanouk expressed his position quite clearly in his abdication speech of March 2, 1955, and in a subsequent radio broadcast to the country at large on March 9, 1955:

> I want to renounce the throne in order to show that I do not cling to power, authority, and privileges for my own person, for my happiness, and for my personal well-being. (Abdication speech.)

> As King, it was difficult to keep informed. Every time I was on a tour I was received with a solemn reception prepared in advance. I could only see the flowers and hear the lies. The true face of the people was hidden from me. (Broadcast to the country.)

Although now a politician, and theoretically a "private person," Sihanouk continues to have at his disposal most of the country's newspapers, the press agency, and the radio network and he uses the royal palace grounds for political meetings of the party he founded. Sihanouk's effectiveness as a vote-getter and campaigner were demonstrated in the 1955 elections when his party so completely overwhelmed the opposition that neither the Democratic party (Pracheathipatey) nor the People's party (Pracheachon) won a single seat in the National Assembly.

Sihanouk created the Sangkum to be the tool with which he would reform Cambodia's political life and institutions. He and the group around him refuse to call the Sangkum a "party." In the words of its statutes: "Our movement is not a political party. It is an expression of the will of the poor classes who have decided to group themselves together to fight against all abuses of power by the local authorities." (Another part of the statutes does, however, refer to it as a party.)

Membership requirements are fairly liberal but at the same time make certain demands of loyalty that fit well with what a Cambodian expects from a strong leader. A new member of the Sangkum cannot belong to another party "at the moment" he joins, he must have a clean judicial record, he must be ready "to support the party's program," and he must "observe strictly the discipline of the party . . . and . . . place the interests of the people above everything else."

An additional feature that makes the party attractive to its followers is its financial tactics. No fees are asked from the members, and the party's resources come from lotteries, festivals, or "donations from the government and others." It is obvious that such a privileged situation gives the Sangkum a tremendous advantage over any other party—the more so as the Cambodian government has been made up of homogeneous Sangkum elements, capable of seeing to it that civil service jobs and other advantages go first and foremost to the areas or persons that have shown loyalty to the party.

Moreover, no Cambodian can forget that the present leader of the Sangkum is also the former king of the country and, no doubt, the future successor of his own father and mother to the throne. Opposing the Sangkum today may well mean opposing the king tomorow, while serving the Sangkum today might be called foresightedness.

Such a situation is not without immediate advantage for the country itself. Sihanouk really has united behind him a great majority of the Cambodians. It seems likely, however, that the

Sangkum's present popularity does not result so much from its program, as such, as from popular confidence that a party headed by the former king is more likely to favor the people. As for the old-line politicians, riding on Sihanouk's coattails greatly simplifies political life.

Son Ngoc Thanh

One other man, Son Ngoc Thanh, has rivalled Sihanouk as a political organizer and a popular figure. He first gained attention when he organized the protest march of Buddhist monks in 1941. When the French dispersed the demonstration he escaped arrest, going first to Thailand, then to Japan, where he stayed for three years. In 1945 he returned to Cambodia with the rank of captain in the Imperial Japanese Army.

When the Japanese overthrew the French colonial administration in March 1945 and allowed Sihanouk to proclaim the independence of Cambodia, Thanh became minister of foreign affairs of the new government. By V-J day he had become prime minister. His tenure in office, however, was short, for the French returned in September 1945 and arrested him in Pnompenh the following month. He was flown to France, tried before a French military tribunal on charges of high treason, and sentenced to twenty years at hard labor. The sentence was commuted to house arrest in France.

During the years 1941 to 1947, Thanh managed somehow to stimulate a nationalist movement against Sihanouk's government. During his brief stay in Thailand in 1941 and 1942 he had been instrumental in organizing and leading the Khmer Issarak movement, and the Democratic party which emerged victorious in the 1947 elections appears to have considered him its nominal head, although he was not personally on hand to lead it.

To counter Communist propaganda efforts, to appease his Democratic party opponents, and to gain popularity, King Sihanouk arranged for the return of Son Ngoc Thanh from France. On October 29, 1951 Thanh came back to Pnompenh and was welcomed by five thousand Cambodians. He had pledged to abstain from politics but two months later, appearing before a Cambodian audience in Takeo province at the side of Pach Chhoen, Cambodian minister of information, he stated that only the departure of French troops could insure both the independence of Cambodia and the return of peace and order in the country's political life.

Son Ngoc Thanh founded a newspaper in Pnompenh, *Khmer*

Krok (Khmer People Awake). Toleration of his activities by the royal government ended in February 1952, and publication of the newspaper was suspended. Broadcasting on his own illegal radio transmitter from somewhere in the forests of Siemreap province, he chose March 9, the anniversary of the 1945 Japanese coup that had displaced the French, to announce his plan "to carry on the struggle for the freedom of Cambodia." At his right hand was Ea Sichau, the 28-year-old director of customs, a well-known, dynamic young Cambodian political leader.

Son Ngoc Thanh attempted to consolidate the forces of the Khmer Issarak, at that time believed to number about three thousand men, half of whom were armed. He is known to have been successful only in establishing an alliance with Keo Tak, the rebel chief in Battambang province. Subsequently, French officials repeatedly charged that he had merged his forces with the Vietminh but Son Ngoc Thanh's supporters vigorously denied any Communist connection, nor did the Communist radio ever claim him as an ally. It is clear that he remained the spiritual leader of the more nationalistic members of the Democratic party, if not the actual director-in-hiding of their activities. Student demonstrations in May 1952 in Pnompenh were generally attributed to his influence.

The popularity of Son Ngoc Thanh was only slightly undermined by his flight from the capital. In fact, he gained an even wider audience when, in 1952, King Sihanouk dismissed the National Assembly, controlled by the Democratic party and friendly to Thanh, and ruled under the Royal Mandate (see chap. 2). Recently his appeal has been to students and other young people who feel that the older men in government fail to open up to them positions to which they feel they have a claim.

Son Ngoc Thanh's success in attracting younger people has given his Democratic party the reputation of being the young, dynamic party of Cambodia, although the People's party has also been successfully seeking support from the younger generation. A comparison of the ages of the candidates presented by these two opposition parties and by Sihanouk's Sangkum for the September 1955 National Assembly elections shows dramatically the polarization of Cambodian politics that this activity could bring about. Roughly one-half of the Democratic party candidates and two-thirds of the People's party candidates were thirty-five or younger whereas about one-third of the Sangkum slate, which included most of the older politicians and government officials, were over fifty-six.

The Khmer Issarak Movement

The origins of the Khmer Issarak (Free Cambodia) movement go back to 1941. Thailand, seeking to make up its 1904 territorial losses to Cambodia had attacked the French in Indochina in August, 1940; after several weeks of inconclusive fighting the Japanese had intervened and compelled the French to agree to a peace treaty with Thailand. By this treaty, signed on May 9, 1941, Cambodia was stripped of the border provinces it had regained in 1904.

According to certain sources the people living in these provinces felt they had been "liberated," since Thailand was an independent state and Cambodia was not. From 1941 until 1945, these provinces became the center of the Khmer Issarak movement, sponsored by the Thai and composed mainly of Cambodian nationalist *émigrés* under the leadership of Son Ngoc Thanh.

With the return of the French to Cambodia in 1945, Thailand was forced to return these provinces to Cambodia; the Khmer Issarak leaders removed to Bangkok where they were joined by other Cambodian nationalists who had remained in Pnompenh during the war but now had to flee.

Subsequent events strengthened the Khmer Issarak. In December 1946 hostilities broke out between the French and Vietminh forces. Thailand, until it finally committed itself to the anti-Communist side in 1950, served as the major transit base for weapons and supplies to the Vietminh and concurrently supported the Khmer Issarak in the hopes of embarrassing the colonial powers. By September 1947 the Khmer Issarak felt strong enough to set up a "Free Cambodian Government."

This "Free Cambodian Government" enjoyed the recognition of the short-lived, left-wing Thai government of Pridi Phanomyong (since 1954 a resident of Red China). The return to power of the conservative Marshal Pibulsonggram in Thailand forced liquidation of most Khmer Issarak activities there and the return of the rebels to Cambodian territory.

The Khmer rebels now sought to consolidate their positions by forming a single unified force, known as the Khmer National Liberation Committee, under Dap Chhuon Nghul Pech, leader of one of the larger Issarak bands. The committee, however, never truly operated as a single force or government. There were at least half a dozen Khmer leaders operating in various areas; their political objectives became less and less clear, and they acted more and more like war lords, exacting tribute from the population in the form of "voluntary contributions," raiding truck convoys and railroad trains. They also received a certain amount of financial aid and arms from the Communist Vietminh, although refusing to accept its military command.

To the Communist forces operating in South Vietnam and to those in the north that had, until the Chinese Communists reached the Vietnamese border late in 1949, depended largely upon supplies smuggled in from Thailand, the undisciplined behavior of the Khmer Issarak created a dangerous factor of uncertainty along their own supply lines. Late in 1947 the Vietminh began to sponsor rival Khmer forces, which at first operated in Kandal and other areas close to the Vietnamese border.

With the establishment of this rival, Communist-sponsored rebel organization, the Issarak themselves broke into two major factions: those who for various reasons maintained relations with the Vietminh, and those who broke with them and responded to a rise in Communist strength by efforts to enlarge their own forces throughout Cambodia. There occurred several clashes between the Vietminh and Issarak forces under the command of Dap Chhuon and Puth Chhay as these leaders sought to cut down the size of the territories held by the Vietminh.

The government succeeded in obtaining at least the temporary cooperation of Dap Chhuon but was less successful in conciliating Keo Tak and his forces operating in Battambang province. Periodic military operations were launched against him without result, and he was left to control a small area of the province. Throughout 1952 and early 1953 the situation remained precarious. The nationalist guerrillas presented more of a threat to the security of the country than the Communist guerrillas, for, while the former were determined eventually to take over the government in Pnompenh, the latter were for the time being preoccupied in keeping their own supply and communication lines to the main battlefield in Vietnam as undisturbed as possible.

The situation considerably improved after the nationalist rebels heard of King Sihanouk's demands for full independence in the spring of 1953. The first indication of a break in the nationalist rebel front occurred when the redoubtable Puth Chhay surrendered with his forces on May 2, 1953 and was brought into the Cambodian army with the rank of major. On May 13, 1953 Ouch Nilpech, another leader in the Battambang area, also surrendered and was commissioned in the army with the rank of captain. The government clearly hoped to reconcile the remaining dissidents. King Sihanouk himself indicated that every effort would be made to bring Son Ngoc Thanh back into the "national community," charging that Thanh's failure to return would "prove definitely that he is a vassal of the Vietminh."

The integration of Puth Chhay's men into the national forces created difficulties for the Cambodian government. Assigned in June 1953 to the defense of Pnompenh, they apparently employed terroristic methods in dealing with the city's population. A number of killings were attributed to them and in September 1953 the King finally was forced to order them out of the city. Puth Chhay withdrew to the south of Pnompenh and maintained an uneasy truce with the government.

On September 11, 1953 Prime Minister Penn Nouth again appealed to the remaining dissidents to cease combat. He offered total amnesty to the Khmer Issarak and called attention to the October 1, 1953 deadline that had been set for surrenders. He promised the use of "the sternest measures" thereafter "to punish traitors to the country." He also asked the Vietminh forces to vacate Cambodia.

The determined drive to cope with Cambodia's internal security problem began to show marked results. Emissaries of the two rebel Khmer Issarak chiefs Chantarangsey and Savangvong arrived to contact the Prime Minister. Their submission was particularly significant since they were the leaders of forces numbering almost 5,000 men. Moreover, they were known to have maintained relations with the Communist-led movement of Son Ngoc Minh. The surrender ceremony took place on February 20, 1954, in Kompong Speu province. The government incorporated into its armed services 1,000 of Chantarangsey's force of 2,700 men, and 800 of Savangvong's 2,000.

With the military situation well in hand, King Sihanouk set about consolidating his political control at the outset of 1955. He was not willing to allow his Issarak and Communist opponents to win through elections what they had failed to gain through guerrilla fighting. He used his control of the government to launch a political offensive against the former dissidents.

After the creation of the Sangkum party, the Democratic party under Son Ngoc Thanh lost ground, especially as Thanh preferred a mountain hideout to remaining in the capital, though he did not again resort to open rebellion. After Sihanouk's 1955 victory at the polls, there was, toward the middle of 1956, a certain resurgence of political activity around Son Ngoc Thanh, but there was no evidence until the Bangkok Plot in early 1959 that he might be induced to again go into open rebellion against the established government.

The Communist Rebel Movement

The objective of the Vietnamese Communists in Cambodia was two-fold: a short-range aim to keep lines of communication open; a long-range aim to establish, if possible, a Communist-dominated government in Cambodia that would be a sympathetic Vietminh supporter and eventually become a protectorate of North Vietnam, as the government of Cambodia had been a Vietnamese protec-torate prior to arrival of the French.

The short-range objective was entirely assigned to Vietminh units themselves, while responsibility for the long-range objective was placed in the hands either of Khmer or, preferably, of mixed Khmer-Vietnamese Communist leaders.

The Vietminh began to organize its political activities in Cam-bodia in 1949 with the creation of the Canvassing Committee for the Creation of a Revolutionary Cambodian People's Party (Ban Van Dong Thanh Lap Dang Nhan Cach Mang Cao Mien). The com-mittee was composed almost entirely of carefully selected Viet-namese with considerable experience in Khmer affairs. In con-formity with the old Komintern directive to unite first of all the "activity of the various national revolutionary organizations," the committee's action was at first entirely limited to promulgating simple Khmer nationalist slogans.

The next step was the creation of special Vietnamese armed units under the command of the South Vietnam Interzone, known as Vietnam Troops to Help Cambodia. Such units completely took over what became the Southwestern Zone (Kampot and Kompong Speu), and soon the whole South Vietnam Zone Command of the Vietnam People's Army (the Vietminh armed forces) transferred its headquarters to Preyveng province in Cambodia, finding it quieter than tightly controlled South Vietnam. It was soon fol-lowed by the Central Office South, commanded by Sieu Heng, a revolutionary of mixed Khmer-Vietnamese ancestry, and the bulk of the Vietminh's regional commands.

In 1950 began the installation of a complete network of Cadre Committees (Ban Can Su) under the over-all direction of Nguyen Thanh Son (Hanilakiri). Cambodia was split into three zones (*mien*); several sectors (*vung*); and numerous local units (*srok, khum, phum*). At zone level, the Ban Can Su Southwest had no Cambodian members, while the two other zone committees had one Cambodian member each on a seven-man committee. Intercell branches (*lien-chi*) and other subdivisions were set up just as on Vietnamese soil.

To make up for the lack of experienced Cambodian leaders, the Communists established schools in Cambodia for both political and military personnel. On June 11, 1950 the Achar Hem Chieu political school was formally opened "at a certain base in the Southwest War Zone of Cambodia." "More than 140 pupils comprising cadres of the *khum* and *srok* grades in southwest Cambodia and a number of other cadres from northeast, southeast, and northwest Cambodia" were reported in attendance. The Khmer People's Liberation Army school had its opening ceremonies "in a liberated area" on August 14, 1950, enrolling "nearly 100 Cambodian partisans." Other facilities to provide personnel for government services, including police, information, economics, and education, were established in Takeo province.

The emphasis throughout was on training youth. To placate the Buddhist clergy, monks who had also been given special schooling by the Communists figured prominently in all the public meetings and ceremonies. To allay fears of Vietnamese domination, propaganda was conducted in the Khmer language and edited by Khmer. Vietnamese units were transformed into mixed Khmer-Vietnamese formations and attached as volunteer troops to the Khmer People's Liberation Army.

Communist Propaganda among Minorities

The principal ethnic minorities in Cambodia were given distinct attention by the Communists. *Emigré* Vietnamese sections of the adult, youth, and peasant Associations for National Salvation of Vietnam were established in Cambodia. In Pnompenh, the Vietnamese, who comprise the city's principal labor force, were organized into unions subject to heavy Communist pressure. In the provinces particular consideration was given to gaining control of the Vietnamese rubber workers and their union, for the Communists were bent on disrupting rubber production to weaken the French economically. Further agitation was conducted among the Vietnamese fishing population living in the Tonle Sap lake region and along the river basins; such action provided funds as well as food supplies for the guerrilla forces.

There was similar activity among the Chinese. An Overseas

Chinese Liberation Association was formed; its functions were to recruit new cadres and above all to levy taxes on rich Chinese merchants and the Chinese operators of the pepper plantations, rice mills, and salt installations. The greatest success in this respect was achieved in Kampot province.

Communist efforts with respect to the Cham-Malay population were directed at mobilizing Cambodia's third largest minority against the royal government and the French, provoking Malay desertions from the French and royal armies, and recruiting Malay fighters for their own ranks. The Communists reportedly were least successful among this Moslem element—a stable, homogeneous, and strongly hierarchical community. They did capture the well-known Malay "Viceroy" Toun-Sles, and for some five months in 1951 issued numerous tracts and propaganda leaflets in his name. But Toun-Sles escaped in June 1951 and the effect of the propaganda apparently lasted only as long as his imprisonment.

These activities were paralleled by intensive attempts to mobilize the large Cambodian minority in Vietnam in the provinces bordering Cambodia. Numerous meetings were held in the fifth interzone (southern-central Vietnam), bordering the Cambodian provinces of Stungtreng, Kratie, and Kompong Thom, as well as in the ninth zone (southern Vietnam), bordering Kampot and Takeo provinces. The Issarak Mutual Aid Committee was set up to raise funds and enlist recruits for the Khmer People's Liberation Army. Communist propaganda which emphasized the unified character of the struggle throughout the Indochinese peninsula was transmitted through such organizations.

The Khmer Resistance Government

With the creation of the Vietnam Lao Dong [Communist] party in 1951, the DRVN (Democratic Republic of Viet-Nam) possessed an adequate political tool to create a brother-revolutionary party in Cambodia—making due allowance, of course, for the lack of political sophistication among the Cambodian masses. This new party, the Dang Nhan Dan Cach Mang Cao Mien or Revolutionary Cambodian People's party, was not only entirely created by the Lao Dong but its very name and statutes were drafted in Vietnamese and had to be translated into Cambodian. A pseudo-revolutionary government—the Cambodian National Liberation Committee—was set up with Sieu Heng, head of the Central Office South, as its president. A year later a "Khmer Resistance Government" was set up under Son Ngoc Minh; it was recognized by the DRVN and the "Free Laotian Government"—but by no one else.

The Khmer Resistance Government established at the outset, as an operational principle, its complete support of the policies and aims of Ho Chi Minh's DRVN, but the Cambodian government had undercut the movement with its own successful struggle against the French, and without Vietnam Communist support, Cambodian Communism was, despite its pretensions to governmental status, an isolated minority movement.

To further integrate Communist policies in Cambodia with those of the DRVN and to begin the process of achieving recognition in the Communist world and elsewhere for Son Ngoc Minh's Khmer Resistance Government, Sieu Heng was officially dispatched to North Vietnam. There in November 1950 he participated in a meeting of the Vietnam Committee of World Peace Defenders, indicating Cambodian support of its activities and resolutions. Subsequently he attended a three-day conference, November 21-23, 1950, as the representative of the Cambodian National United Front in concert with the representatives of the National United Fronts of Laos and Vietnam. This meeting avowedly was designed to discuss the setting up of a joint bloc of the three National United Fronts.

Sieu Heng remained in northern Vietnam where he was received formally by the Standing Committee of the DRVN National Assembly on February 20, 1951. That month he also participated in the deliberations resulting in the open re-establishment of the Communist party in Vietnam, now called the Vietnam Workers' party (Vietnam Dang Lao Dong), and was listed among those who "enthusiastically hail the establishment of our Party and approve the united resistance program." Explicit recognition of the Vietnam Communists as the political leaders of the war against France thus was confirmed by all the participating elements in the three resistance movements. The subsequent merger of the three National United Fronts on March 11, 1951, and the adoption of a common program was merely ceremonial. Effectively, the Vietnamese Communist leadership was empowered to act for all in any subsequent negotiations.

This dependence of the Cambodian Communists on the Vietminh was a fact that both the Issarak and the royal government never failed to exploit. Son Ngoc Minh, the Cambodian Communist leader, was forced to attempt to counter this charge publicly.

The stigma of being a "Vietnamese puppet" stuck, however, and greatly contributed to the eventual failure of the Cambodian Communist movement.

Communist Withdrawal

By early fall of 1953, the security situation in Cambodia had deteriorated to the point where Prime Minister Penn Nouth made his appeal to the Vietminh to evacuate the country.

> You who operate in the Kingdom on the pretext of helping our country to realize its independence, I can tell you that we have obtained it by our own means. While we are not Communists, we have no quarrel with Communism as long as it does not seek to impose itself on us by force.

The Paris edition of the *New York Herald-Tribune*, September 12, 1953, asserted that the Cambodians had offered neutrality to the Vietminh in exchange for the withdrawal from Cambodia of all Vietminh forces, then estimated at about ten thousand.

This statement elicited pained comment from French and American representatives in Cambodia, who deplored its manifest neutralism and threatened withdrawal of economic aid to Cambodia. The statement was promptly reversed by Foreign Minister Sirik Matak, who assured the French and Americans that "Cambodia is ready to give its support to the Free Nations' fight against Communism"; nevertheless the Prime Minister's declaration had indicated that there were influential Cambodians prepared to pay the price of accepting a neutral status for Cambodia in return for the evacuation of alien Vietminh troops. The Vietminh's only known response to this overture was the release of a communiqué from the "High Command of the Khmer People's Liberation Army" which stressed that "guerrilla warfare has been intensified in southwest Cambodia during the past few months."

The return to Pnompenh of King Sihanouk from his voluntary exile in the border provinces, the subsequent mobilization of the "Live Forces of Cambodia," and the return to legality of several nationalist rebels somewhat improved the security situation with regard to the Communists. By December 1953 Communist forces had evacuated most of the area north of the Battambang-Pnompenh railroad line and had retreated into the southwestern hill and mountain area.

Effects of the Geneva Conference

As the French began to implement the "Navarre Plan" early in

1954, the Vietminh high command sought to alleviate the pressure on its northern key positions by launching several diversionary offensives in secondary theaters such as Laos and Cambodia. In Cambodia this resulted in the Cambodian and Vietnamese Communist rebel forces being merged into one single force known as the Khmer People's Liberation Army.

The offensive in Cambodia brought about a sharp increase of guerrilla operations against communications throughout the country and a sudden Communist offensive out of the Laotian and Vietnamese plateau area into the northeastern sector of Cambodia, resulting in April 1954 in a temporary occupation of the important northeastern road hub of Voeune Sai, and an attack on the Pnompenh-Battambang train. Some one hundred civilians, including thirty bonzes, were killed. Public opinion was aroused, and on April 23, 1954 the Cambodian government reported these aggressive acts to the United Nations.

At Geneva, the Khmer Resistance Government was advanced by the Communists as a legitimate voice entitled to a hearing in peace negotiations, but when Son Ngoc Minh, President of the Khmer Resistance Government, demanded on May 3, 1954 that the Geneva Conference formally seat a delegation representing his government, he was not supported by the Communist bloc.

The political aims of the Cambodian Communists were completely defeated as a result of the agreements reached at Geneva. Little remained for them but to make their peace with the royal Cambodian government or to be evacuated north to the Vietnamese Communist zone, thereby clearly showing their allegiance to a foreign cause, that of the Vietnamese Communists. For a time, Cambodian Communist forces sought to obtain through the channel of the International Supervisory and Control Commission (ISCC), recognition as an independent force and possession of an autonomous area such as that obtained by the Laotian Communist forces. The royal government authorities refused, however, to grant them any recognition whatever and insisted that they surrender, indicating that they might be pardoned of they took an oath of loyalty to the royal government.

On September 24, 1954 the Cambodian Communists submitted six proposals to the Joint Armistice Commission, attempting again to get recognition. Again they failed; the royal government refused to negotiate with them.

The Cambodian Communists then threw in with the Vietnamese Communist forces operating in Cambodia. Although most of the low-ranking guerrilla fighters simply slipped away, the hard core of the movement withdrew from Cambodia toward North Vietnam along with the Vietnamese Communist forces that had operated in Cambodia and that now, under the terms of the cease-fire, accepted evacuation. On October 25, 1954 Nguyen Thanh Son —a full colonel in Ho Chi Minh's Vietnam People's Army—left Pnompenh, where he had acted as the head of the Communist delegation to the Joint Armistice Commission, and evacuated to North Vietnam with about 2,500 troops. (Some reports indicate that up to 4,000 troops were evacuated.) The number of evacuees was considered unsatisfactory by the Cambodian government, which estimated that at least 4,000 to 5,000 Communist rebels had remained behind, hidden their weapons, and merged with the surrounding Vietnamese population, ready to rise again should the opportunity occur.

The Present Communist Threat

Cambodians in general tended to look upon the war against the Vietminh as something of a "private affair" between the French and the Vietnamese rather than an effort of the governments of the three Associated States against a common invader.

The cease-fire and the subsequent evacuation of Communist rebel forces from Cambodia did not, however, eliminate the threat of Communist political or even military subversion in the area. In view of the conspicuous success of the nationalist independence policy of Sihanouk, Cambodians now tend to underestimate the potential threat of Communism in their country, the more so as the Communist Vietnamese government in North Vietnam has repeatedly expressed its peaceful intentions toward Cambodia and even promised to give favorable consideration to the status of the Cambodian minority in South Vietnam in the event of a total occupation of all Vietnam by the Communist regime. Communist-line Cambodian newspapers such as *Pracheachon,* along with Chinese Communist newspapers (see chap. 12), now circulate freely in Cambodia.

Cambodian Vulnerabilities

The Chinese in Cambodia, as in other countries where there is a substantial Chinese population, are highly sensitive to political changes in the host country, particularly when they affect relations with the Chinese Communist and Chinese Nationalist governments.

The recent *rapprochement* between Peking and Pnompenh has resulted in a large-scale turnabout among the Chinese community, away from the Chinese Nationalist government and toward the Red Chinese government.

If there is a final break between the Cambodian government and the Chinese Nationalist government in Formosa, it is very likely that the majority of the Chinese community of Cambodia will serve the aims of the Peking government. Since the cease-fire of 1954 there has been evidence of a great amount of Chinese Communist propaganda circulating throughout the Chinese community.

The Vietnamese in Cambodia are now in an even more ambiguous position than the Chinese in view of the fact that their own homeland is just across the border. Many of them still consider Cambodia a semibarbarian colony whose eventual annexation by the Vietnamese mother country is both justified and desirable. Therefore they tend to be loyal to whatever Vietnamese authority makes a strong claim for their allegiance. In the past such a claim has come from the Communist Vietnamese guerrilla forces. Now similar strong appeals are made by the Vietnamese Nationalist government in Saigon, although it is certain that Communist appeals have far from completely disappeared.

The neutral attitude professed by succeeding Cambodian administrations since late in 1954 have created a climate in the country that somewhat encourages lowered resistance to Communist influence. On the other hand, the Cambodians have always taken a firm stand—including successful military operations—whenever they recognized Communist subversive activities as a danger to their system of government, particularly when such activities were openly backed by alien elements, such as the Chinese or the Vietnamese; anti-Communist resistance is less likely to be effective, however, if the subversive force succeeds in attracting a hard core of Khmer and passing itself off as a "Cambodian" movement.

Other Political Groups

Prior to 1955 there were three smaller political groups of some importance: the Liberal party, the National Recovery party and the People's party (Pracheachon).

The People's party was the only one of these to survive the 1955 elections. In mid-1956 it had the allegiance of many of the most left-wing Khmer Issarak ex-guerrillas but has apparently lost ground in recent years. It publishes a newspaper in Pnompenh that constantly espouses a strongly anti-American and pro-Red Chinese viewpoint, although it professes fidelity to Sihanouk and attachment to the Cambodian crown.

Other political "parties" participating in this early phase of Cambodia's development of parliamentary institutions are at present little more than coteries of special interests. For example, the Provincial Guard and the civil servants of Kratie and of certain other provinces were given an electoral precinct of their own during the September 1955 election and naturally elected a candidate who was entirely a servant to their wishes. Other more or less local groups exist but often do not survive the elections for which they seem especially created. Such groups include the several independents that, in the last elections, ran in such areas as Takeo, Battambang, and Stungtreng, and such splinter parties as the Ekareach, which ran candidates in Kratie, Soairieng, Takeo, Preyveng, Kandal, and Kompong Cham.

Deprived of voting rights by the Cambodian Constitution, bonzes as such have no particular political representation. (They were, however, especially authorized to participate in the 1955 referendum confirming Sihanouk's Royal Mandate.) As representatives of a religion that partly depends on the state in its present monarchical form, they have, however, a stake in the continuance of the present Cambodian institutions. Their influence as molders of public opinion should not be underestimated. Any political measure that arouses the outright hostility of the bonzes may be difficult to carry through—if not altogether doomed.

A few bonzes support left-wing activities, and there are some who openly collaborated with Communist Vietminh elements in Cambodia.

Trends

The years 1957 and 1958 saw a series of border incidents with both Thailand and South Vietnam, but the Cambodian government had not openly implicated either the Khmer nationalists or Communists in these, ascribing them rather to Thai and Vietnamese activities on behalf of powers endeavoring to force Cambodia out of its neutrality and into an alignment with SEATO.

The Bangkok Plot, however, is seen by Sihanouk as directly related to the border troubles with Thailand. In a series of public statements following its exposure, Sihanouk has implicated the

Khmer Issarak, pro-American leaders in Thailand and South Vietnam, and a certain "great western power," all of whom he sees as
joined in a united effort to remove him by *coup d'état* if necessary.
He has also accused the Thai of directly supporting the Khmer
Issarak with money and arms received from this same "western
power."

In February 1959 Dap Chhuon, military commander of Siemreap province, rejoined the rebels, taking arms and men and pre-
sumably joining Son Ngoc Thanh, whom Sihanouk claimed had
installed his forces in a border village in October 1958. The Cambodian army claims to have found, in Chhoun's abandoned villa,
a powerful radio transmitter manned by two men in the uniform
of South Vietnam officers.

Summing up the situation recently, Sihanouk stated that Son
Ngoc Thanh had entered Siemreap province with his forces, that
several "commando traitors" in the Locninh region were prepared to
attack, and that he expected further trouble in the provinces of
Battambang, Kampot, and other provinces neighboring South Vietnam. He does not state or imply that any of the recent or impending
disturbances are Communist-inspired; on the contrary, he has per-
sistently laid them at the door of his Khmer opponents, whom he
claims are jealous of his power and are acting as misguided agents
of the West.

There is, on the other hand, evidence that the Cambodian
government is alarmed over Communist influence among Khmer
students in Paris, Khmer Buddhist monks, and the Chinese community. In an article published in March 1958 Sihanouk noted that
Communists were distributing to workers books and reviews in
Khmer which glorified the Soviet revolution and that they were
beguiling the monks with prospects of a "people's democratic republic," nostalgically called Kambuja, which would be under
their spiritual guidance. Though not accusing Son Ngoc Thanh of
being a Communist, he has said that the Communists profit from
the "young," the "religious," and the "democratic" who support
the opposition leader. He has been particularly vocal in laying
most of the blame for Communist influence and propaganda in
Cambodia to what he has called "American bungling."

Apart from the recent resurgence of antigovernment guerrilla
activity along the borders, the government considers that the
greatest threat to public order lies in the Chinese and Vietnamese
communities. In spite of statements made by Chou En-lai to the

Chinese community, appealing to them to support the Cambodian government at least by refraining from political action, and in spite of the government's attempts to stop immigration, the Chinese, among whom Communist activity has steadily increased, remain a source of potential trouble.

THEORY AND STRUCTURE
OF GOVERNMENT

CAMBODIA, ITS PEOPLE WILL PROUDLY TELL YOU, is the oldest organized state of the Indochinese peninsula: the Cambodian monarchy traces an almost unbroken succession of kings from the beginning of the Christian era.

Though time and changing circumstances have through the centuries brought modification of Cambodia's political system, many ancient political concepts and practices have persisted up to today. The early belief in the divine nature of the king is reflected in the reverence toward the present monarch exhibited by most of the people. The early kings were worshiped as divine beings and, as such, subject to no formal restrictions on their powers. Advising the king, however, were the Royal Family Council (existing today, though restricted to a mainly ceremonial role), high-ranking bonzes, and the court astrologer. These advisers, particularly the astrologer, often had a profound influence on the king's decisions.

A new concept, that of devaraja or god-king, followed the introduction of Indian cultural influences, as veneration of the deities Siva and Vishnu was combined with worship of the reigning king in many religious ceremonies.

It is primarily this ability to adapt itself to new circumstances and a certain resiliency that has made the Cambodian monarchy capable of surviving social and political change, war, and even long periods of foreign domination without ever fully losing its authority in the eyes of the majority of Cambodians.

The people of Cambodia have long had ways of conveying their views to their government. During the period of the Royal Mandate, Sihanouk repeatedly sought to obtain popular approval for his acts and in one case held a popular referendum for that purpose. More dramatic is the present function of the old institution of popular audiences granted by the king in the Royal Palace. To these audiences come citizens from all walks of life to air their problems and voice their complaints. Often several thousand people congregate and questions are forwarded to King Suramarit or to Sihanouk, who as the King's son has retained many of his kingly prerogatives.

Since 1955 national congresses of Sihanouk's party, the Sangkum, have followed a similar practice. The third congress, held in April 1956, had a formal agenda that included questions on foreign policy, agriculture, progress in foreign commerce, foreign aid to Cambodia, Japanese immigration, punishment of civil servants in cases of corruption, and plans for the election of provincial legislators. Entrance to the royal grounds was open to all comers. The questions, however, had to be submitted in advance to the Central Committee of the Socialist Community in order to be placed on the agenda.

Meetings such as these are announced in advance over the national radio network, often by a proclamation of Sihanouk himself, and attract participants from many parts of the country, including remote settlements. According to recent reports, this form of direct popular participation in national affairs has brought about much greater interest in governmental matters among Cambodians generally.

It seems clear to observers that the present governmental system, the constitutional monarchy, is well adapted to Cambodia's current needs. There is growing agitation from a large part of the population for a greater development of local self-government— in the form of elective municipal councils and mayors, and elective provincial assemblies and governors—but there is nothing in the information available to suggest that the Cambodian administration, given a few years of peace, will stop short of these objectives.

In May 1958 a French member of the High Council of the French Union in Cambodia reported in Paris on the state of the Cambodian government and administration. In this report he stated that there was an excessive proliferation of echelons in the administration, with complicated pay scales, and that a large part of the problem of administration, aside from corruption, was the fact that many of the services and agencies were still governed by obsolete and contradictory legislation and regulations. The government is now making an effort to rid the governmental services of some of these defects through the Royal School of Administration, which trains cadres for civil service, and through the Ministry of Purification, which attempts to root out corruption. Given its brief experience with representative government. Cambodia has made considerable progress toward coping with the problems that attend the establishment of democratic rule.

As was demonstrated by the period of the Royal Mandate (see chap. 2), the actualities of Cambodian government are not always what the Constitution provides. The Constitution as such, however, enjoys considerable respect, and May 7, Constitution Day, is an official holiday throughout Cambodia.

It would be futile at the present time to expect full and formal compliance with the Constitution by the citizens and the government of Cambodia at all times. Nevertheless, the Cambodian Constitution has become a living element of Cambodian politics. Its fundamental principles have received wide publicity throughout the country and are often and appropriately invoked by persons who have dealings with the government. The Cambodian Constitution, by its very shortcomings in western eyes—its rudimentary definition of the role of the judiciary, its taking into account Buddhist dogmas and the sacredness of the king—seems "Cambodian" to the people of the country. To them, it is a permanent symbol of their independence and an ever more important part of Cambodia's political and historical tradition.

Creation of Representative Government

By virtue of the French-Cambodian Protectorate Treaty of 1863 and the subsequent Franco-Cambodian Convention of 1884, the French resident-general acquired most of the lawmaking and administrative prerogatives of the Cambodian king. No royal command could become the law of the land without the countersignature of the resident-general, who also, as in the other Indochinese protectorates of Annam and Laos, acted as the president of the Royal Council of Ministers, or prime minister of the kingdom.

The king's powers were in effect limited to his spiritual role as head of all Buddhist religious activities in the country and to the exercise of his traditional right of granting pardons. The latter, however, was applied only to those of his subjects who had committed offenses against native law and had been sentenced by a Cambodian court. That the king's importance in the religious field remained fairly undiminished throughout the whole colonial period gave him a certain amount of influence beyond what the French were willing to concede him, and kept alive the allegiance which Cambodians to this day feel toward their sovereign.

Prior to the establishment of the French protectorate, there was no legislative assembly in Cambodia. Upon urging by the French, King Sisowath enacted in March 1913 an ordinance providing for the establishment of a Consultative Assembly to be elected by restricted suffrage. Only Cambodian government officials—retired or active—were eligible to vote and to be elected to the Consultative Assembly; a certain number of its members, however, were appointed directly by the Cambodian government.

The Consultative Assembly met every year for a ten-day session, prolonged if necessary, to discuss budgetary and taxation matters and questions pertaining generally to social and economic affairs. All discussions of political matters were (as in the case of similar assemblies in Vietnam) strictly prohibited. The Assembly functioned regularly throughout most of the colonial period. In view of the limited scope of its responsibilities it did not exercise a broad influence upon Cambodian public life, but it did acquaint a limited number of Cambodians with the workings of a legislature.

The Khmer legal code, although often very detailed in its description of legal cases like most Asian legal codes of the pre-colonial period, on the whole lacked precision and left great latitude to the judge. Corporal punishment, from whipping to outright mutilation, was the order of the day, and punishment by death for what Europeans would consider minor offenses was quite frequent. To a Buddhist, however, death with its aftermath of reincarnation seemed preferable to a long prison term or—what to a Cambodian was worst of all—deportation to a prison camp far from his native soil; should he die while away, his reincarnation would be hindered.

The French colonial administration did away with the most obvious elements of harshness and injustice in the old system and, with the help of Cambodian jurists and advisers, codified the ancient Khmer laws into a single uniform body of jurisprudence published in both French and Cambodian. Care was taken not to offend local custom by introducing radical changes, but wherever possible the code was brought into line with European legal concepts. French magistrates did not directly control the Cambodian court system, but the local French administrators informally saw to it that the new code was applied.

9. Creation of Representative Government

Persons not considered Cambodian were not subject to a Cambodian court; they were tried under French law by the court system of the French protectorate.

When, after the upheavals that attended the collapse of Japanese power at the end of World War II, the Cambodian government was given a measure of autonomy by the French, it sought to consolidate this by basing it upon a popularly elected regime.

On May 31, 1946 King Sihanouk promulgated an electoral law for the convening of a Consultative Assembly—elected by universal suffrage and direct vote—to approve a constitution. This constituent assembly was elected in September 1946 without opposition by the French and without major incident, and was presented with a draft of a constitution elaborated by the King and his personal advisers, which it debated for several months before ratifying. On May 6, 1947 the Constitution of Cambodia—the instrument under which the country is now governed—was promulgated by King Sihanouk.

The system of government it established is a constitutional monarchy, consisting essentially of the king and his Crown Council, the ministries or "the government," a bicameral legislature, and a judiciary. It is based fairly closely on the draft constitution prepared by the French Constituent Assembly in 1945 but rejected by the French electorate in May 1946 because of the extensive powers it granted the president.

"Every Cambodian," says the Constitution, "owes loyalty to the king, must respect the laws, defend the country, and help the government by paying his taxes." These are basic duties. The citizen is at the same time guaranteed basic freedoms of the sort stated in the Bill of Rights of the United States Constitution.

All residents of Cambodia regardless of race are guaranteed freedom from arrest and prosecution without due process of law. They possess a limited right of habeas corpus and enjoy the protection of the principle that "any accused person is presumed not guilty until he has been proved guilty."

Taking into account the religious basis for the old Cambodian aversion toward deportation from the homeland, the Constitution prohibits punishment by exile. Private property is protected from infringement without due process of law. Everyone is guaranteed freedom of religion, although the same article of the Constitution identifies Buddhism as "the state religion." Freedom of speech and of other forms of expression, freedom of assembly and association, and the inviolability of home and correspondence are also guaranteed. Cambodian citizens are also guaranteed full equality in the right to aspire to public office and the right to petition for redress.

Some of the civil liberties protected by the Constitution—*i.e.*, regarding detention, freedom of speech and assembly, and secrecy of letters—may be suspended temporarily in case of an emergency. But a state of emergency may not exceed six months and all acts committed by government authorities during that period are subject to later claims for redress on the part of those who were affected.

Amendments may be initiated by the king or the prime minister or the president of either House. The latter two may request an amendment only after approval by at least one-fourth of the members of the respective Houses over which they preside. The rights reserved to the king under the Constitution may not, however, be curtailed by constitutional amendments.

Amendments become effective only upon approval by three-fourths of the National Assembly. In order to avoid undue pressures upon the Assembly, that body may consider amendments "only when no state of emergency exists in the realm."

Three amendments have thus far been made: one in September 1955, in which the constitutional description of Cambodia's political status changed from "self-governing state belonging to the French Union as an Associated State" to "a sovereign and independent state"; one in October 1955, giving a measure of self-government to the provinces by authorizing the establishment of elected provincial assemblies; and a third, made by royal decree in January 1956, giving Cambodian women the vote at all levels and making them eligible for such positions as village mayors. If implemented effectively, this latter measure will put Cambodia in the forefront of Asian countries that have granted equality of political rights to women and will no doubt eventually produce great changes in the society.

The Executive

The King and the Royal Councils

The king, who must be a male descendant of King Ang Duong (reign: 1846 to 1859), considered the head of the present dynasty, is the supreme head of the state and "his person is sacred." He must, however, swear allegiance to the Constitution. His powers under that Constitution are for the most part those normally associated with

STRUCTURE OF THE CENTRAL GOVERNMENT
(January 1959)

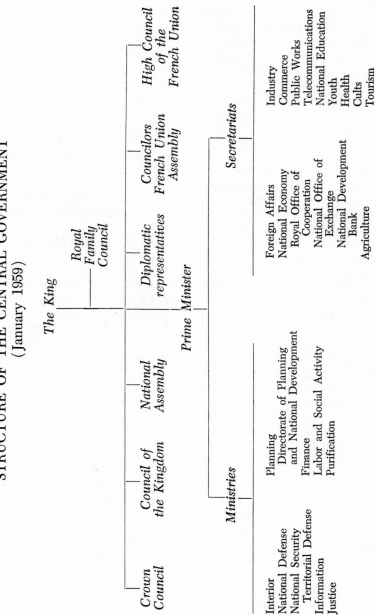

The King

Royal Family Council

Crown Council — Council of the Kingdom — National Assembly — **Prime Minister** — Diplomatic representatives — Councilors French Union Assembly — High Council of the French Union

Ministries

Interior
National Defense
National Security
Territorial Defense
Information
Justice

Planning
Directorate of Planning and National Development
Finance
Labor and Social Activity
Purification

Foreign Affairs
National Economy
Royal Office of Cooperation
National Office of Exchange
National Development Bank
Agriculture

Secretariats

Industry
Commerce
Public Works
Telecommunications
National Education
Youth
Health
Cults
Tourism

the functions of a constitutional monarch, such as promulgation of laws and the appointment of a prime minister and other ministers on the basis of the political majority of the National Assembly. He signs the treaties negotiated by his government, officially receives and appoints ambassadors, and summons and dissolves the National Assembly upon advice of his ministers. He is the commander in chief of all Cambodian armed forces. Executive, legislative and judicial power are exercised in his name. He has the power, with the advice of the Crown Council, to name an heir to the throne and to cancel such a nomination.

The Constitution also gives him the power to initiate legislative deliberations, and he may in practice exercise a powerful political influence if he has such inclinations or if he can be manipulated by the people around him. Sihanouk did have such inclinations when he was king and was able to exceed his constitutional powers without severe opposition by the legislature.

The king is assisted in his duties by the Crown Council, composed of the president of the Royal Family Council (see below), the president of the Council of Ministers (generally referred to in English as the prime minister), the president of the National Assembly (lower House), the president of the Council of the Kingdom (upper House), the leaders of the two major Buddhist sects, and the president of the High Court of Justice. The president of the Royal Family Council is also chairman of the Crown Council. Under the Constitution the Crown Council exercises a great influence when the king is absent from the realm or incapacitated—for it may appoint a regent or, after declaring the throne vacant, determine the succession.

The Crown Council must meet within three days after the throne vacancy occurs and designate an heir to the throne or a regent if the heir is a minor. Its functions other than jurisdiction over the royal succession are rather limited, but its members are generally men of such great influence in the kingdom that their advice is likely to be highly respected by the reigning king on other matters as well. In time of a ministerial crisis, the Crown Council is an important stabilizing factor.

The Royal Family Council is an advisory body composed of all male members of the king's immediate family. While its function is mainly ceremonial, the influence of its members upon the king may be very considerable. It meets regularly, at the behest of its president—usually one of the senior members of the family but not the king himself—and may volunteer advice to the king on various

problems. The king may request the convening of the Family
Council for such purposes.

The Council of Ministers

The leader of the majority party in the National Assembly becomes the prime minister and is confirmed in office by the king.
He in turn chooses his ministers. The Cabinet can begin to function,
however, only after it has received a vote of confidence from the
Assembly.

In practice the executive power in Cambodia is in the hands
of the Council of Ministers, headed by the prime minister. The
prime minister and his Cabinet constitute the Royal Cambodian
Government, which as a collective body discusses all problems
relating to the general functioning of the governmental machinery
and is empowered to execute the laws passed by the National
Assembly. This it does by issuing ministerial decrees (*kram*) and
regulations (*kret*). The government is collectively responsible to the
National Assembly for the general policies of the administration.
Between 1949 and 1955, however, when the king exercised direct
emergency powers, the government was primarily responsible to
the king rather than to the legislature.

In general the powers and duties of the Cambodian Cabinet
follow fairly closely the French pattern. Cabinet ministers may be
selected from the national legislature, or from outside it. Ministers
selected from outside the national legislature have the benefit of
immunities accorded all members of the National Assembly. The
Constitution limits the number of Cabinet ministers to twelve.
While in office, its members may be tried for crimes and offenses
by the High Court of Justice upon complaint of the National
Assembly.

As in France, a motion of nonconfidence or censure by the
National Assembly brings about the collective resignation of the
Cabinet. In the case of such a crisis (in the past such crises often
have tended to last several weeks) the outgoing government is in
charge of the "expedition of current affairs" until a new one has
been accepted by the National Assembly.

In case of a dissolution of the National Assembly, the Cabinet,
with the exception of the prime minister and the minister of the
interior, remains in office to carry on the ordinary business. The
president of the Assembly then assumes the office of prime minister.

The vote of a motion of disapproval by the National Assembly
involves the collective resignation of the Cabinet.

The Administration

Responsibility for government administration is vested in the heads of the various executive departments of the government. While these officers are called "ministers," as in France, some of the agencies of government are now called "departments," as in the United States.

The number of executive departments is subject to change with every transfer of the mantle of government from one political party, or combination, to another. An executive department that is a ministry under one administration may be downgraded to a deputy ministry or even state secretariat, only to be upgraded with the next change in government. In this, the Cambodians follow French parliamentary procedure.

Moreover, two or more departments may be placed in charge of a single minister or secretary of state. In the recent cabinet reshuffling, for example, Sihanouk as prime minister appointed the former ambassador to Moscow as Minister of State for Interior, Justice, Information, Planning, and Purification. Such combinations reflect not only the special qualifications of the minister concerned, but also the desire to coordinate important and related activities.

The functions of most Cambodian governmental departments are clearly indicated by their names. Certain of the more important ones, however, require description.

1. *Interior*: Since Cambodia is centrally administered, the Ministry of Interior is one of the key ministries. It controls all provincial governors and district administrators, passes upon the appointment of most civil servants in the local administrations throughout the country, and exercises strict control over the local and provincial police forces.

2. *National Security*: This is a relatively new ministry which has taken over the functions previously assigned to the Interior Department through its Under-Secretariat for Territorial Defense. The department is responsible for internal security, a function that gives it full control over the semimilitarized forces which deal with subversive groups and other forms of insurrection and lawlessness. Defense against external aggression is the primary responsibility of the Department of National Defense, but there is close collaboration among the departments of National Security, National Defense, and Information, in regard to internal security problems.

3. *Planning*: This ministry is charged with national development programs, such as the recently terminated Two Year Plan.

Under it is the Directorate for Planning and National Development which carries most of the burden of implementing various aspects of the development programs.

4. *Purification*: This ministry, variously referred to also as "General Purification" or "Sanitation," has the responsibility of weeding out corruption in the civil service. The importance attached to this function is indicated by the fact that this department is generally placed in charge of a minister who also carries such other important departments as Interior, Justice, and Information.

5. *National Economy*: This secretariat is charged with controlling aspects of the national economy primarily related to external trade, foreign aid, and the development of internal commercial activities. Its three most important divisions are: the National Exchange Office, which controls all foreign exchange transactions; the National Development Bank, which serves as a repository for all foreign aid funds; and the Royal Office of Cooperation, the central agency for consumer, producer, and credit cooperatives.

The Civil Servant

Cambodia has a very limited staff of "professional" civil servants. Some of them—particularly those at higher levels—have been trained in France, but the majority have been trained on the job, learning from elder Cambodian civil servants or from French supervisors.

As Cambodia moved toward independence, more and more of the higher administrative jobs were transferred from the French to Cambodians. In such cases political appointments were made by the king and his immediate entourage. This gave rise to a spoils system, a development that became particularly strong when the opposition Democratic party took over the government in October 1951. Most civil servants who were out of sympathy with the party in power were replaced. For a period of two years the spoils system was in full force, with a consequent lowering of administrative standards. Only some of the lower posts were filled through competitive examinations.

After Sihanouk assumed direct power in 1952, a Civil Service Study Commission was set up; in August 1953 a series of decrees brought most government jobs under civil service and established five major civil service categories, whose posts are now filled primarily through open competitive examinations:

1. *Administrative Corps* — including regular civil service office

workers and also encompassing the national and municipal police forces and the prison system.

2. *Medical Corps* — including all medical officers of the civil administration, druggists, dentists, and "sanitary agents," as well as the personnel of the psychiatric hospital of Takhmau.

3. *Educational Service* — including all professors, school inspectors, technical instructors, teachers of the Buddhist Institute, and physical education coaches.

4. *Financial Service* — including inspectors and controllers, customs staff, personnel of the Treasury, and staff of the records and real estate administrative services.

5. *Technical Service* — covering public works personnel, post office and telecommunications staff (including radio broadcasting), personnel engaged in agricultural, land survey, water, forestry, hunting, and fishing services, and the statistical and veterinarian services.

Cambodians consider corruption of some kind one of the normal prerogatives of administrative power. All except the western-educated members of the younger generation consider it natural that gifts be given a civil servant from whom services are desired. This was openly recognized by the administration of King Sihanouk, and cases of corruption that had been dealt with by his government are spelled out in great detail in Sihanouk's official report on the achievements of his reign under the Royal Mandate. But punishments do not appear to be very severe.

A marked improvement has taken place since the Geneva cease-fire of 1954, the return of an organized government, and the strengthening of the administrative structure. The new cadres trained in France and the United States have brought back a new concept of public service. In February 1956 the Institute of Public Administration was opened in Pnompenh; eventually it ought to provide the country with a corps of trained civil servants. As noted above, a Ministry of Purification now is responsible for detecting corruption in the civil service.

The National Legislature

The Council of the Kingdom

The Council of the Kingdom is the upper house of the Cambodian legislature and is partially elective. Its members are to a large extent "elder statesmen" of the kingdom. While the Council has no direct legislative powers, its advice on legislation under consideration is very important. Since it includes members of the king's family and entourage, its influence over the king is likewise very great and often likely to be more intensive than that of the National Assembly.

The Council is composed of both elected and appointed members who must be more than forty years old. There are twenty-four members in all. Two members of the Council are appointed by the king from the royal family itself. Two members are elected by the National Assembly, but not from among its own members. Eight others are elected by local government authorities: seven of them by the provincial councilors of each of the seven administrative regions, and one by Pnompenh's seven borough chiefs and the members of its municipal council. Another eight members representing the major trades and professions, are elected by their trade or professional organizations, and another four are elected by the civil servants.

The Council of the Kingdom is elected for four years and its members enjoy privileges similar to those enjoyed by members of the National Assembly. The powers of the Council are fairly similar to those of the former colonial Consultative Assembly, that is, mostly advisory.

The National Assembly

There is thus far only one fully elective legislative body in Cambodia—the National Assembly, provided for by the Constitution of 1947. Several elections for the National Assembly have already taken place and according to official Cambodian statistics a high percentage of the eligible electorate participated. Representation is proportioned on the basis of approximately one deputy for every twenty thousand voters. In 1955 ninety-one deputies were elected to the Assembly; in 1958 only sixty-one seats were filled. There have been several proposals calling for an increase in the number of deputies by reducing the apportionment ratio to one deputy for every fifteen thousand voters.

The powers of the National Assembly resemble in many ways those of the French National Assembly. It is vested with all law-making powers in the country; no other government body or even the king can vote laws into existence. The Assembly ordinarily meets at least twice a year for sessions lasting about three months each. Like other legislatures throughout the world, it works in small committees which report out proposed legislation. All its proceedings are public with the exception of executive sessions, which are fairly rare. Members are elected for four years, but seats vacant through death, resignation, or expulsion may be filled through off-year elections. Members enjoy the usual parliamentary immunities and privileges. To be eligible for election to the Assembly a Cambodian must be at least twenty-five years old, and, as in the United States, a civil servant seeking election must give up his job in the administration. The members of the National Assembly are the representatives of the whole Cambodian nation and not only of those by whom they have been elected. They cannot be bound by any imperative mandate.

To be qualified to vote for representatives to the Assembly, Cambodians must be at least twenty years of age. Military personnel on active duty, however, are not allowed to vote. Buddhist monks also are denied the ballot.

Like the French constitution, the Cambodian constitution contains a clause providing for the automatic dissolution of the Assembly and a new election if the Assembly overthrows a government through a vote of nonconfidence twice within eighteen months.

The Judiciary

When French colonial administration was established in Cambodia, responsibility for the administration of justice was divided between the new French courts and the native Cambodian judicial system. Cambodians who perpetrated a crime against Cambodian nationals or who committed other violations of Cambodian law were left in the hands of Cambodian courts. Cambodians who had violated French laws or committed crimes against non-Cambodian nationals were tried by French courts under French laws.

A French tribunal, composed of career judges of the French judicial system, sat in Pnompenh. The tribunal was under the jurisdiction of the Court of Appeals in Saigon. There were also resident tribunals in each of the Cambodian provinces with the exception of Kandal, in which Pnompenh is located. The provincial tribunals were manned by colonial civil servants operating under the authority of the French provincial residents. In general a provincial court had the final say in minor cases in its area; in serious criminal cases, however, the criminal court at Pnompenh was given jurisdiction. Cases involving non-Cambodians were brought before the criminal court in Saigon. In appeals, when a case involved only Cambodians the court in Saigon had final jurisdiction; other litigation could be carried to the Supreme Court of Appeals in Paris.

The native court system was reorganized and standardized during the French colonial period and has remained substantially unchanged since, at least at the local level.

Section VIII of the Constitution defines the present judicial organization, particularly that of the High Council of Magistracy. This Council, a type of disciplinary court dealing especially with offenses committed by members of the Cambodian court system, is composed of the Minister of Justice as chairman, two members appointed by the king, two members elected by the National Assembly, and two members elected by the Cambodian magistrates.

The highest tribunal in the land, however, is the High Court of Justice, composed of five members: one elected by the National Assembly, two elected by the Council of the Kingdom, and two high magistrates.

A court of appeals (*sala outor*) has appeals jurisdiction in civil cases and in most criminal cases. A court of review (*sala vinichhay*) is another court of appeals but acts almost like the United States Supreme Court. Its authority is particularly important when judgments are contested on charges of procedural error. The court examines the facts and determines whether or not the statutes have been properly adhered to.

At the next level are the one-man provincial tribunals of first instance (*sala dambaung*). The judges are civil servants appointed by the national government. Their jurisdiction encompasses all criminal and civil cases, and the judge also exercises first appeals jurisdiction over cases that have been tried previously by a *sala lahouk*.

At the lowest level, *i.e.*, the village or municipality, there are justices of the peace or conciliatory justices (*sala lahouk*). In many cases, the jurisdiction of a *sala lahouk* is extended over several *srok*. In other communities, where there are only a few cases to handle or where the population is sparsely distributed, the district chief simultaneously handles the job of conciliatory justice. The competence of the *sala lahouk* is of necessity very limited and in many cases comparable to that of the American justice of the peace. He can impose only small fines and very brief prison sentences, and even those can be appealed to higher authority. At the same time, he acts as sheriff: he makes inquiries and searches and effects seizures and arrests for higher authorities if the accused is located within his jurisdiction.

Until recently there was only one criminal court (*sala okret*); it was located in Pnompenh. In view of the small size of the kingdom and the comparative rarity of serious criminal cases, this does not seem to bring unusual hardship to the accused. In cases where the number of witnesses to be summoned to Pnompenh becomes too great, the court itself moves to the provincial seat of the area where the crime was committed.

The achievement of full independence brought all foreign nationals in Cambodia within the jurisdiction of the Cambodian courts. Extraterritoriality had been a particularly sore point with the Cambodians because all the Chinese, Indian, and Pakistani inhabitants of Cambodia—as well as the Europeans—had enjoyed an almost complete immunity from Cambodian law. The shift from mixed jurisdiction to full Cambodian control took place in August 1953.

Since then Cambodian efforts in judicial administration have centered mainly on simplifying the existing codes and judicial procedures. A decree of November 1955 greatly reduced the expenses of judicial procedure at the lowest levels of jurisdiction, and the establishment of a justice of the peace in every *srok* was planned for 1956. In 1952 King Sihanouk issued a special ruling instructing the Ministry of Justice and the Ministry of Interior to have their subordinate authorities (the courts and the police) show greater leniency in cases where the charges consisted of insults or remarks against the king; enforcement of such legislation had led to many abuses by overzealous local officials.

Law Enforcement

The National Police

The Cambodian government places a strong emphasis upon the paramilitary assignments entrusted to the Cambodian police. Such assignments are important particularly in view of the numerical weakness of the country's regular armed forces.

The scattered pattern of population distribution in Cambodia —thousands of tiny villages and only a few large cities—makes it difficult for any level of government to operate an efficient police system. The difficulty increases as one reaches the lower units of government where policing is most needed: a village of 300 inhabitants cannot afford to maintain an effective police force. The National Police is controlled by the Ministry of Interior through the Secretary of State for the Interior and Territorial Defense. Its standards of fitness, equipment, and recruitment are set by the Ministry. Its major operational units outside of Pnompenh (where the National Police is also the municipal police) are units of the Provincial Guard, formerly known as the Provincial Police.

During a Cabinet meeting held on June 8, 1956, the Cambodian government decided on changes in the nation-wide organization of the police, with the Secretary of State for the Interior and Territorial Defense simultaneously assuming the duties of director of the National Police. New decrees concerning police ranks and the establishment of additional police precincts were adopted.

The deactivation of ten companies of the Provincial Guard Auxiliary, announced by the Ministry of Interior and Territorial Defense on May 31, 1956, also seemed to indicate that the police would be adapted to less warlike duties as the security situation in Cambodia improved. In the meantime, operations of the Cambodian police were divided into two major and distinct activities: regular police duties and "pacification."

The police, in cooperation with the provincial administration, have full powers over the issuance of identification cards, which every Cambodian over sixteen, male or female, is required to carry at all times, and over the issuance of passports for travel abroad. Other general functions include the control of hotel registers, which every hotel manager must submit daily to the police and must have ready for inspection at any time. The duties of the police have also included the control of illegal traffic in arms and other contraband, control of immigration, and a general security maintenance aimed at stamping out rampant banditry.

Since the end of the Indochina hostilities in 1954, the sudden rise in road traffic—due both to improved security and increased imports of automobiles—has created special traffic problems and hazards. In the spring of 1955, the special motorized Brigade de Circulation Routière (BCR), or Road Traffic Brigade, was activated to maintain order on the highways outside the cities.

Cambodia's police force is recruited on a local basis through public competitive examinations. An applicant must be able to write either Cambodian or French, and have completed at least grade-school education. Examinations are held at irregular intervals in the major cities. Higher police officials are appointed by the Ministry of Interior upon the recommendation of the Secretary of State for Interior and Territorial Defense. Although any Cambodian citizen may become a police officer, in actual practice only Cambodians of Khmer or mixed Khmer ancestry seem to apply for positions with the regular police forces. On the other hand, many of the Malay, Vietnamese, and mountain tribe minorities serve in the Provincial Guard Auxiliary and other village self-defense units.

A National Police Academy has recently graduated its first class. It will unify training methods and provide training in such specialties as fingerprinting, anthropometry, and communications; in the past, police students have been sent abroad to study these specialties and police inspectors have been sent to Thailand for advanced training. A Provincial Guard school, with a capacity of 350 students, has operated in Kompong Chhnang since 1953.

Until contemplated improvements are fully implemented, the Cambodian police will continue to suffer from severe shortages of trained personnel.

The Cambodian police are empowered to act as a summary court and may fine citizens for violations of police or traffic regulations. Contrary to American, but similar to French practice, the Cambodian police may also exercise direct jurisdiction in traffic and other cases and levy fines from 15 up to 40,000 riels (from about 40 cents to $1,100). When fines cannot be paid, prison terms in lieu of payment may run up to two years for any one fine—at the rate of one day of jail per 50 riels up to 10,000 riels, and one day of jail for every 100 riels fine above 10,000. Simple violations of the Traffic Code, involving fines from 15 to 50 riels, can, as in most European countries, be settled on the spot, with the policeman issuing a receipt to the violator.

This summary court system has been much criticized, since it permits the police to harass the population almost at will. In September 1952 Sihanouk addressed a memorandum to all members of his government, all provincial governors, and the chief of the Pnompenh police, noting that members of the police force too often were prone to exact special privileges from the population. Road traffic control personnel, for example, frequently stopped public conveyances at check points to collect an imaginary "tax" from the drivers. The practice had become a virtual institution on the much-traveled Pnompenh-Saigon highway—the policemen delivering valueless lottery tickets as "receipts" for the money taken.

Abuses of police power led to the creation in October 1954 of a Bureau of Study and Investigation for the Defense of the Interests of the People. Known from its French initials as BEI-

DIPER, its function is to receive direct complaints from people who feel they have been wronged by arbitrary action of the police or other government agencies. According to Cambodian sources, within seven months of the Bureau's inception more than 3,600 such complaints were received and acted upon. The Cambodian government has taken serious steps, including the dismissal of important police officials, to reduce corruption in the force, but the problem cannot yet be considered solved.

The National Police itself has created two special sections to cope with abuses of authority: the Investigation Section, responsible particularly for the investigation of abuses or frauds committed by government officials; and the Station Police, given the ill-defined responsibility of taking over "all police duties which another section of the police has not been able to fulfill."

Banditry and the subversive activities of various guerrilla groups have constituted Cambodia's most serious public order problem. Until 1952 the task of "pacification" was almost entirely in the hands of the French Expeditionary Forces, with but uncertain success. In the summer of 1952 the Cambodian government created the Under-Secretariat of State of the Interior for Self-Defense (*Auto-Defense*) and the pacification effort became a joint French-Cambodian operation, with the Cambodians taking a steadily increasing part.

The plan of operations was simple: the regular army forces would first break the back of guerrilla resistance and do a mopping up; then the Provincial Guard would be sent in to organize self-defense units in the larger villages by arming reliable civilians. To police the areas between villages, mobile and semimobile Provincial Guard units would be stationed at centrally located points. Independent Infantry Companies (Compagnies Autonomes d'Infanterie, or CAI) would step into the picture for "external defense" when an enemy attack proved to be more than a temporary probing stab.

At the national level, the anti-guerrilla effort was coordinated in the High Committee for Pacification, presided over by the king. Provincial pacification committees, each presided over by a provincial governor, implemented pacification policy at field level. In these committees all military operations were coordinated with the civilian authorities, to obtain a maximum concentration of effort with the least possible harm to the civilian population affected by the operation.

Subordinated to the Ministry of Interior—hence considered as a police force—the Provincial Guard in 1956 was stabilized at a manpower level of about 5,500 men equipped for the most part with small arms; a few heavier weapons, such as light machine guns and BAR's, were also available. Most units were motorized and equipped with mobile radios.

Toward the end of 1953 the Provincial Guard and their auxiliaries in the villages (5,000 in 1953 and about 8,000 in 1954) had assumed almost full control of local defense, but the problem posed by the sudden Communist Vietminh invasion of northeastern Cambodia in 1954 created a dangerous situation by siphoning off almost all the available Cambodian regular army forces and CAI, leaving the defense of the rest of the country in the hands of the police units. (By October 1953 the French Expeditionary Corps had evacuated all of Cambodia west of the Mekong.)

Since it was obvious that the Provincial Guard would not be able to cope with the situation alone, King Sihanouk initiated a new program—the "Mobilization of the Live Forces of Cambodia" (known in Cambodia as Comchivapol, or by its French initials MFVC). This amounted to the mobilization of everyone, man or woman, willing to come to the defense of the country.

Within a few months, more than 100,000 Cambodians had responded to the call. They could be seen drilling in the market squares and along the roads, often with wooden replicas of rifles or of other weapons. About 15,000 recruits were armed in time to constitute an important adjunct to the existing police units.

From the organizational point of view, these various steps were consummated by the activation of a Territorial Defense Staff (the French term is Etat-Major pour la Défense en Surface) within the Ministry of Interior. Grouped under its command are all non-military forces operating against the internal enemy throughout Cambodia.

The activation of the Territorial Defense Staff took into account the fact that fighting an internal enemy was a problem entirely different from that of fighting an alien invader and that it required not only different weapons but different tactics and, most important, an entirely different strategy.

The creation of the Comchivapol permitted the first effective policing of villages and districts, hitherto entirely outside police control. At present both the Comchivapol and the Provincial Guard auxiliaries police the villages in which they reside, somewhat in the manner of sheriff's deputies in the United States. Their role is considered essential to the maintenance of public security in the face of new guerrilla activities in the border provinces.

The Prison System

The prison system—inadequate by western standards—suffers from the fact that it was once part of the prison system for all Indochina: the French moved their prisoners as they saw fit within Vietnam, Laos, and Cambodia. Since the number of criminal cases in Cambodia (with its then fewer than 4 million people) was insignificant during the colonial period, Indochina's largest facilities—Poulo Condore Prison Island, Tourane penitentiary, and the forced-labor camp of Son La—were located in Vietnam.

At present the only adequate Cambodian prisons are the few in Pnompenh and other larger centers. In the villages a bamboo cage set between the stilts of the village chief's hut may serve as a jail; all but the most lackadaisical prisoners could break out at will, but very few Cambodians do. Families usually bring food to relatives confined in the village jail.

Serving a prison term is considered degrading but does not necessarily make one a permanent social outcast. Many people in Cambodia have been outlaws of one type or another—nationalist rebels against the French, then against the king; warlords; bandits —and as a consequence the term "criminal" carries little lasting stigma. After the accession of King Suramarit to the throne in 1955 more than 500 prisoners (with scarcely two years of their sentences served), whose crime records ranged from homicide with robbery to multiple first-degree murder, were amnestied. They will probably be quickly reintegrated into Cambodian society. In general there is characteristically a low rate of violent crime as compared to nonviolent offenses. Of the latter, a major proportion involved business transactions; it seems more than likely that these had to do with Chinese and Vietnamese rather than Cambodians as such, given the preponderance of these minorities in the business picture. No figures, however, are available to compare the crime rates of the various ethnic minorities with that of the Khmer majority.

Regional and Local Government

There are several levels of local executive government in Cambodia: regional, provincial, district, and village or town.

While regional government is thus far limited to representation in the Council of the Kingdom (see above), provincial government is more fully developed: it is, in fact, the major unit of lower-level government in Cambodia. At this level sit various provincial representatives of national government departments, overseeing the local execution of government orders issued from Pnompenh. The provincial governor and most of his important colleagues are appointees of the Ministry of Interior. They are regular civil servants who may be shifted from one province to another at the behest of the central authority.

As is usual in such cases, service far from the national capital is considered undesirable and even a sort of "punishment." Thus, very often only civil servants without influence in central political circles or those noted for poor performance or even dishonesty have been shifted to remote areas near the country's borders. Since it is particularly the critical border areas which raise the most serious problems, this policy is not conducive to good government. Sihanouk, in a policy speech on February 29, 1956, advocated that the provincial civil servants sent to the remotest provinces and border regions be chosen from among those possessing the highest qualifications and that they be given priority for advancement.

District government is not a fully developed institution. It serves merely as an intermediary between provincial government (which receives orders directly from the central government) and the city and village mayors—*mekhum*—who ultimately have to execute all orders that have been channeled to them from above. Some of the *mekhum* are elected, but most of them are still selected by the village councils, subject to approval by the provincial governor. A Ministry of Interior directive of October 20, 1955, stipulates that in cities or villages where *mekhum* have thus far been appointed to office they should be replaced by election as posts become vacant.

There are at present sixteen provinces (*khet*) each of which is headed by a governor (*chauvaykhet*). Two of these provinces were created only recently and apparently as a means of more effectively organizing the policing and security system in the northwest area along the Thailand border. In May 1957 the offshore island of Koh Chang was designated as the province of Koh Kong, and in June 1958 a section of Battambang province, south of Poipet, was designated as the province of Ratanakiri, with capital at Andaung Pich, between Poipet and Sisophon. In turn each province is divided into a varying number of districts (*srok*). Each *srok* is headed by a *chauvaysrok*, or district chief. Both the provincial and district administrators are appointees of the central government and are civil servants of the Ministry of the Interior and Territorial Defense.

The districts in turn are subdivided into village groups, known as *khum*, which are somewhat comparable to New England townships. Each village has a "Council of Notables," who usually select a mayor (*mekhum*) from among their midst; the mayor is responsible to district and provincial administrators. The larger cities, such as Battambang and Kratie, are autonomous municipalities with a city council.

The capital, Pnompenh, is organized like a province. It is administered by an appointed governor, assisted by a municipal council. The city is divided into seven boroughs.

The recent war years in Indochina brought about a considerable degree of isolation of the outlying areas from the capital. In order to consolidate the control of the central administration over the outlying provinces, all provinces were grouped into seven administrative regions. These regions have no administrative organization of their own; they are nominally controlled by a provincial councilor, a representative of the central government who acts through the provincial governors of the region and reports back to the central government on major occurrences in the area. Though not endowed with well-defined powers, he is generally a person of great influence in the kingdom. His role may become important in such sensitive border areas as the First Region (Battambang and Siemreap).

There has been very little reshuffling in the Cambodian regional and local administration in recent years. While some of the present provinces may seem somewhat large in view of the existing paucity of communications, the present territorial organization permits fairly adequate administration and control.

While no local legislatures have thus far developed in Cambodia, several resolutions toward that end have been introduced, and in 1955 a constitutional amendment authorized the formation of provincial assemblies. Sihanouk and his People's Socialist Community (Sangkum Reastr Niyum) have made the establishment of provincial legislative assemblies the first plank of their platform. In his February 29, 1956 speech, Sihanouk indicated that such provincial assemblies would provide a more efficient supervision of the administration of the provinces and a more effective control of the provincial civil service by the local population.

DIFFUSION AND CONTROL
OF INFORMATION

THE MAIN CHANNELS OF PUBLIC INFORMATION in Cambodia are informal media that have developed as a natural, integral part of Cambodian society: the "grapevine" and the local, nonprofessional "news analyst." Newspapers do reach most parts of the country, but the total circulation of daily papers is less than 10,000, in a population of five million. There are three radio stations, but relatively few receiving sets; what sets there are are found chiefly in the cities and towns.

French is the only European language understood by more than a few people; French books are thus the chief foreign publications available in Cambodia. These reach mainly the governing group, the well-educated classes, and the bonzes; these groups in turn are among the sources of informal news dissemination.

Cambodians tend to consider "information" as reflecting the point of view of the disseminator. They like to be reasoned with and to hear discussion. They have to be convinced that a particular action or idea is to their advantage and in line with their basic philosophy and religion. They feel insulted if they are lied to. Cambodians say they don't bother to read Vietnamese political tracts, for instance, because they know they are lies. Their confidence can be gained by strict honesty about facts and about limitations of knowledge. If a proverb is cited inaptly, a Cambodian is likely to categorize the speaker or writer automatically as pretentious and "unqualified."

Propaganda in Cambodia has in the last few years gained an importance which it never had before. The major groups vying for attention are: the Cambodian government and its ruling majority party, Sihanouk's Sangkum; the opposition parties, principally Son Ngoc Thanh's Democratic party and the leftist People's party; the United States government, which seeks to support the democratic and anti-Communist elements in Cambodia and to this effect largely cooperates with the Cambodian government; the French government, which seeks to create a climate favorable to the economic and, particularly, cultural objectives of France in Cambodia; and, lastly, the Chinese and Vietminh Communists, who seek to exploit current neutralist sentiment among the Cambodian intelligentsia so as to keep Cambodia from becoming too friendly with the West.

Cambodian official propaganda is organized on a fairly simple basis. The Cambodian Ministry of Information has in every provincial capital an information hall, generally maintained by one or two local employees of the Ministry. In the smaller towns and villages the propaganda effort is usually limited to a billboard in the vicinity of the city hall, on which official communications are posted by the mayor, sometimes along with posters he may receive from the Ministry of Information.

The Ministry itself has several sections: radio, press, propaganda, etc. Its organization is not very stable and even its title is subject to change; at times—as in mid-1956—it is attached to another government department, such as Religion and Cultural Affairs, or even Education. Its basic functions, however, remain essentially the same.

There are no "information specialists" in the American sense of the term, and the western concept of public relations is unknown in Cambodian government circles. Government propaganda thus operates mostly on a hit-or-miss basis, as its results sometimes demonstrate.

Informal Channels and Patterns

Foreigners have said that Cambodians are tight-lipped, and it is true that they do a very good job at keeping information away from anyone when they choose. But among themselves there are very few secrets. Everyone in a community soon knows what is going on, although no one seems to spread the information.

Cambodians also have a reputation for seeking "hidden" meanings in speech and action. Part of this may result from the subtlety and consequent flexibility of their language: there may be a dozen ways of expressing a particular thought, and the Cambodian chooses his words according to his judgment of the social situation. Context and knowledge of the personality of the speaker tip off the listener as to the meaning intended. Allusions to symbols and legends which are commonly known by Cambodians also enrich the "hidden" understanding. Sihanouk, for example, often refers to legends and uses allegories in his speeches.

Communication between people of different status is often a matter of nuances—in effect, of what sophisticated westerners call "psychological cues," which can be picked up by both the speaker and the listener. Cambodians talk frankly and openly only with others of the same status. In discussions with people of superior status they are affable but discreet.

The pagoda is a key point in the relay of information and in opinion formation. Its officials are popular figures and their advice is sought. The traditional pattern of religious instruction of boys serves to establish the bonzes' influence in later life, since fairly close personal ties are formed. At times the bonze acts as a channel for complaints which the peasant is unable to express directly.

The people gather at the pagoda, as the focal point of community activity, to read the bulletin boards, books, perhaps newspapers; less frequently, there is a radio. The pagoda is a bridge between the community and the external world beyond the village, as well as between the community and the "other world" of the spirit.

Chinese resturants or sidewalk cafés are popular spots in the cities for casual conversations. And most villages have a Chinese-operated store—which by virtue of a few stools and tables may also qualify as a resturant—where information is exchanged. Community markets are ideal for the exchange of information: every village has its market. The upper strata of society meet and talk at sports clubs.

Information is carried from one community to another by government officials, schoolteachers, truck drivers, chauffeurs, drivers of pedicabs ("the peasant's taxi"), and other itinerants. Cambodians have always moved freely within their small kingdom, perhaps because of the extensive waterways.

The Vietnamese in Cambodia have a reputation for being gossipmongers, it being unkindly said that Vietnam rids itself of undesirables and gossip-spreading women by expelling them to Cambodia.

Information is sterile in Cambodia until it is interpreted, usually by the local "news analyst"—either a bonze or an elder of the village. The elders are respected both within their community and by outside officials. An American reports that once when he arrived in a village with a provincial governor, the governor immediately went over to where the elders were standing "to tell them the news of the city."

Popular opinions and grievances are brought to official attention in a number of ways. The king holds regular audiences where complaints can be registered. Cambodians do protest against the actions of their officials. On one occasion three letters addressed to the governor, the military governor, and a cabinet minister respectively were placed in the truck of an American observer. Each letter was signed, and each complained that a village chief was taking undue advantage of his authority. Complaint was possible; but the people apparently felt that the local mail system was not to be trusted. In some instances, villagers have paraded in front of the Royal Palace in protest against some governmental measure. There have also been mass demonstrations of approval —more often than not staged by the government to impress foreign diplomatic observers that a particular act has popular support.

Newspapers

Daily newspapers have only about one-fourth the circulation of journals issued biweekly, weekly, or monthly. As shown in Table 4, of the sixteen published papers only three are dailies—one in the Cambodian language, the other two in French. The fact that daily papers are so few in number may be due to the high unit cost of publication and the paucity of qualified journalists.

The daily with the largest circulation in 1952 was the *Cong Thuong Pao*, a Chinese publication with fewer than 2,000 subscribers. Founded in 1950, it is a four-page journal of commerce and industry. It is now published only three times a week. Of all Cambodia's publications, *Pracheathipatay*, the biweekly spokesman of the Democratic party has had the largest circulation—9,000 in 1952.

The front page of a recent issue of a typical French-language newspaper covered important Cambodian news such as the inauguration of the bonze hospital at Pnompenh by the King and the policy speech made by Sihanouk upon his return from Pnompenh. Other news given front-page attention was of regional importance: SEATO, a new cabinet in Laos, the departure of French troops from Indochina, and arms traffic for Chinese Nationalist guerrillas along the Thai-Burmese border.

News from France comprised the bulk of overseas news: heavy

snowfalls, a government crisis, a discussion of the French Union, and Morocco's claims for independence. Only three small items had a non-Cambodian or non-French context: a new Russian "peace offensive," border incidents between India and Pakistan, and the crash of an airliner that carried French passengers from Indochina.

Pages 2 and 3 carried news that was closer to the immediate personal interests of Cambodians. On page 2 were the movie programs of Pnompenh; an announcement by the Khmer Tobacco Manufacturing Corporation to its stockholders of a meeting of the Board of Directors; a commercial advertisement for dancing lessons. Page 2 also carried an extensive review of the British press; a general information article based upon a United Nations World Health Organization report to the effect that birds may be carriers of infectious diseases; an extensive daily report of the activities of the National Police; and a Paris stock exchange report giving the official and black-market prices of important currencies, as well as the stock quotations of Indochinese corporations.

Page 3 contained many important administrative announcements, classified advertisements, and the program of the government radio network. Among the official announcements was one by the governor of Pnompenh chastising the habits of certain poor people who simply abandon the bodies of dead infants instead of incurring the expense of burying them properly, as required by rules of hygiene and by the Buddhist faith.

An announcement by the Ministry of Commerce and Industry asked merchants and industrialists for cooperation with the Ministry when they are interrogated for the purpose of compiling commercial statistics. An announcement by the city police of Pnompenh informed an American citizen that his wallet containing official papers had been found and was being held for him at the police precinct.

The majority of the other official announcements were calls for competitive bids to be submitted to various government agencies for work to be undertaken on behalf of the government. Among the commercial advertisements on the page, one advertised the drawing of the national lottery and another the services of a doctor—with "special rates for civil servants and students." There was also a notice, which was being carried daily, of the drugstore in Pnompenh that is assigned emergency duty and must remain open for business all hours of the day and night—a practice borrowed from the French.

A national news agency, the Khmer Press Agency, was set up in 1951. Daily newspapers, government ministries, other government offices and some private commercial concerns subscribe to the service.

A 1951 law gave everyone the right to print and publish in Cambodian or any other language, provided a license was obtained from the Ministry of Information. There is no proclaimed official censorship, but the Ministry may withdraw such a license at will, and there is little chance of appeal. For example, the French magazine *Match* in 1953 published an article which was judged uncomplimentary to King Sihanouk; its circulation in Cambodia was forbidden, and the ban was not lifted until February 1956. The art of public criticism is not highly developed in Cambodia, and extremes of adverse criticism of the government are met with drastic punishment. On occasion, however, suppressed newspapers have changed names and continued publication.

The status of newspaper reporters and editors has not been clearly established. Newspapers are often organs of political parties, and they capitalize on the prestige of the political leaders.

Early in 1957, the government passed a law which was a codification with certain modifications of the 1951 law and subsequent regulations. The first article of the new law states that "except for infractions of laws and regulations then in effect," the following were permitted: (1) printing and libraries, (2) the possession, distribution, and sale of all original writing, recordings, and drawings whatever the language or the method of reproduction, (3) the introduction, distribution, and sale in Cambodia of all writing, recordings, and drawings originating abroad. The article also states that, under the same conditions, it is permitted to disseminate and defend any idea, whether political or religious.

The government issues various official publications and also has some measure of control over all nongovernmental publishing in Cambodia. Foremost among the official publications expounding the government's official position is the daily forty-page mimeographed press bulletin of the Agence Khmère de Presse (AKP), the only Cambodian news agency. The AKP is owned and operated by the Ministry of Information. Since AKP news bulletins form the basis of most newspaper features throughout the country (it seems highly unlikely that any Cambodian newspaper has a direct subscription to a foreign press service), all the news published is apt to be written in the same vein, with variations in style according to the target public.

The government also operates a French-language weekly, *Realités Cambodgiennes*, which is of a fairly high tenor. Since it contains policy editorials as well as news from the various embassies and other missions accredited to Cambodia, apparently it is addressed to the foreign colony.

Books published by the government constitute an important propaganda medium. These recently have included several large books, most of them containing official Cambodian documents (some that formerly had been classified) which show what the policy of the government has been with regard to some of the most urgent problems at present facing Cambodia. These books are intended to influence educated, key people rather than the masses.

Leaflets are used in specific instances, particularly in the struggle against rebels and Communist guerrillas. The printing and distribution of these leaflets are handled by the Royal Khmer Army's Bureau of Psychological Warfare, with the help of the United States Information Agency (USIA) and the French Information Service. There are also leaflet-distribution activities in the field of hygiene and public health.

Intensive poster campaigns are waged about public issues. The government publishes a large number of posters to promote such concepts as good health, public service, and patriotism. USIA has been instrumental in helping the Cambodian government solve technical problems of production and layout for propaganda material. Posters are kept as simple as possible to maximize their impact.

Radio

The use of radio is expanding in Cambodia, as government officials adapt modern techniques to the age-old Cambodian reliance on word-of-mouth communication. Until the end of 1954 the French controlled the radio system; it has since been operated by the Cambodian government Department of Information. Collective listening stations are set up in many of the "information halls" of the principal towns. Many of the pagodas have receiving sets, thus adding to their role as centers of information and discussion. The government owns the broadcasting stations and controls the programs.

Radio Cambodge was pieced together from old Japanese equipment in May 1946. By 1951 this apparatus was replaced by a new and more powerful American transmitter. Four stations were reported in Pnompenh in March 1955—two of 1 kilowatt and two of 10 kilowatts. In 1958 the *World Radio Handbook* listed only one station—Radio Cambodia, a 10-kilowatt station, which broadcasts news in French and Cambodian, language lessons in English and French, national music, and press reviews.

A 20-kilowatt radio transmitting station, gift of the Chinese People's Republic, is being constructed in Pnompenh and will be completed sometime in 1959. Once in operation it will be known as the Royal Khmer Radio Broadcasting Station (Station Royale du Radio Diffusion Khmère).

In 1958, 7,000 receiving sets were registered. A license fee is collected for each, but pagodas and some other institutions are exempt from the payment of the fee. Inadequacy of electric power seriously restricts the use of receiving sets away from the large towns.

The Khmer National Radio Broadcasting System—which operates Radio Cambodge—is on the air only five to six hours daily, the operating time being from 7 to 8 A.M., from noon to 1:45 P.M., and from 6 to 8:30 P.M. About two-thirds of the programs are devoted to music, which consists of both "live" presentations of Khmer songs and instrumental works and recordings of Khmer and European compositions. News, talks, and religious broadcasts make up the balance of the programs, most of this being in Khmer, some in French, and a little in Vietnamese and Chinese.

Since it owns and operates the entire radio broadcasting system the government has at its sole disposal the medium with the biggest potential for instantly reaching people throughout the country. But given the still small number of radio sets actually available and the relatively few electrified urban centers, the effectiveness of radio broadcasting as a government propaganda medium would be negligible if it were not supplemented by the extremely well-developed system of word-of-mouth transmission of news and information. It can be assumed that every owner of a radio set keeps his whole neighborhood informed of the latest news (with himself as "news analyst"), if only for reasons of pride of ownership. In certain small towns where the mayor owns a set, a public address system may be connected with it, so that people by collecting in the market square may listen to news and entertainment.

The more important pagodas and the quarters of senior bonzes usually have radio sets. The receivers are likely to be powerful and far-ranging because the bonzes like to listen to the Buddhist programs that are broadcast by stations in Burma and Thailand. Since the bonzes are important molders of opinion—perhaps the most important single opinion-forming group in the kingdom—the Cambodian government finds it useful to keep them informed on certain actions it contemplates. It did so very successfully in 1953, for example, in its "Mobilization of the Live Forces of Cambodia" effort.

Motion Pictures

Motion pictures in Cambodia are agents of cultural as well as ideological change for urban dwellers but are seen by very few country people. The French authorities, when still in control, issued an ordinance that French films be shown at least five out of every thirteen weeks. This reflected the importance attached to motion pictures as a medium of communication—and possibly a public preference for other than French films. The American, French, Indian, and British governments for some years have promoted the use of their respective films in Indochina.

Indian films generally are modern representations of old legends and are loved as such; in these, good always triumphs. American "Westerns" are liked for their sweep of action and scenery; other films, American or European, portray the life of modern cities. Cambodians thus are impregnated with western ways; city children, impressed by American films, have combined two standard prototypes into a Cambodian "cowboy-gangster" role in their games. Some 400 feature films were imported in 1950, 41 percent of them American, 36 percent French, 13 percent Chinese, 6 percent British, and 2 percent Italian.

There were thirteen movie theaters in Cambodia in 1951, ten of them in Pnompenh. Their total seating capacity was 5,464, with a combined annual audience estimated at 1.5 million. The theaters are reported to be packed at almost every showing. The two major circuits controlling eight of the theaters—the *Société des Ciné-theatre d'Indochine* and the *Société Indochine Films et Cinémas*—both were financed by French capital; the other five theaters are said to be controlled by Chinese. Each theater has a 35-mm. projector; ten of them also have 16-mm. projectors.

The programs usually consist of a feature, a newsreel, and a documentary or a cartoon. Gaumont Newsreels and the French edition of Fox Movietone and Pathé Journal are shown in the French circuits. The Chinese theaters show no newsreel.

Limiting factors in the use of movies are the lack of theaters in outlying areas and the inability of many people to understand foreign languages or to read Cambodian subtitles. The Ministry of

Information has a mobile radio-cinema unit equipped with a 16-mm. projector, but details as to its use are unavailable.

American Information Activities

American government information activities in Cambodia are in the hands of the United States Information Agency, which has a main office in Pnompenh and a branch office in Battambang.

As noted above, the USIA has lent its support to Cambodian government propaganda operations—its production of leaflets in the operations against the Vietminh in Stungtreng and Kratie were particularly effective and appreciated—but it also pursues its own, specifically American, objectives. It operates a small book-translation program, a weekly wall newspaper, a Cambodian version of the magazine *Free World*, a lending library and bookmobile program, film shows, and English classes. Some of the English classes are especially for bonzes who want to participate in Asia-wide Buddhist conferences where English is the main medium of communication. USIA also participates with exhibits in such events as fairs.

Most USIA activities are effective and appreciated by the Cambodians; others sometimes miss the mark. The International Fair in Pnompenh in November-December 1955, dedicated to "Peace, Freedom, and Progress," included a well-attended American civilian exhibit, showing United States technical achievements in various fields from housing to television. But it also included (courtesy of the local U. S. Military Assistance Advisory Group) an exhibit of rifles, mortars, light machine guns, and land mines supplied Cambodia under the Mutual Defense Assistance Program. Communist propaganda exploitation of this military exhibit as "warmongering" nullified an appreciable amount of the effect created by the civilian aspect of the exhibit.

The Voice of America operates a Cambodian section in Washington manned entirely by Cambodians under the direction of American personnel. Programs are informative and geared toward entertainment rather than open propaganda.

Cambodian "neutralism" has handicapped American action mainly in that this phenomenon requires particularly delicate handling. The goal of USIA is to educate Cambodians about the United States and to persuade them that Americans are not simply trying to take the place recently occupied by the French. Short-range programs are aimed at the governing group; a long-range program is directed toward the peasant as well. The Voice of America broadcasts in Cambodian, and its Vietnamese broadcasts are also received in Cambodia.

French Information Activities

France considers Cambodia its cultural preserve; especially since its loss of influence in neighboring Vietnam, it has considerably intensified its cultural efforts in Cambodia. Some of the broadcasts of the Cambodian national radio network still are in French and French educational activities have considerably increased their scope in recent years through new installations as well as through a great number of scholarships to France for Cambodian students.

France's approach to influencing Cambodians differs somewhat from that used by USIA. Instead of attempting to "explain" or "sell" France, the French Information Service often brings exhibits of specifically Cambodian interest, such as picture exhibits concerning special Cambodian ceremonies—religious holidays, cremations, etc. These seem to be received favorably. French economic aid is also played up, important particularly in contrast to France's former colonial policies in the area.

The French Information Service in Vietnam publishes an official daily, the *Journal d'Extrême-Orient*, which contains Cambodian news and has distribution in Pnompenh.

An agreement negotiated between the French and Cambodian governments in 1950, under which the 1954 transfer of Radio Cambodge took place, permitted France to establish a French broadcasting and television service in Cambodia. (The Cambodian government was allowed to establish its own facilities in France.) The French have not yet set up a broadcasting service; they have a temporary arrangement with Cambodia authorizing them to use Radio Cambodge for the broadcasts of the French Information Service. This arrangement gives French a preferred position over other foreign-language broadcasts on the Cambodian network; it is specified that 50 percent of the network's spoken broadcasts in a language other than Khmer shall be in French, and that 75 percent of recorded modern music, other than Khmer, shall be from French recordings.

Communist Propaganda

Communist propaganda in Cambodia lost most of its strength with the signing of the Geneva cease-fire in 1954. The Cambodian government could no longer be called a French "puppet," and the subsequent general elections—with results that were accepted by the International Supervisory and Control Commission (ISCC)—eliminated the other major line: "lack of true democracy."

By 1956 the only major Communist argument in Cambodia was "neutralism" or "friendly coexistence" with the Communist camp. As a corollary, Communist propaganda attacked all Cambodian elements hostile to such a policy as "undemocratic" or as "American puppets," and sought to discredit American activities in the country.

The Vietnamese and the Chinese within Cambodia are particularly vulnerable to Communist propaganda. Their homelands are largely under Communist control, and pressures may be exercised against relatives. In addition, their own loyalty to the Cambodian state is often less than complete.

Since Sihanouk's recent attempts to foster friendlier relations with Communist China (see chap. 11), Red Chinese propaganda has taken a sudden spurt in Cambodia. There are now Chinese Communist newspapers, and Communist radio broadcasts are beamed at the Cambodian Chinese community. It was also discovered last year that cigarettes and other products from Communist China had made their appearance in Cambodia, their wrappings covered with anti-American slogans in Chinese.

Evaluation of Media and Themes

Word-of-mouth persuasion is by far the best means of getting a message across in Cambodia. Use of the Cambodian language, therefore, is essential. Radio is less effective than face-to-face, word-of-mouth transmission. Loud-speakers have been used very effectively by Cambodians in political campaigns. Portable loud-speakers are considered the most effective means of persuading groups of people in villages or cities. There appear to be no taboos affecting the location of mobile units in Cambodian villages, and operators are understood to get the full cooperation of local officials. Bonzes and elders play influential roles in interpreting information to the common people and in reporting the popular views to officials.

To influence national policy, only a minority of the population needs be reached. Decisions are made at the top and passed down along the line. But Cambodian officials are very anxious that their subordinates like them, so a great deal of care goes into explaining measures and attempting to persuade the common people that an act is right. Moral correctness, in terms of the

Buddhist standards, is extremely important to Cambodians.

The average Cambodian has a preference for clear, uncomplicated images, such as those used for the traditional dancing masks: the "good man" and the "bad man" or good or bad spirits are clearly recognizable types. Used in propaganda posters and slides, such clear-cut "good-bad" ideas meet with considerable success. With the exception of the western-educated intelligentsia, most Cambodians are unsophisticated; they are not credulous, however, and they like to see what makes things "tick."

Indian-made films based on Buddhist legends are immensely successful in Cambodia because they represent symbols that are part of the cultural heritage of the majority of the people, regardless of social rank and education. American-made cowboy and crime films have also had great popular success throughout the country, showing that, in spite of Buddhist precepts, scenes of violence are not entirely objectionable.

The present Cambodian government propaganda program on the whole can be considered effective—but it is a fragile edifice, being built entirely upon the present nation-wide popularity of Sihanouk. The Cambodian masses are taught to believe or to do things because this would be pleasing to Sihanouk. Issues being pushed at the present time, outside of fidelity to the former king and his Sangkum party, are largely negative: neutrality on one hand, and anti-Vietnamese, anti-Thai, or anti-American feelings on the other. A Cambodian regularly reading his own government's press statements or hearing its information over the radio cannot help but feel "encircled" by a group of big, bad, predatory nations. Being what he is, however, the Cambodian is probably not overwhelmingly concerned about this situation, and therein lies one of his major weaknesses as well as one of his major strengths.

FOREIGN RELATIONS

EVER SINCE THE ONCE MIGHTY CAMBODIAN KINGDOM was destroyed by Thai invaders in the fourteenth century (see chap. 2), Cambodia's major foreign policy problem has been to counter the ambitions of two rival neighbors—Thailand and Vietnam—bent upon colonization and annexation of the fertile and prosperous country around the Tonle Sap and the Mekong delta.

As the French consolidated their control over the Indochinese peninsula in the nineteenth century, both Thailand and Vietnam were eliminated as political factors. During the ensuing period of French protectorate administration (1864-1949) Cambodian foreign affairs were entirely in the hands of France. At first the situation was not without benefits for Cambodia. Although its border with South Vietnam was fixed along a line that did not follow ethnic patterns, France did, on the other hand, espouse Cambodian claims against Thailand for restitution of the provinces of Siemreap (which contains the Cambodian national shrine of Angkor Wat) and Battambang. Both provinces were returned to Cambodia in 1904.

Since Cambodia was not a colony but a protectorate, its relations with France were in some aspects "foreign" relations. They were so considered by the Cambodian government, whose Ministry of the Palace, Finance, and Arts handled official relations with the French resident-general. Most such contacts were hardly more than formality, but the existence of such a channel kept alive the concept of "foreign" relations between the two countries. Official correspondence of the time shows that such channels were respected in the exchanges of views between Cambodian and French authorities.

French control of Cambodia, interrupted during World War II, was reasserted in 1945, but by November 1949, after a constant struggle for a wider range of powers, the Cambodians achieved the first prerogatives of sovereignty (see chap. 2). In a treaty with France, Cambodia was promised limited diplomatic representation, but France in fact never insisted on the limitations and Cambodia soon sent ambassadors to Paris, Washington, Bangkok, Tokyo, New Delhi, and London, in that order. Full independence was achieved in December 1954. January 1, 1955 saw the dissolution of the joint arrangements between France and the former Associated States of Indochina in monetary, customs, and foreign economic affairs, and the last limitations on Cambodia's independence in the economic field were removed. Economic relations between Cambodia, Laos, Vietnam and France were put on a bilateral basis, with each of the former Indochinese states assuming complete authority over its economic policies both at home and abroad. The achievement of full sovereignty afforded Cambodia its first opportunity to reevaluate its international position as an equal among nations. Mindful of its weak military and political position—and keeping to a path chosen by India in joining the British Commonwealth— Cambodia chose to stay in the French Union if it could. The terms it set were fulfilled in September 1955 when all references to Cambodia's adherence to the French Union were eliminated from the Cambodian Constitution so that the association could become a subject for bilateral Franco-Cambodian agreements, negotiated by two sovereign states dealing with each other on the basis of equality.

Sovereignty has brought about a considerable improvement in relations between Cambodia and France. Cambodians participate actively in the discussions of the French Union Assembly in Versailles and also are represented in the High Council of the French Union. United States Senator Mike Mansfield wrote in October 1955, after one of his several visits to Cambodia:

> The improvement in relations between the two countries is now very evident. At present, French prestige in Cambodia is probably at its highest level in the postwar years. This change is attributable, in my opinion, primarily to the achievement of independence, to the principle of national equality which now governs relationships between the two countries, and to the prompt adjustment of French policy to the change. . . . France has a sizable economic aid program in Cambodia which includes the construction of port facilities on the Gulf of Siam. French military technicians are playing a major role in training and advising the royal army.

The opinions expressed in Senator Mansfield's report were confirmed by Sihanouk in an article published in *Réalités Cambodgiennes* in March 1958: "French culture, of all foreign cultures, has our preference. France is one of our best friends."

It is likely that France's future role in Cambodia, particularly in view of the extensive influence of French culture (see chap. 19), will remain a major one.

Cambodia and Its Neighbors

Although Cambodia's relations with both Thailand and Vietnam have been tense, the Thai are cultural brothers of the Cambodians while the Vietnamese are not, and the Thai do not occupy an important place in the economic and ethnic picture of Cambodia as the Vietnamese do. This accounts for many differences in the attitudes Cambodians have toward their two major neighbors: a quarrel with Thailand is something of a family affair; in a quarrel with Vietnam, national honor is at stake.

Relations with Thailand

Culturally, the Cambodians consider Thailand a sort of "older brother." Until recently Cambodian Buddhist monks had to look to Thailand for higher Buddhist education, and Cambodia still looks to Thailand for the necessary linguistic westernizations when new technical words are needed for which there is no equivalent in Cambodian (see chap. 4).

Thai occupations of Cambodian territory, extending over long periods, are not deeply resented today. The people in areas under Thai occupation during World War II were well treated, so that the Cambodians tend to look upon the incident as one between the French and the Thai rather than between Franco-Cambodians and the Thai. Since the restoration of the *status quo* at the end of World War II by the Treaty of Washington, November 17, 1946, Thai-Cambodian relations have been generally friendly.

Recent tensions between Thailand and Cambodia have two major causes: Sihanouk's neutralist policy, which the Thai feel will deprive them of an anti-Communist buffer, and Thai beliefs that, in view of the disappearance of colonial influence in Indochina, Thailand can now reassert its traditional ascendancy over Cambodia, and also Laos, perhaps in the form of an anti-Communist "Buddhist bloc" of states which might even include Burma.

Feelings on both sides were exacerbated in 1953 by the Thai

occupation of a Cambodian Buddhist temple, Phra Viharn, allegedly in contempt of signed treaties. Cambodian troops ejected the Thai, who retaliated by closing the border and instituting what amounted to a blockade of Cambodia. Tensions later eased but the border issue was never fully resolved, and troops of both countries continued to occupy a disputed area near the ancient ruins of Angkor Wat.

In July 1958 Sihanouk, upon resumption of the premiership, paid a visit to Bangkok for the purpose of a "man-to-man" exchange of views with the Thai leaders. At this meeting he arranged for Thai-Khmer negotiations in Bangkok in August to discuss: (1) joint action for the prevention of crime at the border, (2) agreements on railway connections and customs, (3) extension of commercial intercourse, and (4) cooperation for the control of epidemic and epizootic diseases. Before opening these negotiations he visited Nehru in India to ask his advice on handling Cambodian relations with Thailand and South Vietnam. Reports from Pnompenh attributed part of the Thai-Cambodian trouble to the fact that Cambodia had recognized Communist China whereas Thailand was a member of SEATO.

Negotiations in Bangkok got off to a bad start. The Thai claimed that Cambodia was serving as a base for Communist infiltrators while Cambodia claimed that Thailand was not respecting its neutral position. Negotiations ended with little accomplished and there was an anti-Cambodian demonstration in Bangkok the day after the departure of the Cambodian delegation. Three months later Cambodia decided to recall its ambassador and embassy personnel from Bangkok. This action was explained in a communiqué dated November 29, 1958 in which the Cambodian government reviewed the events leading up to the break, claiming that the Thai, in the midst of the negotiations, had denounced the agreements on free movement of people living along the border and had posted armed forces there under the pretext of stopping Communist infiltration. The communiqué closed with the statement that the recall was only temporary and that relations could be renewed when both parties could come to an amicable agreement.

Since the November recall there has been a new series of border incidents accompanied by vigorous press and radio campaigns directed by each country against the other. An impending explosion was averted in February 1959 by mediation on the part of the United Nations special representative, Swedish Baron Johan Beck-Friis.

Relations with Vietnam

Relations with the Republic of Vietnam (South Vietnam) seriously deteriorated after the Geneva cease-fire of 1954. There are several persistent sources of friction between the two countries.

Cambodia has never relinquished its claims to the rich Cochin China provinces that once were part of Cambodian territory but were awarded, over strong Cambodian protests, to Vietnam by the French in the Elysée Agreement of March 1949. A large Cambodian minority, nearly half a million Khmer, still lives in these provinces and Cambodia has resisted the establishment of a permanent border between the two areas, decrying what it saw as Vietnamese oppression of these people or attempts to "Vietnamize" them. Overcrowded South Vietnam, on the other hand, has always coveted the open and thinly populated plains of the Mekong-Tonle Sap basin and Cambodia has been peculiarly sensitive for this reason to any movements of Vietnamese troops on the border.

A series of border incidents involving the flight of Vietnamese planes over Cambodian territory and the capture of Cambodian fishing vessels by Vietnamese patrol boats culminated in March 1956 in the closing of the Cambodian-Vietnamese border. This had the effect of almost totally blockading Cambodia from the outside world, since its only deepwater port, Sihanoukville, was not completed. In view of its neutral position Cambodia had refused to establish diplomatic relations with South Vietnam on the grounds that if it did so it would also have to recognize the Communist regime of North Vietnam. On May 17, 1956, however, the Cambodian government not only reopened the border but also announced its decision to exchange diplomatic representatives with South Vietnam. Normal commercial relations were again established.

Since early 1957 a new series of border incidents has been reported by both sides, the last serious one occurring in June 1958 when the Cambodian government received reports that South Vietnamese troops had crossed the border, had occupied several Cambodian villages, and were moving the boundary markers.

The Cambodian minister of foreign affairs issued a royal proclamation accusing the South Vietnamese of twenty-seven violations since January 1957 and urging the United States to intervene as a friend of both nations. This was followed by a vote of censure in the National Assembly and by an appeal to the International Truce Supervisory Commission. In spite of this trouble diplomatic relations were not severed and Cambodia has since vigorously denied that it might take such action. Recently friction between the two countries has been overshadowed by troubles with Thailand.

As of January 1959 Cambodia had not yet reached a decision to exchange diplomatic representatives with the Democratic Republic of Vietnam (DRVN, North Vietnam). There have been indications, however, of a growing *rapprochement*. In a 1956 interview the DRVN premier said that in the event of total DRVN control of Vietnam "the rights of the Cambodian minorities will be given full consideration." This statement, while completely theoretical at the present time, places the northern regime in a favorable light, the more so as the southern government has adamantly refused to reconsider in any way the status of the Cambodian minority in Vietnam.

In late 1958 Ho Chih Minh offered 200,000 riels to the Cambodian and Vietnamese victims of a fire in a border village, and a DRVN trade delegation to Cambodia concluded a commercial agreement between the two countries. In spite of Cambodia's insistence that it will not recognize DRVN until both parts of Vietnam are unified, recent exchanges between Cambodia and North Vietnam reflect an interest in further friendly relations.

Relations with Laos

Laos has nearly always been powerless to endanger Cambodian security, and wars fought in common against the same Thai and Vietnamese enemies have given the two countries historic bonds of friendship. Relations between the two countries in recent years have been peaceful and largely uneventful. Both countries have exchanged ambassadors and have recently concluded a commercial agreement. Laos has also expressed an interest in gaining access to the Cambodian port of Sihanoukville on the Gulf of Siam, an interest which has been favorably received by Cambodia.

Cambodia and the Communist Nations

Relations between Cambodia and the Communist nations have varied in proportion to western blunders in dealing with the Cambodians. To each western pressure—whether real or fancied —to join the western camp, Cambodia has reacted with a friendly move toward the Communists, both to repair injured pride and to maintain the neutral line it has traced for itself since the Geneva cease-fire.

11. *Cambodia and the Communist Nations*

As a rule of thumb it can be said that relations are closest with those Communist countries that are farthest away and least likely to interfere directly in Cambodia's affairs. This has been clearly evident in Cambodia's relations with Russia and Communist China.

Relations with Communist China

Chou En-lai himself initiated improved relations between Cambodia and his country when, at the Bandung Conference of April 1955, he declared in his policy speech that he "wished to repeat assurances made to Nehru and U Nu [Prime Minister of Burma] between sessions of the 1954 Geneva conference that [Communist] China had no intention whatever of interfering or intervening in the internal affairs of Cambodia and Laos."

Matters remained at an apparent standstill for nearly a year, until Sihanouk, at the invitation of Red China, visited Peking in February 1956. He returned with glowing accounts of what he had seen there and with the outline of a Sino-Cambodian economic assistance treaty. But in spite of many press reports to the contrary, Sihanouk had not been convinced of the benefits his country would derive from imitating the Communist example. On the contrary, upon his return Sihanouk made a speech at the Pnompenh airport which was broadcast throughout Cambodia and which expressed his impressions as follows:

> In a Communist country, the people work without respite day and night in the factories and on the construction sites; teams of workers succeeded each other one after another. Women and old people cannot remain inactive. Over there, human life is of little importance. . . . Cambodia is faithful to the worship of Buddhism; it is thus impossible for it to accept such a regime. You can thus be entirely assured on this point. Let us content ourselves with the present regime of our country.

To anyone familiar with Cambodian mores this statement constitutes a grave indictment of Red China; compulsory, regular, and monotonous work is abhorrent to the Cambodian, and not being entitled to a life of leisure in one's old age is well-nigh a calamity, a condition of utmost misery. The disrespect for human life cited by Sihanouk would constitute for a Buddhist country such as Cambodia—where any life form is deeply respected—a key reason for not accepting such a regime.

Sihanouk amplified his view of Sino-Cambodian relations in his speech at the investiture of a new Cambodian government on February 29, 1956:

> We must observe a policy of neutrality and wisdom. . . . We cannot establish diplomatic relations with Peking and abandon [the Chinese Nationalist government of] Mr. Chiang Kai-shek. The powers favoring Chaing Kai-shek will accuse us of partiality. Mr. Chou En-lai, after having listened to my explanations, has told me that he would not insist upon the exchange of ambassadors between his country and Cambodia.

Sihanouk's visit to Peking and the impending economic agreements with Red China brought immediate reaction among the Chinese community in Cambodia. Ever sensitive to policy changes, it began to veer to the new "line": a Chinese Communist lending library was set up in Pnompenh; the Chinese newspaper *Mekong Yat Pao* (Mekong Daily) changed its name to *Jen Minh Jih Pao* (People's Daily) and began to carry the program schedules of Radio Peking; a wealthy Chinese businessman imported Red Chinese films to be shown in local theaters; and the Chinese Nationalist consulate in Pnompenh, according to the local Chinese newspaper *Cong Thuong Pao* (April 20, 1956), ran out of visa forms for Chinese citizens desiring to leave Cambodia for "neutral" areas such as Hong Kong and Macao.

With the signing of the economic aid agreement in June 1956, delegations of Chinese technicians and advisors arrived in Cambodia, followed shortly by the first shipments of construction materials and consumer goods. In November, Chou En-lai visited Pnompenh where he and Sihanouk affirmed Nehru's Five Principles (*Panch' Shila*) of coexistence and appealed to the Chinese community to support the Cambodian government. By the end of 1957 Chinese influence in Cambodia had so alarmed Sihanouk that on January 3, 1958, in a closed session of the Sangkum party, he delivered a bitter attack on the Communists, concluding with the remark: "I know the Communists are going to cut my throat, but I am ready to die for my country."

In mid-1958, however, Sihanouk sent a letter to Chou En-lai recognizing as *de jure* the People's Republic of China; in August normal diplomatic relations were established between the two countries. On this occasion Sihanouk and Chou En-lai issued a joint statement in which Chou called again on the Cambodian Chinese to abide by the laws and respect the customs of Cambodia and to refrain from political activities, while Sihanouk declared that the participation of Communist China in international organizations and conferences would be an "important and necessary factor in the settlement of international issues and hence also in the maintenance of peace in Asia and the world."

In December 1958, addressing a gathering at the Communist Chinese agricultural exhibit in Pnompenh, Sihanouk called on the Cambodian people to emulate the progress made by the people of Communist China. Recognition of Red China, which brought an immediate protest from the United States, appears to have ushered in an era of resignation on the part of Sihanouk and his supporters in the government. Recent rumblings of a plot to overthrow him may, however, indicate that other members of the elite are not happy with the present situation.

Relations with the USSR

Relations between Cambodia and the Soviet European bloc are on an entirely different basis from those between Cambodia and Red China, for here no precedent existed and, unlike the case of China, no rival Russian government could claim to have been recognized earlier by Cambodia. Furthermore, Russian Communism carries an air of "remoteness" unlike that of Chinese Communism; as a European import it does not—to the Cambodians—seem likely to infiltrate the national body as insidiously as the Chinese variety.

Recognition of the USSR (May 17, 1956) and later of Poland and Czechoslovakia met with no opposition in Cambodia. The USSR and Cambodia have announced that ambassadors will be exchanged. Sihanouk visited the USSR, Poland, and Czechoslovakia in the summer of 1956. But again, Sihanouk sought to establish a delicate balance by coupling this visit to Communist countries with a visit to anti-Communist Spain and by sponsoring Spain's entry into the United Nations.

Cambodia and the Greater Asian Area

With full independence, Cambodia sought to establish close bonds with both the young, ex-colonial nations and the older nations of Asia. The Bandung Conference of African and Asian Nations provided the perfect opportunity.

At Bandung, Sihanouk made his country's entry into world politics by advocating a peace and nonaggression plan. He finally endorsed the *Panch' Shila*, the Five Principles of coexistence, which

Nehru had agreed upon with Chou En-lai in 1954. His attempts to establish friendly relations with the Philippines failed, however, probably because of poor handling of the initial steps.

Relations with India

Throughout much of Cambodia's history India has played a role of "elder brother." In the past Cambodian politicians have been prone to say that, if abandoned by France or the United States, Cambodia would rely upon India for economic and perhaps military help.

The Cambodian struggle for independence received warm support in India, and since independence Nehru has been sympathetic to Cambodia's avowed policy of neutralism. Sihanouk has been well received in Delhi whenever he has gone there to seek Nehru's advice.

Relations with Japan

Japan's role in initiating the independence of Cambodia has not been forgotten and today Japan is perhaps more popular in Cambodia than in any other country of Southeast Asia. Japanese occupation in the last days of World War II, when Japanese forces were urgently needed on active war fronts, was very lenient, so that Cambodians today do not tend to resent the Japanese as do, for example, the Filipinos. To the Cambodians (as to the Indonesians) Japan is more a liberator from colonial control than a military oppressor.

The results of this attitude have been shown in recent years. In November 1955, Cambodia waived payment of the one million yen (about U. S. $12,800) that Japan owed to Cambodian nationals as war compensation. On December 9, 1955 Japan and Cambodia signed a Treaty of Amity which laid the groundwork for economic and technical cooperation, cultural exchanges, and a limited immigration of Japanese settlers into Cambodian frontier areas. Both parties agreed to develop mutual financial, economic, and cultural cooperation; to exchange scientific and industrial knowledge; and to accord facilities to immigrants. This last general point related in fact to the immigration of Japanese into Cambodia; although the treaty did not specify numbers, a plan to permit 2,000 Japanese per year over a five-year period was discussed. In April 1956 the Congress ratified the Treaty of Amity but approved only a total immigration of 2,000 Japanese and on condition that they be installed in unoccupied and unexploited areas. Shortly thereafter a

Japanese mission arrived to prepare the way for immigration. In November 1956 the Japanese government announced its decision to allocate in 1957 a sum of 1,500 million yen (about 150 million riels) for the construction of an agricultural experiment center and health research institute on the Kirirom plateau 114 kilometers from Pnompenh. At the same time the Japanese press was indicating that Japan would be especially interested in developing the lumber resources of Cambodia.

Cambodia maintains an embassy in Tokyo and relations between the two countries appear to have been unruffled by the issues of "neutralism" and "coexistence."

Cambodia and the United States

The characteristics of Cambodia's relationship with the United States changed within less than two years from extreme friendliness to almost outright hostility. This radical change came about after the Geneva cease-fire had revealed two new factors: the collapse of French military and political power in the Far East; and the certainty that, despite statements to the contrary, American public opinion would not permit U. S. troops to be committed in the area. The delicate equilibrium that had existed in Cambodian-American relations was broken and neutralism appeared on the Cambodian scene. The problem of how to maintain Cambodian independence despite the pressures of the cold war became the major focus for foreign policy.

From the American point of view, Cambodian independence was in large measure assured by the creation of the Southeast Asia Treaty Organization (SEATO) in September 1954. Although Cambodia, like Vietnam and Laos, did not join the organization, all three are under the "protective umbrella" of the treaty, since the member powers have agreed to consider a Communist attack upon one or all three states of Indochina as an attack against themselves. The treaty does not, however, guarantee intervention by U. S. forces in case of such an attack.

Cambodian leaders felt that to react favorably to such a "protective umbrella" would leave them open to Red Chinese or even Indian charges that they had become American puppets. This charge could, without necessarily improving its security situation, deprive Cambodia of the moral support it was getting from most other Asian countries. Such a reading of the international situation was further reinforced by what the Cambodian delegation (led by

Sihanouk in person) heard at the Bandung Conference early in 1955.

Cambodia consequently embarked upon a policy which the Cambodians prefer to call "neutral." Rather than comparing their position with that of Indonesia and Burma—countries which are considered "soft" to Communism—the Cambodians feel that they are in the position of Switzerland or Sweden: uncommitted to either side, but repressing Communist subversion at home and taking a pro-West stand on all major problems outside the military field.

Contrary to American expectations (especially since American economic aid has been, as Sihanouk put it on April 5, 1956, "the oxygen that keeps Cambodia alive"), Cambodia has not evidenced any desire to join a clearly pro-West treaty arrangement that would mark it as a target of the Communists without increasing the economic advantages it already draws from its aid agreements with the United States and France. In the words of a British observer in the *Economist*, May 5, 1956:

> . . . like all nations in the area, Cambodia is exposed to the winds that blow from Peking. Sihanouk realizes well enough that the Americans are bound to continue their aid to his country, and secure in this knowledge he can assert his independence to the point of public insult.

Here again appears the underlying Cambodian value of "collaboration on a basis of free consent": independence must be asserted—the more so because most Cambodians recognize their dependence upon United States aid. Pressures to endorse or sign a declaration favorable to the West—allegedly exercised upon Sihanouk during his 1956 stay in the Philippines—definitely ran against the grain not only of Sihanouk himself but of Cambodians in general.

Sihanouk's stormy departure from Manila was followed by a series of incidents between Cambodia and its neighbors, Vietnam and Thailand, which Cambodians tended to attribute to American machinations. Then came further Cambodian accusations against the United States, this time over the terms of military and economic aid. The Cambodians accused the United States of practicing a "go-slow" attitude until Cambodia adopted a policy more amenable to the West. Whatever the truth may be, the coincidence of such incidents was sufficient to create a hostile reaction in Cambodia and contributed greatly to the possibility of closer relations with Communist China and the Soviet bloc.

In April 1956 relations between Washington and Pnompenh nearly reached the breaking point. There were rumblings that Cambodia had accused the United States of making economic and military aid conditional on Cambodia's joining SEATO—an accusation which was refuted by the United States and disclaimed by Sihanouk. The subsequent resignation of Sihanouk from the post of prime minister brought about a considerable lessening of tension. And statements at about the same time by Secretary of State John Foster Dulles and U. S. Ambassador to Cambodia Robert Mc-Clintock that the United States respects the neutrality of Cambodia and that American aid is unconditional met with a favorable response in Cambodia.

Since 1956 two incidents have threatened the improvement of Cambodian-American relations. The first was Cambodia's recognition of Communist China in July 1958, an act which brought expression of deep concern and regret from the United States and an indication that the American economic and military aid program might be reconsidered. Sihanouk has since expressed the hope of being able to steer a middle course and called upon the United States to show more flexibility in its policy.

The second incident was the purported discovery in January 1958 of a plot to overthrow the Cambodian government. Claiming that the American intelligence agencies already knew of the plot and the identity of its leader (Sam Sary—see chap. 8), Sihanouk accused the United States of failing to warn Cambodia: "I cannot name those who informed me of the conspiracy but I can say who abstained from doing so." He implied that the United States was hoping to draw Cambodia into the "anti-Communist front."

Whatever the validity of this charge, it is clear that Sihanouk is still highly sensitive to American actions and that Cambodian leaders will still resist strongly any attempt to draw Cambodia into alignment with SEATO.

International Organizations

Since 1949, when its independence within the French Union was first recognized, Cambodia has been a member of many United Nations specialized agencies and organizations. Pending full membership in the United Nations, it was able to join only those agencies that were open to nonmember states. Full membership was several times delayed by Soviet opposition, and the Philippines once opposed Cambodia's admission on the grounds that it was

French-controlled—one reason perhaps for Cambodia's present animosity toward the Manila government. Cambodia was finally admitted in 1955, under a sixteen-nation "package deal" in which the USSR agreed not to oppose the entry of western-sponsored countries provided some of its own candidates were admitted.

Since the Geneva cease-fire, Cambodia has begun to participate more extensively in international affairs of both a private and a governmental nature. An international fair, for example, was held in Pnompenh in 1955; many western and Asian nations were represented.

The existence of direct airline connections with foreign countries and the completion of the deepwater port of Sihanoukville will further increase Cambodia's contacts with the outside world. Its participation in United Nations affairs and in regional Buddhist activities such as the Buddhist Congress of Rangoon in 1954-56 also serves to expand its international contacts.

Patterns of Diplomacy

In contrast to their neighbors the Vietnamese or the Chinese, who seek to attain their objectives through suppleness and maneuvering, the Cambodians up to now have been prone to adopt an attitude of smiling but dogged determination.

In the course of a lengthy negotiation, it might appear that a point acceptable to the Cambodian negotiator had finally been made, only to find that he later raises an almost identical point requiring further negotiation. It is of primary importance to discover the actual objectives of the Cambodians, then to proceed slowly toward a middle ground acceptable to both sides.

Cambodians are apt to be unyielding if they feel an essential issue is at stake. This has been one of the major reasons for the deterioration of relations between France and Cambodia in the 1949-54 period. While France negotiated to retain as much control as possible, Cambodia wanted nothing less than full independence; once full independence was attained, Cambodia felt ready to negotiate with France on a basis of equality about various privileges France desired to retain in the area. The French negotiators had failed to recognize the essential point of Cambodia's position: "independence first—negotiations later." A similar breakdown in communication seems to have occurred in Cambodian-American relations in 1955-56.

There is perhaps no better example of Cambodian behavior

in international negotiations—outside of the direct negotiations with France on the particular problem of independence—than that provided by the events of the Geneva cease-fire conference in 1954.

Throughout the conference the Cambodians proved tough and astute negotiators. Undaunted by the fact that they represented the smallest nation attending, they refused to be pressured by the representatives of the bigger nations into accepting compromise solutions which would endanger their nation's sovereignty or its unity of territory and government. Their first success was in the refusal to deal with the Communist-led "Khmer Resistance Government," which they contended was nothing but a puppet of the Communist bloc. This stand was supported by all western powers present, and the Communists finally accepted it.

The second victory for the Cambodian negotiators—and further evidence of their willingness to fight for objectives they consider essential—related to national unity with the Cambodians living in South Vietnam. Though they knew this issue would not be settled at Geneva, they objected to the clause of the Final Declaration which calls for "respect for the territorial integrity of Vietnam." Tep Phan stated over the objections of Sir Anthony Eden, then chairman of the conference, that "this provision does not imply the abandonment of such legitimate rights and interests as Cambodia might assert with regard to certain regions of South Vietnam." The Cambodian delegation then proceeded to circulate a memorandum on its stand to the other conference members, in spite of the objections of the chairman that the point raised was irrelevant to the problems to be settled by the cease-fire conference.

The third firm stand the Cambodians took occurred on the very eve of the cease-fire agreement. The treaty, to be signed at 9 P.M., included provisions for the complete neutralization of Cambodia and Laos. According to reports at the time, the Laotian delegation, certain that the treaty could not be further amended, had retired; the French would sign on behalf of both the Laotian and the Vietnamese delegations. At the last moment, Tep Phan, Cambodia's civilian delegate, despite last-minute entreaties by all major parties to the conference, refused to accept the section dealing with the total neutralization of his country. Surprisingly, the Communists gave way, and Cambodia obtained for itself and for Laos (whose delegates learned about the windfall in the morning) the right to maintain effective national armed forces and to retain foreign training missions. The treaty was finally signed at 3:42 A.M. on July 21, 1954—with Cambodia winning on every point.

The position taken by the Cambodian delegation at Geneva—particularly when compared with the role of the Laotian and the Vietnamese Nationalist delegation—is noteworthy. Apparently the Cambodian delegation, independently of France and other powers, had arrived at a clear notion of what Cambodian national objectives were, then never once departed from its stand. This is an important characteristic of the Cambodians as negotiators and always to be reckoned with.

Cambodia's performance on the world diplomatic stage shows that its rulers know what they want for their country and know how to get what they want, often on their own terms. This quality of persistence in negotiation, regardless of the odds, has driven to desperation many a western negotiator—including Soviet Foreign Minister Molotov—who has had to face Cambodians at the bargaining table. This ability, which they know well how to conceal beneath a docile appearance and which is firmly allied to their pride in their nation, makes them tough opponents in any diplomatic negotiation.

BASIC FEATURES OF THE ECONOMY

THE ECONOMY OF CAMBODIA is essentially agricultural and its backbone is the small family enterprise. Rice, rubber, timber, and fish are major products, much of which is exported.

Until recently, industry in Cambodia was confined mostly to processing of agricultural products, to handicrafts, and to such small industries as forging, blacksmithing, tile and brick manufacture, coking plants, and potteries.

Rice is grown almost exclusively on small, privately owned tracts of land, just large enough for a farmer and his family to work. Few farmers show any interest in becoming big landowners, though this attitude can be attributed in part to a scarcity of labor for hire and to the fact that in Cambodia extensive landownership per se brings little if any social distinction. Accumulation of financial wealth is not a goal for most Cambodians.

Rubber is produced on French plantations, which constitute the largest French investment in Cambodia. Rubber workers, who make up the country's biggest labor group, are a predominantly transient group, most of them coming from Vietnam.

Timber areas are worked by concessionaires—usually Chinese or Vietnamese, occasionally Cambodian—who lease the forest areas from the government; trade in timber is mainly in the hands of Chinese.

Most Cambodian rice farmers are also fishermen, but organized fishing is controlled by Chinese concessionaires, whose employed labor force is made up mostly of Vietnamese and Cambodians.

Chinese control of most of the country's commerce, both domestic and international, causes the government and educated Cambodian citizens considerable concern. The government is attacking the problem, however, by giving every possible advantage to the increasing number of Cambodians going into business.

This new willingness among Cambodians to try commercial ventures seems to have developed in the decade since 1946 and is due no doubt in part to increased western education. The primary motivation, however, seems to be a drive for independence. Once political independence had been achieved, the dependence of the Cambodian economy on "foreigners" became a conspicuous and humiliating, as well as dangerous, factor in the life of the new nation.

"Cambodianization" of the economy has been sparked to some extent by individuals. The more sophisticated Cambodians stress that it is important to the nation and its independence that Cambodians make money and invest it in productive enterprises. The use of savings for the embellishment of pagodas has recently been criticized by some of the western-educated, who charge that the pagodas are untaxed havens for "the idle." Some of these intellectuals also believe reforms in public administration must precede any real economic progress.

But the elite do not have a monopoly on concern for speeding economic development. Some farmers are becoming aware of the need to increase crop yields and to improve water control and show signs of being anxious to learn how to do their part in the development of their country. And, though their number is still small, more and more young Cambodians are showing interest in learning modern agriculture and industrial techniques.

The government is also playing an important part in the effort to "Cambodianize" the country's foreign trade. The development of alternatives to Saigon as Cambodia's principal port and the imposition of import controls are vital steps toward freeing its international trade from foreign domination.

In the agricultural sphere, the government is trying to free the Cambodian farmer from the clutches of his "banker"—the Chinese moneylender, who is also usually the sole outlet for surplus crops —through the development of agricultural cooperatives and a system of cheap rural credit. Land is no problem in Cambodia, but a sound system of agricultural credit is needed as a basis for agricultural reform.

The government's financial resources are not sufficient to develop all the needed facilities—roads, ports, dikes for flood control, and irrigation works. Cambodia is therefore dependent to a considerable extent upon foreign aid to balance its budget and its accounts with the rest of the world. The need for private investment—to broaden the base of the economy and to expand the Cambodian sector of the business community—is great but the concept of long-term private investment has been slow to take hold in Cambodia's own business community. Where private savings are available, they are often inadequate to the purpose and the government has undertaken to augment these savings and encourage investment by furnishing low-interest credit to both large and small business firms. The government would also like to attract foreign capital but the likelihood that foreign companies would be asked to accept certain conditions—*e.g.*, hire a fixed percentage of Cambodians—may prove a real obstacle to large-scale foreign investment.

Early in 1956 the Cambodian government endeavored to make a long-range, comprehensive assault on its economic problems, outlining a Two Year Plan for technical, economic, educational, and social development. Also in 1956 the government greatly increased, and diversified the sources of, its foreign aid, notably adding aid from the People's Republic of China. Under the Two Year Plan imports of consumer and producer goods were rapidly increased, and considerable amounts of rural credit and investment funds for industry were made available to the Cambodian population. Foreign private investment was encouraged, particularly in those areas where Cambodians were not prepared to develop large plantations or industrial enterprises. Two important agencies—the Royal Office of Cooperation and the National Development Bank—were created to handle most of the operations of the Plan.

Results of the Plan, which was officially terminated in June 1958, cannot as yet be fully evaluated, but the evidence seems to be that progress was uneven. The most persistent problems are: difficulty in exporting products that have been priced out of the world market; shrinking customs receipts; tax evasion; lack of adequately trained technical and administrative personnel; and delay in repairing and improving the transport and communications systems.

Government officials were satisfied that over-all progress had been made in the two-year period but admitted there had been insufficient response from the private sector to the financial and investment facilities made available by the government. It was generally agreed that conditions necessary to expansion of private enterprise did not yet exist in the country. Education in modern skills appeared to be the crux of the problem, and the lion's share of the new national budget was accordingly allocated to educational programs.

ORGANIZATION AND USE
OF MANPOWER

LACK OF A TECHNICALLY TRAINED LABOR FORCE is probably the most apparent obstacle to the economic development of Cambodia, but the retarding effects of the Buddhist religion and of the country's great wealth of arable land must be considered at the same time. Buddhism, by its emphasis on nonaccumulation of worldly goods and on acceptance rather than manipulation of nature, tends to reduce the kind of personal ambition that has played a vital role in western economies; one does not attain the "good life" by amassing material things. Also tending to reduce the Cambodian's incentive for change and development is the ease with which he can meet his minimum needs by the simplest farming of the rich and plentiful land.

Whereas the American or European will devote considerable attention to improvement of work techniques, the average Cambodian gives little thought to these matters. Such modern agricultural methods as are to be found in use in Cambodia were developed mainly by foreigners—French, Chinese, and Vietnamese. The French, for example, introduced and built up large rubber plantations, side by side with Cambodians who seemed little interested in improving their methods of rice culture or the productivity of their land.

The very limited achievement by Cambodians in industry is even more marked. They have thus far shown little inclination toward industrial employment and have few of the skills and work habits such activity requires. This is not a matter of incapacity—most of the country's truck drivers are Cambodian—but of absence of motivation. The technician, whether industrial or agricultural, has traditionally held low rank. A definite social gap exists between the man who works in a technical capacity and the professional man or anybody occupying a white-collar position. Education is considered a means of rising above the low social level associated with manual or semimanual labor, and young Cambodians fortunate enough to acquire an education seldom think in terms of engineering or the other sciences, which to them belong to that level. Even a very limited education will be used to get clerical work in an office rather than work in a machine shop or factory.

This prejudice is part of the over-all attitude toward commerce and industry long characteristic of Cambodian thinking but is becoming noticeably less pronounced as Cambodia moves to make itself economically independent.

Labor Force

In recent years the government, under the personal leadership of Sihanouk, has instituted various kinds of measures designed specifically to change these basic attitudes and provide an adequate supply of technically trained Cambodians. Students were sent overseas for specialized technical training while at home the government tried to improve the domestic technical facilities. Specialized technical schools have been created in such fields as commerce, banking practice, public administration, police, railroads, and arts and crafts. Realizing the need for a broader base, the Superior Council of Technical Education in mid-1958 adopted a program of agricultural and commercial instruction in the secondary school system. Attitudes toward manual and semimanual labor were attacked directly and personally by Sihanouk. In August 1958, upon his return from a visit to Peking, he convened a special session of the Cabinet in which he outlined a plan of compulsory labor for white-collar workers, one similar to that instituted in China. Civil service and military personnel were to work thirty days per year on farms and in factories, students were to work a half day per week in private enterprises, and "unemployed intellectuals" were to be absorbed in a special unit with the purpose of reorienting them toward the "productive sector."

Though this combination of measures may in time produce a significant increase in the supply of technical personnel, as well as a change in attitude toward commercial and industrial occupations, for the present and near future Cambodia will have to rely heavily on technical experts brought in under foreign aid for implementation of its development programs.

Composition

At least 80 percent of Cambodia's male population is engaged in agriculture—most as peasant farmers, the rest as wage laborers and people employed in the marketing of agricultural produce. Women and children are also frequently employed in farm work, though often on a part-time basis. Women generally work full-time in the fields until they become mothers. Agricultural pursuits are the main occupation of most Cambodians, but many of them also engage in fishing and the manufacture of handicraft products to supplement their incomes. A number of the country's major industries—for example, the weaving of *sampots*—are carried on throughout the country as part-time activity.

Industry and the manufacture of handicraft products employ only a minority of the population on a full-time basis—at most, no more than 100,000. Workers who on the basis of employment in large factories can be classified as industrial workers in the western sense number no more than 6,000; the majority of this industrial labor force is Chinese, Vietnamese and Cham (see chap. 3). Practically all the rubber plantation workers are Vietnamese, and at least 50 percent of those engaged full-time in fishing and industrial pursuits are Vietnamese or Chinese. Foreign groups—the Chinese in particular—also have come to dominate the country's commercial life.

Although there are relatively few doctors, lawyers, or engineers in Cambodia, the country's professional class is made proportionally large by the number of civil servants and religious and lay teachers. There are over 5,000 teachers—a large number of them bonzes—and close to 20,000 people are employed in the various government services. The Cambodian economy also supports an armed force of approximately 30,000 men and a police and permanent militia force of about 15,000.

Agricultural Labor Force

Agriculture in Cambodia is to a considerable extent a family enterprise, with the single important exception of the large rubber and pepper plantations, where hired agricultural laborers do the work. The abundance of land and the traditional system of land ownership, giving property rights to the man who works the soil, generally make it unnecessary for one man to work for another. Rice farming is normally sufficient to provide food and a small cash surplus for clothing, taxes, and festivals. The subsidiary activities of the peasant and his family, such as fishing and handicraft work, are sources of extra income. Frequently, however, the Cambodian farmer is heavily in debt. He may not have the money to pay for a funeral or a marriage ceremony, or for a trip to a festival; perhaps one year his crop was poor. To see himself through these problems he goes to the moneylender, who is usually the broker to whom he sells rice. Once in debt, he rarely returns to a state of financial solvency, frequently becoming no more than an agent of the moneylender to whom he is indebted.

Though tenant farming and sharecropping are rare in Cambodia, there is some employment of hired labor, particularly during the harvesting period. In the majority of cases, the hired help live in the village where they are employed and are able to return to their homes after their day's work. It is, however, incumbent upon the employer to provide them with lodging if their place of work is far from home. The employer is also in many cases responsible for feeding his workers. Pay usually is in money although frequently a portion of the salary is in kind.

A high degree of unreliability is reported for hired agricultural workers; this may be in part explained by the fact that many of them are working off debts contracted by their fathers or even their grandfathers.

Cambodia's plantation labor force consists of about 11,000 men. Approximately 10,000 are employed on the French-owned rubber plantations. The others are Chinese workers on the country's pepper estates, most of which are owned by Chinese.

More than 80 percent of those who work on rubber plantations are Vietnamese, recruited specifically for such work. About half the remaining 20 percent are Cambodian, the other half Chinese. The predominance of Vietnamese labor on the rubber plantations is largely explained by the conviction of the French that Cambodians do not possess and are not capable of acquiring the skills and meticulous work habits required in plantation work. On the other hand, the Chinese, who do possess these qualities to a high degree, are not favored by the French because as a rule they demand higher wages and are more difficult to manage than the Vietnamese.

The Vietnamese on the rubber plantations have for the most part been recruited from Vietnam, where labor is plentiful. Early recruiting practices, largely conducted by a Vietnamese *cai* (labor recruiter), subjected the worker to considerable abuse and hardship, but major abuses have recently been corrected. Recruits now are asked to sign for only eighteen months, instead of three years.

After completion of the contract, the workers may sign on for an additional period or simply stay on as "free laborers." As a free laborer the worker enjoys the same status as a contract laborer, except that he does not participate in the deferred-payment fund set up to provide the employee with enough money for the return trip home.

On the whole plantation workers enjoy conditions of employment that are denied most other Cambodian workers. Free medical care, educational and recreational facilities, and free housing are among the many advantages offered to attract workers to the plantation. Money wages alone—ranging from 10 riels a day for woman and child labor to 20 riels a day for a first-class male tapper —compare favorably with those of the industrial worker. Fringe benefits and frequently additional payments in kind represent added inducements. On the other hand, it seems improbable that the workers would be permitted to take or even advocate labor action in an effort to correct grievances.

Industrial Workers and Artisans

The majority of the 5,000 to 6,000 people who make up the industrial labor force (excluding handicraft workers) are Vietnamese, Chinese, Sino-Cambodians, and Chams. Of an additional 2,000 coolies and other workers regularly employed in public works and another 1,000 employed in various railroad occupations, the greater part probably are also non-Cambodian.

To overcome the shortage of technical workers the government, in addition to promoting technical education in schools, has passed legislation requiring every industrial establishment employing more than thirty workers to hire one apprentice for every ten trained workers employed. These efforts have to date produced only meager results, however.

The handicraft industries play an important role in the economic life of Cambodia (see chap. 16). Although the majority of those engaged in handicrafts as a full-time occupation are located in Pnompenh and other large cities, work of this kind is also important in the rural areas.

There are various types of specialization among Cambodian artisans. For example, men dominate crafts dealing with metals, wood, and precious stones; women exercise a virtual monopoly over the country's *sampot* and other textile enterprises. The Cambodians control operations devoted to silver work; the Chinese and Vietnamese are most prominent in jewelry work, which requires a greater initial investment. Although there is little village specialization, both pottery making and metal work appear to be somewhat localized.

White-Collar Workers

A Cambodian fortunate enough to rise out of the peasant class will direct his efforts to getting a white-collar job, preferably in the civil service. The prestige and job security that go with a government position make the civil service a particularly attractive profession.

In a recent speech, Sihanouk criticized the civil service as corrupt and lacking initiative: "The civil servants must get rid of all such bad habits as oppression, bribery, and so forth." Referring to the role of the civil servants in the cooperative movement, he continued: "Civil servants will not be authorized to hold shares in these cooperatives; indeed certain of them only think of their own advantage, while others might make off with the cash boxes."

Officeholding in Cambodia still has the character of the awarding of a contract to the highest bidder. An official will frankly announce the sum his office has cost him. The literal translation of the Khmer verb for "reign" is the "king eats his royalty," and as the king does, so does the busy official. Abuse and graft are considered natural and inevitable, except by young, western-educated Cambodians.

Wages and Benefits

In comparison with other forms of nonagricultural employment, industrial employment in Cambodia brings relatively low wages, in terms of both money and purchasing power. While the money wages of the industrial worker have increased twentyfold in the fifteen years following the outbreak of World War II, the cost of living has increased almost twice as fast, with the result that real wages have been cut in half. Although industrial money wages frequently exceed those received on the rubber plantations, the fringe benefits on the plantations far outweigh the additional money paid industrial workers.

There is considerable variation in industrial wage rates, depending upon the skill of the worker and upon sex and age. A skilled worker receives almost twice as much as one who is unskilled, a situation resulting partly from the fact that farmers or agricultural laborers during off-seasons often willingly accept work in the cities at exceptionally low wages. Women's wages average more than 25 percent below the wages paid men in the same position; wages received by children are even lower. Although there are no exact statistics on this subject, it has been estimated that workers engaged in transportation and commercial pursuits receive the highest wages and those engaged in the processing of agricultural goods, the lowest. It is possible, however, that workers engaged in the processing industries receive greater benefits in kind, thus compensating them to some extent for their low money earnings.

With the exception of workers employed on the rubber plantations, Cambodia's labor force is not covered by any minimum-wage legislation. Legislation looking toward the establishment of a minimum wage was at one time proposed by the Ministry of Labor, but it was never enacted into law. The failure of the proposed legislation has not, however, prevented the establishment of a system of wage scales. This system, designed initially to facilitate the determination of family allotments, has come to serve as the basis for regulating wages.

According to western observers, the Cambodian government has as yet no clear concept of the purpose of wage legislation. The Inspector of Labor, who pushed wage legislation, looked on it more as a handy guide to those who hire labor rather than as a means of protecting the workers.

Various forms of fringe benefits contribute significantly to the income of Cambodian workers. The food, lodging, medical, and educational benefits received by the rubber plantation workers have already been mentioned. Most nonagricultural workers receive similar benefits, though on a smaller scale and not as systematically. Payment in kind is not as common in nonagricultural employment as in agricultural work, but in times of stress nonagricultural employees have received part of their wages in rice.

Of greater importance is the system of family allotments, introduced by the French in all of Indochina in 1948 and established as a national institution by Cambodia in 1955. Under this system, which covers industrial and commercial employment (and, according to some evidence, the civil service as well), employers are obliged to contribute to the welfare of the worker's family. They make these contributions monthly to the Interprofessional Compensation Fund for Family Allowances, whose governing body (Administrative Council) is composed of the labor inspector, a representative of the Labor Ministry, a representative of the employers, and a representative of labor. The Chamber of Commerce has been designated to select the employers' representative, while the Administrative Council itself is authorized to select the workers' representative from a list of three names submitted by the labor inspector. Workers' and employers' representatives are chosen for a three-year period and are eligible for re-election.

Payments are made from the fund in the form of allowances for the worker's wife and children on the following basis regardless of the worker's salary: 15 percent of the base salary for his wife, 5 percent of the base salary for each of his first ten children.

The system of allowances created since Cambodia achieved full independence has not yet become fully operative and statistics on the number of employees covered are not yet available.

Labor Relations

As has been said, with the exception of the civil servants the majority of wage earners in Cambodia are Vietnamese, Chinese, or Cham. As a result, the interest of the government, the press, and the public in labor problems is less than it would be if the bulk of the labor force were Cambodian.

Labor Laws

Standards governing relations between employers and employees are the subject of two major laws passed by the French between World War I and World War II. The legislation of October 25, 1927 is still the basic law governing plantation or "contract" labor; the decree of December 30, 1936 is the basis for regulation of other types of employment. An additional decree in 1937, applicable to European and Chinese workers in Cambodia, has not been converted into Cambodian law since independence. All ethnic groups are now covered by the same labor legislation.

The 1927 law, applying specifically to plantation labor, laid down general conditions of recruitment, prescribed methods of wage payment, and established minimum food and housing standards which included special provisions to safeguard the health and welfare of the worker. It also established special provisions regarding the expiration, termination, transfer, or renewal of contracts, and it provided for a system of enforced savings to make sure that the predominantly Vietnamese workers would have a surplus and sufficient funds for the return trip to Vietnam upon the conclusion of their contract periods.

This law has been supplemented both by additional legislation and unwritten custom. Among the numerous improvements which have occurred in the past thirty years are the introduction of more humane recruiting methods, the reduction of the work day from ten to eight hours, and the payment of wages actually higher than the minimum wages set for plantation labor by legislation. On the whole, the plantation worker receives better treatment and more benefits than do the majority of workers; nevertheless, he seems to be completely dependent upon the good will of his employer and the protection of the government for the continuation of these benefits. In contrast to plantation labor in neighboring Vietnam, the plantation force in Cambodia has no organization of its own to look out for its interests.

The French decree of December 1936 extended the scope of labor regulations, which before then applied exclusively to plantation labor, to include all "wage-earning and salaried employees." Its major provisions deal with the regulation of apprentice labor, conditions of employment, the health and safety of the workers, and compensation for industrial accidents. It also established a system of labor inspection and of consultation between employers and the government's labor inspector, who represents the interests of the workers, to decide general labor policies.

Perhaps the outstanding feature of the two basic labor laws as well as of the labor legislation that followed is the important role assumed by the government in the field of labor inspection and the settlement of labor disputes.

One result of the 1927 French legislation was the establishment of a General Office of Labor Inspection for all Indochina. Its duties —executed in Cambodia by a local inspection office and relating to both "contract" and "noncontract" labor—included: (1) coordination of all measures for the regulation of labor, savings institutions, and social welfare; (2) supervision of the movement of labor; and (3) inspection of the various services dealing with labor and of undertakings of all kinds in which labor is employed. A decree of January 30, 1929 invested the inspectors with police powers enabling them to deal directly with any breaches of the labor regulations.

One of the most important functions of the local inspectors was the conciliation of labor disputes. If the inspector was unable to effect a settlement by conciliation and the parties to the dispute refused to accept his arbitration, the dispute was then submitted to the courts. The parties to the dispute were then bound by the decision rendered.

With relatively few modifications, the Office of Labor Inspection was transferred from French to Cambodian hands in January 1951. One of the major factors that keeps it from functioning effectively is its lack of an adequate staff, in terms both of numbers and training. Government officials dealing with labor affairs lack experience, are underpaid, and work only part time at their official tasks; they are hardly capable of carrying out the necessary inspection and enforcement functions.

Labor Organization

Until January 1, 1956, the formation of labor unions in Cambodia was not permitted. French labor legislation for Cambodia avoided any reference to the subject. This attitude may have stemmed partly from French fear that union organization would provide a focal point for nationalist or Communist agitation, and partly from the strong political influence of the principal French employers.

In 1920 the French sponsored the formation of artisan organizations which came to be known as the Cambodian Guilds. All local craftsmen were organized into one of five major guilds. Each guild appointed one of its members to represent it on a committee empowered to discuss quality standards, wages, and other questions with the government. The guild did not, however, enjoy any of the prerogatives of a trade union. Its primary function was to improve the quality of Cambodian handicraft production and facilitate the marketing of the goods produced.

The guild system served, nonetheless, as a sort of forerunner for the law of January 1, 1956, which permits labor union organization in Cambodia. Under the terms of this law, unions (to be known as "trade associations") could be formed by persons working in the same trade. There is to be no more than one union per trade in each of the provinces. Each union is to appoint an officer to direct its activities and to represent it in discussions with employers and with the government.

A union's major responsibilities are: (1) to secure employment for its members; (2) to propose price and wage scales; (3) to see to it that decisions reached in negotiations with employers and the government are complied with by the workers. There is very little information available on this subject, but there is reason to believe that unions are considered part of the government's apparatus to facilitate its dealings with an increasingly important segment of the population, rather than independent organizations free to act to improve the working conditions of their members.

The exclusion of all foreign nationals from official positions in unions may provide a clue to a secondary objective. In view of the dominant influence of foreigners—the French, Chinese, and Vietnamese—in the industrial and commercial life of the country, the government may well look upon unions as one method of counterbalancing "foreign" economic control—"Cambodianizing" the labor organizations and supporting their demands in any future dispute with foreign entrepreneurs.

Thus far there has been little if any union-organizing. Inadequate labor leadership in this field may be one of the handicaps, but the government has also discouraged unionization by denying the right to strike. In the middle of July 1956, faced with an impending strike for pay increases on the part of water and electricity utility workers in Pnompenh, the Minister of Interior served notice to all concerned that the right to strike was not admitted in Cambodia, that the government would not tolerate strikes whatever the motive, and that any foreigners involved in promoting a strike would be expelled from the country.

Conversely, the government appears to have adopted a paternalistic attitude toward labor. It has passed laws relating to such things as installation of infirmaries in public, semipublic, and private enterprises, the according of rest periods to female employees and the granting of paid annual leave to employees in all branches of the economy. By a decree of December 26, 1957 the government also created a separate Department of Social Action and Labor. There is no evidence, however, that any of these measures were in response to the demands of organized trade unionism.

Forced Labor

Forced labor—defined as "all means or methods of direct or indirect compulsion for the purpose of engaging any individual or retaining him at a work-place without his consent"—was forbidden throughout the French Union by an act of April 11, 1946, and made the law in Cambodia on October 30, 1947. Though it was alleged as late as 1953 that vestiges of various forms of forced labor were still to be found in Cambodia, these charges have been denied by both the French and Cambodian governments and it seems unlikely that forced labor still exists.

Slavery and other forms of forced labor have had a long history in Cambodia, and undoubtedly they left their mark on the country. Evidence pointing to the early existence of slavery is found in the sculptures at Angkor Thom and Angkor Wat, in references in both Khmer and Sanskrit inscriptions, and in the account of the Mongol ambassador to Cambodia in 1296: "The grandees and rich people . . . employ in their houses at least a hundred slaves, who do all the work. Even middle-class families possess from ten to twenty [slaves] per household and only the poorest have none. . . . These slaves are aborigines from the mountain solitudes."

During the period of Cambodian expansion, the Cambodians used a slave labor force composed of both mountain people and natives of neighboring countries; later they themselves fell prey to conquest and subsequent bondage as the power of their kingdom waned. The seventeenth and eighteenth centuries in Cambodian history were dominated by the rivalry of Thailand and Vietnam for possession of Cambodia, both its land and its people. In many cases Cambodians were actually carried off into slavery. Those who escaped this fate suffered a different kind of forced labor—rendering unprecedented labor services to their own overlords who sought to ward off foreign encroachment. Serfdom during this period became an integral part of the Cambodian economy. Prior to the penetration of the French, every able-bodied member of the male population between the ages of twenty-one and fifty owed the government up to ninety days a year of free labor service.

A second form of slavery was debt slavery—the enslavement of Cambodians by other Cambodians. This had its origins in the ransom paid by prisoners of war to escape perpetual slavery for themselves and their descendants. It carried with it much of the debasement of status and personality formerly connected with conquest and captivity. Debtors not only served their master, but also the king. The creditor or master was often obliged to have the debtor serve a given portion of his time on public works. Referring to the system of debt slavery, King Norodom (reign: 1859-1904) stated: "This enslavement for debt is one of the foundations of the Cambodian state. Our subjects reduced to that servitude are the happiest of all."

The French abolished these forms of slavery—a step resisted by Cambodia's rulers—in the late nineteenth century. But the French were primarily responsible for the establishment of a system of contract labor which in practice incorporated many of the features of forced labor. Workers recruited in North and Central Vietnam to work on the rubber plantations of Cambodia enjoyed few of the rights commonly associated with the status of a free laborer and were openly exploited by the plantation owners. Legislation of the past twenty years, however, has corrected the major abuses of the contract labor system. Conditions of employment on the plantations have improved considerably, and the worker has free recourse to government protection. He is now free to resign if he feels he has been treated unjustly.

FINANCIAL SYSTEM

ONE OF THE THORNIEST PROBLEMS facing the government has been the reluctance of Cambodians to pay taxes, a reluctance which greatly increased when the French left. Under French colonial administration the government had been able to collect 80 to 90 percent—one more conservative estimate puts the average closer to 60 or 70 percent—of the revenues expected. When Cambodia gained its independence the collection rate dropped sharply, in some provinces to as little as 10 to 15 percent of expectation. Possibly a misinterpretation of the economic implications of independence caused Cambodians to think of taxes as a thing of the colonial past. Whatever the explanation, collection of taxes has been extremely difficult. It has been further hampered by a shortage of honest, well-trained tax officials and by the general confusion that attended the transfer of authority from the colonial administration to the independent Cambodian government.

The Two Year Plan

With the inception of its Two Year Plan in 1956 the Cambodian government embarked on a large-scale program of spending designed to raise the standard of living of the rural population, repair war damages, expand the communication and transport facilities, improve water control in agriculture, and foster the growth of industry. Total expenditures for this program were initially set at 3,500 million riels, but only an estimated 2,455 million riels had actually been spent when the Plan was officially terminated in June 1958. A continuing program, to run for five years, has been under consideration but had not been put into effect as of early 1959.

The Two Year Plan was financed almost entirely by foreign aid (see Table 5). The less than 5 percent from the national budget consisted of funds reallocated by various departments for projects growing out of the Plan. A small share of the financing came from municipal budgets. The only other sizable financing came from two government agencies with funds other than those allocated to them from the national budget: the Royal Office of Cooperation, which derives half of its resources from the subscriptions of its affiliated cooperatives; and the National Development Bank, which serves as a repository for certain foreign aid funds. These two agencies contributed 117 million riels in 1957 and 121 million riels during the first half of 1958.

The foreign aid funds were used primarily for basic construction—for electrification, water supply, railroad, port, and airfield projects. The funds from the Royal Office of Cooperation and the National Development Bank were used entirely for technical programs, such as those directed toward improving production methods in agriculture, livestock breeding, forestry, mining, crafts, and industry.

Expenditures and Revenues

Expenditures under the national budget rose from 2,250 million riels in 1957 to 2,650 million in 1958 (see Table 6). By far the largest part of this increase involved allocations for educational, economic, and social development. In the two-year period the budget for education showed the highest rate of increase, and is today the highest for a single department.

The next largest departmental expenditure is for national defense, though if internal security is included the total expenditure exceeds that for education. During 1957 and 1958, however, the rate of increase in this category has been comparatively low, and lower for national defense than for national security.

Much of the burden for national defense has been taken off the national budget in recent years by foreign military aid, particularly from France. During the 1952-54 hostilities the government had to make sharp cuts in most civilian expenditures in order to meet its military needs, but after 1954, with a 35 to 40 percent drop in over-all military expenditures, foreign aid covered a much larger proportion. Foreign military aid paid for about 60 percent of the Defense Ministry's outlays in 1954, and for about 70 percent in 1955. The 1955 budget reflected a shift in emphasis from all-out mobilization to the build-up of a balanced, peacetime military force.

To meet its expenditures the government chiefly depends on customs revenue. Direct taxes consist chiefly of income taxes, taxes on land, and business license taxes. Other sources of internal revenue include a national security tax; the proceeds of the national lottery; earnings from government operation of railroads, hotels, and telecommunications; and special levies on certain industries—mainly fishing and timber—to obtain funds for conservation programs.

Indirect taxes (other than monopoly excises) include special sales taxes on items such as alcohol, petroleum products, tobacco, sugar, salt, radios, and livestock, over and above the general sales tax levied on sales of all products. Monopoly excises consist of taxes on the sale of products, such as salt, that are government sales monopolies. The general sales tax is understood to be a levy for national defense. Petroleum products, all of which have to be imported, are subjected to a so-called "per equation" tax, designed to equalize in the Cambodian market the different prices charged by different foreign suppliers.

There is no legal discrimination against ethnic minorities in the administration of the tax system, but in cracking down on possible tax evaders the government has directed its attention mainly toward Chinese business houses. The new requirement that all businesses keep their financial records in Cambodian has most of all affected the Chinese firms, not only because of their number but also because of their practice of keeping their books in Chinese, which had made it easy to hide the facts from the tax examiners, few of whom know Chinese. These firms may still secretly maintain a set of books in their own language, but there is now one set in Cambodian for the government inspector to examine.

Donations to the pagoda, so important in the budget of every family, are not deductible in the computation of income tax. To treat them as deductible might in many cases exempt a family from any income tax obligation. There is no information available on how direct taxes are collected, but it is possible that payments by rural taxpayers are made to some extent in kind.

Currency and the Bank of Issue

Cambodia, like Vietnam and Laos, established its own banking and currency system in 1955; that same year the present currency —the riel—came into existence.

Before World War II the country's official currency had been the Indochina piaster, issued by the private, French-owned Bank of Indochina (Banque de l'Indochine) and linked directly to the French franc. It was a currency in which the people of Cambodia as well as of the rest of Indochina had much confidence. The Japanese occupation changed all that. The cost of the occupation was imposed on the local population. Money was issued in printing-press fashion, and there was little merchandise on which to spend it. The result was acute inflation.

The return of a French-controlled administration after the war found the Indochina piaster thoroughly depreciated. Shops were bare of consumer goods. In an effort to prime the economy, the value of the piaster was set at 40 percent above its prewar value, thus giving it an artificially high purchasing power in relation to the franc. The result was a spate of large-scale, illegal financial transactions, with the French treasury absorbing the loss.

A partial remedy was attempted in May 1953, when the piaster was devalued to bring the official rate of exchange with the franc closer to market reality. Prices, already high as a result of the huge outlay on military operations against the Vietminh, went even higher.

Today the riel has completely replaced the piaster, and its value is fixed at 10 French francs to 1 riel. On this basis the official exchange rate for the United States dollar is about 35 riels to the dollar, or 1 riel to about 3 cents. The unofficial rate is reported to approximate 50 to 60 riels to the dollar. Technically the official exchange rates of the currencies of Cambodia, Laos, and Vietnam are the same, but the riel fares much better than the Vietnamese piaster on the world's free markets.

Note issue is required by statute to be covered to the extent of at least 33 percent by gold or foreign exchange. In practice the monetary reserve has been almost twice as high—reflecting the extensive foreign aid Cambodia has received, the fact that there has been little withdrawal of foreign capital, and the trade surpluses Cambodia enjoyed in the past. This reserve has contributed to the premium the riel enjoys over the Vietnamese piaster in the world's free markets and in the exchange of piasters for riels in Cambodia. News of this sort spreads quickly and has strengthened the people's confidence in their paper money. A large number of transactions, however, are still carried on through barter. (It is reported that bank checks are not fully trusted outside the commercial community in the cities.)

If currency in circulation at any given time is more than 15 percent higher or lower than at the same time the previous year, the governor of the National Bank is required to give the king a report on the causes of the rise or fall, the possible effects on the economy, and suggestions for correcting the situation.

Complete control of Cambodia's currency is vested in the National Bank, which has authority to buy or sell short-term treasury bills or the securities of private institutions in order to regulate the supply of money. Such transactions must conform, however, to over-all government monetary policy, and may not be conducted solely for the profit of the issuing organization.

The government encourages the concept of the riel as a *monnaie-charnière* or "hinge currency," not tied to any particular monetary area and free to move independently of other exchanges. This ideal of monetary independence would appear to be an off-shoot of Cambodia's newly won autonomy, perhaps influenced by its political neutralism.

The Banque Nationale du Cambodge (the National Bank of Cambodia), a government institution, was established in 1955 following the dissolution of the Banque d'Emission des Etats Associés (the joint Bank of Issue of the Associated States). The earlier Banque d'Emission, organized in 1949 by France and the three former colonies—Cambodia, Laos, and Vietnam—had served as the area's first governmental currency authority.

The National Bank of Cambodia has much more authority than did either the Bank of Indochina or the joint Bank of Issue. Like them it is the sole currency authority, but it is in addition charged with central banking responsibilities, including the control of credit, and with the development of private banking in accordance with specific standards.

Aware of the importance of sound currency and banking practices to the country's economic and political stability and of the dangers that would accompany any political tampering with the operations of the central bank, the government in its statute setting up the National Bank placed it directly under the king. The king, with the advice of the Crown Council, appoints the bank's governor, its deputy governor, the head of its National Exchange Office (the division responsible for foreign exchange control), and at least one of its two auditors.

The bank's "board of governors"—to apply the American term for the system's governing council—is the Conseil d'Administration, a committee composed of the governor, the deputy governor, one representative each from the Ministries of Finance and of National Economy, one representative of individuals or organizations holding shares of the bank's stock, and three representatives of the country's agricultural, commercial, and industrial communities, appointed by the government on the recommendations of the groups concerned. Besides making policy in the field of money and banking, the Conseil advises the king on the appointment of a new governor and deputy governor.

There are also advisory groups (Conseils Consultatifs de la Monnaie et du Crédit) made up of men with economic experience and professional stature who serve two-year appointments without compensation. The governor and the heads of the provincial branches of the National Bank are each served by such a committee.

A Center of Instruction in Banking Practice, instituted by the National Bank for its own employees, gives courses in the operations of the Bank and in accounting, financial mathematics, and other related subjects. The courses last three years and lead to a Certificate of Professional Aptitude in Banking. They are open not only to employees of the Bank but to qualified persons in commerce and industry.

The government by law subscribes to 75 percent of the National Bank's capitalization and these holdings are nontransferable. The remaining 25 percent of the capitalization consists of negotiable bank stock which may be acquired by Cambodian nationals or by corporations owned by Cambodian nationals upon approval of the bank's governor. Unsubscribed negotiable stock may be held by the government on a temporary basis.

The National Bank, in its capacity as state bank, can advance money to the Treasury, but such advances may not be in excess of 25 percent of total government revenues in the preceding year. It is also empowered to invest, after due consultation with the Treasury, in other banks set up for the purpose of agricultural and industrial development (including handicrafts) in Cambodia. However, investment by the National Bank is limited to 10 percent of the capitalization of the receiving bank.

The National Bank may advance loans for periods up to 90 days and extend credit for commercial and production purposes up to 300 days. But it deals only with the government and other financial institutions. It sees its loan policies as important instruments for injecting more money into the economy without burdening the borrower with unreasonable rates of interest and combating two major afflictions of the Cambodian economic system, "usury and blind hoarding." In 1955 its various interest rates at no time exceeded 4.5 percent.

The bank still uses the French Union Stabilization Fund in

Paris as a funnel for many of its foreign exchange transactions; the dollars Cambodia receives under the United States aid program are not kept in the Fund, but are controlled directly by the National Bank. The Bank's contact with the Paris money market is administered by the Banque de France, which effects clearing arrangements between the riel and other world currencies.

The National Bank regarded the large franc balance with which it began operations as partly an advantage and partly a weakness because any sudden fluctuation of the franc could importantly affect the backing of the riel. To minimize such vulnerability the bank hopes to build reserves of other transferable currencies—for example, from an expansion of exports to the dollar and sterling areas. The bank has also bought small amounts of gold; all gold produced in Cambodia must now be sold to the National Bank.

The bank would like to see Pnompenh become a recognized gold market, as Hong Kong is. Cambodia has already diversified its overseas money market operations by depositing its U. S. dollar reserves in New York and its sterling in London.

The National Development Bank

When the National Development Bank was created in 1956, its purpose was to serve as repository for foreign aid funds and to handle the financial operations of the Two Year Plan. In regard to the former function it has not in fact been able to divert all of the foreign aid from previous repositories. Its resources in 1958 were as follows:

Allocation from the national budget	100	million riels
Special taxes	300	" "
American economic aid	50	" "

The National Development Bank makes medium- and long-term loans to medium- and large-scale productive enterprises. Between October 1956 and June 1958 the bank had granted loans amounting to 53.6 million riels to some ten enterprises. In addition the Cambodian Electricity Company received 150 million riels and the Khmer Company, a rubber plantation, had received 12 million riels.

The Royal Office of Cooperation

The Royal Office of Cooperation, also created in 1956, serves as the central government agency for credit cooperatives, consumer cooperatives, and various kinds of producer cooperatives in agriculture and small industry. Its capital of 200 million riels is subscribed in equal parts by the government and by the affiliated cooperatives. It has four sections—the Directorates for Credit, Consumption, and Production, and a Commercial Directorate. The Directorate for Credit makes loans to affiliated provincial credit cooperatives which in turn make loans to their individual members and occasionally to nonmembers. It also makes loans to consumer and producer cooperatives. The producer cooperatives in turn make loans to their members but the consumer cooperatives do not.

The Directorate of Credit has absorbed the functions of a former governmental credit institution—the Office of Popular Credit, known as OCP from the French initials.

The Cambodian OCP was established in 1950 to carry on in Cambodia the efforts of the Office du Crédit Populaire de l'Indochine to reduce and eventually wipe out another banking institution —the moneylender. The moneylender in Cambodia is regarded as an evil because his oppressive terms for repayment of both interest and principal seriously retard the growth of a sound economic system.

Set up to provide low-interest financing for the development of agriculture, handicrafts, and small machine-industry, the OCP had been concerned primarily with agriculture, making funds available to small agricultural banks and to agricultural cooperatives (see chap. 15). Its basic capital was supplied by the government itself, but it also received short-term advances from the government and from private and public credit institutions as well.

The OCP loaned money only through the provincial credit institutions—associations to which farmers (or groups of farmers) and villages (or groups of villages) belong, and whose administration was being supervised by the OCP. These associations received deposits from their members, and the deposits were guaranteed by the government. The registered membership of these rural banks has risen steadily, as have deposits and the amount of their loans.

The interest rate charged by these banks was supposed to be 7 percent, though it may occasionally have gone as high as 12 percent. The moneylenders, on the other hand, charged up to 100 percent or more.

Some progress was made in providing low-interest credit to farmers (see Table 7), but most rural credit was still the province of the moneylenders.

Under the ROC's Directorate for Credit, the organization and facilities of the OCP have been improved and expanded. As of mid-1958 there were thirteen affiliated provincial credit institutions with a total membership of 92,489 against 62,123 in 1955. Loans outstanding to individual members of the credit cooperatives amounted to 121,050,000 riels as against 41,574,000 in 1955. In addition the Directorate of Credit had loaned a total of 145,374,000 riels to consumer and producer cooperatives affiliated with the Royal Office of Cooperation. The basic interest rates remain the same but the amounts of the loans have increased and there are modifications in the terms of the loans and in the categories of property acceptable as collateral which have made them more attractive to the rural population.

Commercial Banks

Private banking in Cambodia is for the most part commercial banking; the banking system is very seldom used for private savings. Most Cambodians have little if any spare cash, and what savings or reserves they do accumulate are usually kept in the form of jewelry, religious ornaments, or other objects of personal or household use.

There are seven private banks in Cambodia, all of them commercial institutions: the new Khmer Bank (Banque Khmère); the French Bank of Asia, formerly the Bank of Indochina (Banque Française d'Asie); the National Bank for Commerce and Industry (Banque Nationale pour le Commerce et l'Industrie), owned by Thai and local Chinese; the Franco-Chinese Bank (Banque Franco-Chinoise), a French bank; the Pnompenh Bank (Banque de Phnom Penh), also French; the Chartered Bank of India, Australia, and China, British-owned; and the Hong Kong and Shanghai Banking Corporation, also British. A Formosan bank, the Bank of China (Banque de Chine), ceased operations and liquidated its affairs effective 29 July 1958.

The Pnompenh Bank (said to represent Thai interests) is the only foreign bank with its main office—its only office in fact—in Cambodia.

All commercial banks are subject to government regulation. Branch offices of foreign banks may be established, but only if (a) the foreign country concerned is one with which Cambodia maintains normal diplomatic relations—this requirement is without prejudice to branch banks already operating in Cambodia—and (b) the bank agrees to employ a certain percentage of Cambodians, to be fixed by the Ministry of Finance. The Ministry also decides whether the creation of such a bank would be in the best interests of the Cambodian economy and of the government's effort to "guarantee financial independence."

There are no bank reserve requirements nor any other forms of direct control by the National Bank over the country's private banking system. The private banks do, however, follow the lead of the National Bank in credit policies and general banking practices. They deposit money in the National Bank, use it as a clearinghouse, and handle all foreign exchange matters within the terms of reference the bank prescribes. They also submit their daily balance sheets to the National Bank.

These commercial banks reportedly make it a policy to maintain a highly liquid position, advancing short-term credit against excellent collateral at high rates of interest. The loan financing required for development purposes in agriculture and small industry comes from other sources—the agricultural credit banks in the rural areas, the agricultural and handicraft cooperatives (see chap. 15; chap. 16), and the two government institutions discussed above, the National Development Bank and the Royal Office of Cooperation, both under the Department of National Economy.

AGRICULTURAL DEVELOPMENT

MOST CAMBODIANS EARN THEIR LIVELIHOOD by cultivating rice; processing and marketing rice are the country's most important industrial and commercial activities. Rice is the staple of the Cambodian diet and normally the chief source of foreign exchange. Its cultivation has a certain dignity all its own—a value in the Cambodian shape of things. "To destroy growing rice," says a Cambodian proverb, "is as serious as to insult one's mother and father."

The fact that, providing irrigation facilities are developed, there is more than enough land available for everyone to grow sufficient rice to feed himself and to provide income to pay for the things he needs has much to do with the Cambodian outlook on life in general. The abundance of good arable land which makes it possible with the simplest technology to produce enough rice to satisfy minimum needs is partly responsible for the average Cambodian's lack of interest in improvement of agricultural methods. Since nature provides the basic necessities of life the Cambodian sees no vital need to develop new and more efficient techniques. In contrast, by the middle of 1958, total government expenditures for agriculture under the Two Year Plan amounted to 143 million riels. Of this, 87 million riels was spent on agricultural water development alone, the rest going to agricultural production, animal husbandry, and forestry. No funds allocated to fishing were used.

The Buddhist faith is also a factor in the outlook of the present. Buddhism does not encourage the accumulation of wealth, and Cambodians therefore are accustomed to feel that nothing much is gained from owning more land than a man and his family can comfortably work themselves with the traditional techniques.

Earlier efforts of the French to introduce new techniques into

Cambodia foundered on the indifference and complacency of the peasants. With the exception of the French-owned, Vietnamese-worked rubber plantations, most agricultural operations in Cambodia show little change from traditional patterns. Nor have the official introduction of new crops, development of a number of large rubber and tea plantations, and establishment of irrigation and canal networks had any appreciable effect on the material status or the attitudes of the peasants.

The abundance of land and the dominant belief that nature will continue to be bountiful have been factors in the abusive exploitation of many of Cambodia's natural resources. These factors also offer at least a partial explanation for the attitude of the Cambodian toward the economic penetration of the Chinese, French, and Vietnamese: if rich land will always be available to provide a living and a sense of personal independence, "foreign" industrial and commercial control can be tolerated.

A growing awareness that the resources of the country may after all be limited and that much of the fruit of Cambodian labor is enjoyed by foreigners has resulted in recent years in a stiffening of the Cambodian's attitude toward the presence of powerful foreign elements.

Unlike some of its neighbors, Cambodia suffers no great pressure of population on land resources, and as a result there is little need for Cambodian peasants to work for others. Only about 10 percent of Cambodia's total area of 44 million acres is under continuous cultivation. Sporadic cultivation is carried on in the sparsely forested areas and the large savanna and short grass tracts which constitute about 30 percent of the total. About 50 percent is heavily forested, and the remaining 10 percent is water (see Plate, Agricultural Products).

The continuously cultivated lands are those bordering the Mekong, Tonle Sap, and Bassac rivers and the Tonle Sap lake—lands constantly being built up by the fresh sediment deposited during the high-water periods.

The largest cultivated area is located at the confluence of the three rivers. In this region, most of which lies in the provinces of Kandal, Takeo, and Kompong Speu, approximately 2 to 2.5 million acres are inundated each year during the flood season. Rice and a wide variety of secondary crops are grown here.

The second largest agricultural region is in south central Cambodia, mainly in the provinces of Kompong Cham, Preyveng, and Soairieng. Here the cultivated area parallels the Mekong from

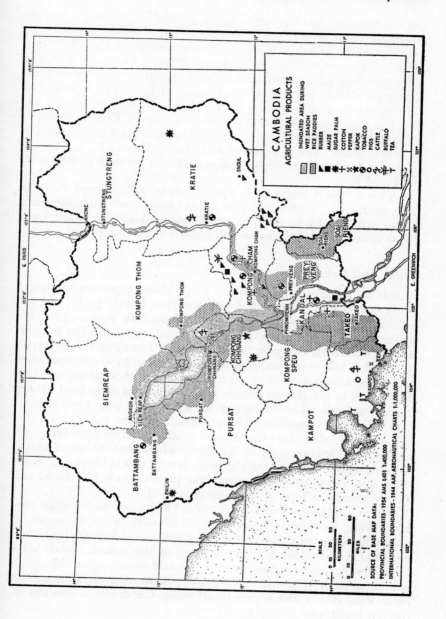

the Vietnamese border in the south to the southern portion of Kratie province in the north.

The third major region—sometimes referred to as the "rice bowl"—is in western Cambodia. The cultivated area here includes those portions of Battambang, Siemreap, Pursat, and Kompong Thom provinces that border on Tonle Sap lake. The richest rice area in this region is Battambang.

The north and southeast sections of Kompong Cham constitute a fourth important agricultural region. The area has a comparatively long dry season, which, together with the fertility of its soil, favors rubber production. Over 90 percent of the country's rubber is produced here.

The rest of Cambodia is very sparsely settled, and there is little continuous cultivation. The tribal peoples who inhabit parts of this area live by hunting, livestock raising, and a slash-and-burn (ray) system of agriculture which quickly depletes the soil.

Crops and Livestock

Rice is by far the most important crop. Three types are produced —wet rice, floating rice, and dry-season rice. Eighty percent of the estimated 2.9 million acres of land devoted to rice culture are under wet rice cultivation, relying on heavy rains and the inundation of rice fields by river floods. About a fourth of the country's rice land is fallow—a condition usually ascribed to underpopulation and to the minimum interest most Cambodians show about exerting themselves to get the maximum production from their land. There is only one general rice crop a year, although a very small second crop is produced with irrigation during the dry season.

Most of the rice Cambodia produces, approximately one million tons, is consumed in the areas where it is grown. The exportable surplus comes mainly from Battambang, Preyveng, Soairieng, and Takeo provinces, where the population is less dense and a more extensive type of cultivation is used.

Rice production since World War II has run higher than prewar levels, reaching a peak in 1956-57 with a total output of 1,478,000 metric tons (see Table 8); of this about 230,000 tons were exported. Insufficient rain at the start of the season, floods after transplanting, and dryness toward the end were responsible for a poor crop in 1954-55—necessitating emergency supply measures to meet local needs and seriously affecting Cambodia's earnings of foreign exchange.

Cultivation is carried on almost exclusively on a family basis, each family cultivating an area generally ten acres or smaller—sometimes only three acres in the case of holdings on river banks. The yield varies from region to region: it is highest in Battambang, Preyveng, and Pursat provinces and lowest in Kratie, Stungtreng, and Kompong Speu provinces. The average yield per acre is about half a ton, not much higher than it was fifty years ago and low in comparison with that of other rice-growing countries in Asia. What little increase there has been in production has been directly paralleled by an increase in the cultivated area.

The production of plantation crops—rubber and pepper—is almost entirely in foreign hands. As noted, rubber plantations are almost exclusively French-owned. They employ about ten thousand workers—most of them Vietnamese, the rest mainly Cambodians and Chinese. On the other hand, with the exception of one large French-owned estate, all the pepper plantations are under Chinese control; the labor force is also exclusively Chinese, on the French estate as well. Rubber and pepper are the only two products in Cambodia that are cultivated intensively.

Over 90 percent of Cambodian rubber acreage is in the northern and southeastern sectors of Kompong Cham, where soil and climatic conditions are especially suitable. Thirteen estates control over 80 percent of the land planted to rubber, and one of the seven French rubber plantation companies—Compagnie du Cambodge, affiliated with the French company, Terres Rouges—owns the three largest estates, which cover 40,000 acres, or more than half the total rubber area. Although the Chinese have been forbidden by law to own any of the red lands on which rubber is produced, they have nonetheless gained control of a number of the smaller plantations by using Cambodians as "straw men."

Rubber production in 1957 was 30,683 metric tons, compared with the prewar peak (1938) of approximately 17,000 tons. Production methods are modern and yields are high. Since 1940 one of the greatest difficulties encountered has been the shortage of labor, because the usual influx of contract labor from Vietnam was seriously diminished as a consequence of both World War II and the Indochina hostilities. The labor shortage severely curtailed the number of trees tapped and limited the maintenance work required for the immature trees. A more normal labor situation followed the cessation of hostilities in the summer of 1954. The cease-fire also brought an end to Communist guerrilla attacks against the plantations.

Pepper is grown almost exclusively in the provinces of Kampot and Takeo, primarily on the mountain slopes between the Gulf of Siam and the Elephant Mountains, where soil and climatic conditions are especially favorable for its cultivation. Most of it is exported.

Markets for Cambodian pepper have been difficult to find since the pepper is poor in quality as a result of plant disease and insufficient use of fertilizer. In recent years, government research organizations have attempted to improve the quality by grafting high-yield strains onto the original stock. There has also been an attempt to eliminate the high cost of plantation labor by encouraging pepper cultivation as a small-scale family venture. The success of these attempts has not yet been determined.

The cultivation of crops other than rice, rubber, and pepper is largely concentrated along the Mekong and the Tonle Sap rivers. These secondary crops include corn, green beans, soybeans, peanuts, sesame, manioc, and castor beans. Their production, for the most part on a family basis, is an important element in village economic self-sufficiency. They are largely consumed in the areas where they are grown but in some cases are also a source of export income. There is, for instance, a better quality of corn produced mainly for export, while an inferior quality is grown for local fodder. Some of the crops have important by-products: for example, the leaves and stem of the peanut plant provide excellent forage, the shells are widely used as fertilizer by the Chinese on their pepper estates, and the seed is an important source of vegetable oil.

Fruit trees—among them, banana, citrus, mango, and coconut —are another important feature of almost every Cambodian village. While most of the fruits (and many of the vegetables) produced are not marketed, commercial truck gardening by Chinese has recently expanded in the vicinity of Pnompenh and other cities.

The major cash crops produced on a family basis are tobacco, cotton, kapok, and sugar palm. There is also some cultivation of silk and ramie. Most of the silk production is exported in raw form; a small amount is processed for use in Cambodia. Ramie is used extensively in Cambodia in the manufacture of fish nets.

Production of several of these secondary crops is lower than before World War II. Cambodia produced 90,000 tons of corn in 1957-58, compared with almost 400,000 tons before the war. Cotton output is down to 200 tons as against 1,500 tons in 1941-42. Assigned reasons for the declines, though not always the same in each case, include the effect of the Indochina hostilities and the falling off of export markets.

Cambodia is one of the few countries in Southeast Asia where livestock raising can be extensively developed. Buffalo and oxen herds are numerous but small. In the lightly populated regions— mainly in Battambang, Pursat, and Siemreap provinces, which appear ideal for large-scale livestock development—the animals are left to roam at will. At times whole herds are decimated by epizootic diseases.

At the present time, livestock raising on a commercial basis is almost exclusively in the hands of Moslems (the Cham-Malays); many of the animals and much of the meat are sold to Vietnam. While Cambodians themselves formerly devoted most of their livestock activities to the raising of draft animals, they have recently turned increasingly to the raising of pigs and fowl, probably for sale to non-Cambodians for slaughtering. Local consumption of meat has increased in recent years.

Cattle "rustling" is reported to be common along Cambodia's Thailand and Vietnam frontiers and has provoked more than one diplomatic incident. In 1957 and 1958 joint veterinary conferences were held between Thailand and Cambodia in an effort to control epizootic diseases.

Techniques

Methods employed in the cultivation of Cambodia's major crop, wet rice, are similar to those in other rice-growing countries of Asia. Planting generally takes place during May and June, although this may vary from place to place and year to year, depending on climatic conditions. With the exception of Battambang province, where the seed is sown directly, rice seed is first planted in nursery beds and transplanted approximately one month later.

In plowing his land, the Cambodian farmer relies heavily on the water buffalo. Of all draft animals the water buffalo is best able to provide sufficient traction power in a slippery field to pull the plow. The plow—made entirely of wood except for the triangular iron blade—turns the soil to a depth of 8 or 10 inches. The plow is the principal farm tool, though cultivators made of fire-hardened wood also are quite common.

The major hazard is that the field may be flooded before plowing and planting have been completed. Some levees have been constructed to prevent early flooding, but the lack of a comprehensive network of dikes has left the majority of Cambodia's rice areas vulnerable to sudden floods.

After the period of sowing and transplanting, the Cambodian farmer devotes little attention to the crop until the harvesting period, about six months later. Extending from late November to early January, harvest is a time of intense activity for the farmer and his family. The rice is cut by sickles, husked, sifted, cleaned, and sorted. These activities are primarily a family affair, although neighbors may help now and then. After the harvest the rice field is drained of all but a small portion of the water and preparation is made for planting corn or dry-season rice.

The average Cambodian farmer shuns thoughts of interfering with what nature has afforded him. Some students of the area contend that Cambodians are not only apathetic toward the introduction of new tools and techniques but frequently hostile to such innovation. Even when the possibilities of better yields through new techniques can be demonstrated, farmers may frequently refuse to apply them. They will often show great curiosity about some new technique, but still refuse to adopt it. After all, the traditional methods have consistently provided at least a subsistence livelihood. Appeals to cooperate with long-range development programs are even less effective.

Even if the Cambodian were inclined to try to influence the natural course of events, he would think in terms of the propitiation of the supernatural rather than in terms of his own efforts. Such an attitude makes it difficult to put across any program of technical improvement in Cambodia. The government's efforts have included free distribution of better quality seeds (15 tons in 1953, 1,900 tons in 1954), instruction in better methods of cultivation, and encouragement of mechanized farming as a way to overcome the manpower shortage. Effective introduction of mechanization has been limited thus far to Battambang province.

Water

Sufficient water for agricultural use normally is no problem in Cambodia. Although much of the land requires irrigation, the water is available; the problem is one of control and most effective use. The country is hit by monsoon rains half the year, and nature has provided not only an extensive system of waterways but also a uniquely automatic irrigation mechanism that floods the Tonle

Sap to several times its normal size and then drains off the excess. Levees have been built along river banks to protect fields from flood waters, but what has been done is neither extensive nor well maintained. In some areas—mainly eastern and western Cambodia —the levees have been constructed in such a way as to allow water to enter for irrigation purposes and to flow back into the rivers when the flood waters subside. Draining the fields is an essential prerequisite for the use of the same land for dry-season crops. Even where canals do exist, effective control is very limited.

In the absence of large-scale water control devices, flood waters often inundate the fields before sowing is completed. Frequently a channel opening may be plugged with sediment so that its drainage effectiveness is vastly reduced. At other times the water level is not high enough to permit the water to flow through the channels and the fields suffer from dryness though water lies just beyond on the other side of the levee. Methods of transferring water to the places where it is needed are generally crude.

Irrigation of individual fields is carried on by primitive means. Instead of developing small individual channels which would allow the water to distribute itself evenly over the flat fields, the Cambodian relies on a combination of his primitive tools and nature's bounty. The annual floods and the rain water that collects in shallow catch basins bordering the rice fields provide water which is then transported to the neighboring fields by wooden buckets and hand scoops. The amount of land under controlled irrigation —where water is brought to the fields by a system of canals or pumps—is not known, but it appears to be extremely limited.

The reconstruction of ancient irrigation works and water-control systems and the construction of new ones had been undertaken by the French and the Cambodians since about the turn of the century. But much of what they accomplished was neglected or suffered military damage when Cambodia was caught in the maelstroms of World War II and the later Indochina hostilities. Important strides have been made since 1951, with assistance from the United States, in restoring the old irrigation systems—based on reservoirs that accumulated water during the wet season—and building new systems of water control. These efforts will permit the restoring to cultivation of large areas that had become useless when the irrigation systems that once supported them broke down.

A five-year program for flood control, drainage, and irrigation was drawn up in 1952. It was estimated that this program would cost close to $2.8 million, to be financed mainly by the United

States. In addition to the construction of dikes at Cheang Prey and on the western Barai Basin—projects that began in 1953—the plan also envisaged the draining of the Angkorborey plain, the construction of a flood gate between the Mekong and the Bassac, and the construction of a number of other water-control works.

Land Tenure

The majority of holdings in Cambodia are less than ten acres each in size (see Table 9). By and large the size of land holdings, aside from the rubber and pepper plantations, corresponds to the working capacity and needs of a family working its own land with a yoke of buffalo. If additional labor is needed during the period of harvest the tradition of mutual family aid is sufficiently strong to fill the gap. Normally the farm is large enough to provide food as well as a small cash surplus for clothing, taxes, and festivals.

There is no communal land subject to periodic redistribution. Tenancy and sharecropping are almost nonexistent, and, with the exception of those employed on the rubber and pepper plantations, there are few hired laborers. The few people who work as hired help generally do so on land near their own villages and live at home. When they work far from their own villages it is the responsibility of the employer to provide them with food and lodging, as it is on the rubber and pepper plantations.

Although, by custom, uncultivated land that is brought under cultivation becomes the property of the tiller, the question of land ownership in Cambodia is a delicate one.

The system of land ownership under ancient Khmer law resembled the system in Europe during the Middle Ages. In theory at least, all land belonged to the sovereign, and his subjects had only the rights of temporary possession and usage. There was not, however, the complex hierarchy of intermediaries between sovereign and peasant that characterized the European system.

In Cambodia the land was legally held by the person who cultivated it. Registration of land was not practiced, being regarded as unnecessary. To claim the right to a piece of land it was sufficient for the peasant to clear it, plow it, and in some cases enclose it. By the same token the negligent peasant who left his field unworked or absented himself from his land for several years lost his right to the land; it went to the first man who was willing to work it.

This system was changed in the nineteenth century. By the

joint Franco-Cambodian Convention of June 17, 1884, "the land of the Kingdom, until this day the exclusive property of the Crown, is no longer unassignable." The confusion and mishandling that followed not only contributed to Cambodian skepticism as to the honesty and the administrative ability of the French but also opened the way for the present unstable situation. The Cambodian peasant saw no incompatibility between the sovereign right of the king and his own individual right to real property, so the French action was received, not as an attempt to develop a system of private ownership, but as an attempt to undermine and defraud the king. Today, much of Cambodia's occupied land remains unregistered.

Credit

The fact that land registration never got very far, together with the reluctance of the administration to grant loans to peasants whose legal title to land had not yet been clarified, forced the peasant into reliance on moneylenders for credit. The result is one of the major problems in Cambodian agriculture—a severe shortage of rural credit on reasonable terms.

The lack of adequate credit has contributed heavily to the slow pace of agricultural advancement. Most of the money the Cambodian farmer borrows is not for land improvement but to tide him and his family over for short periods, or to finance his attendance at some festival. Little of the money borrowed is used for investment. Once in debt, and saddled with an interest rate that often reaches 100 percent, the peasant seldom is free of it. Any subsequent spare cash must then usually be applied to payments on his debt, and little if any is available for investment, even if he were so inclined.

Even after government credit facilities were established, collateral requirements and bureaucratic red tape made borrowing from the Chinese moneylender the path of least resistance. The Chinese, in carrying out their role as moneylenders, have revived a type of contract that has roots in ancient Khmer law. The contract, although detrimental in the long run to the Cambodians, has at least the appeal of being familiar to them.

Under the ancient system the borrower committed his property as collateral. As the property was not transferable, the creditor enjoyed only the right to take it over and work it for a given period of time until the loan was paid off. In substance the Chinese, in addition to charging usurious interest rates, have maintained this system. Instead of taking over the property the moneylender accepts in return for his loan a paper granting him the right to succeed to possession of the land within a certain period of time if the loan is not liquidated. Some Chinese moneylenders are said to anticipate that—when a complete registration of the land is finally carried out and they themselves are allowed to own rice land—they will be able to turn their paper rights (the right to work the property) into actual ownership. Others are satisfied with the present arrangement.

In the meantime moneylenders, who are also rice brokers—and the dual role is usual—content themselves with control of the harvest. The Chinese creditor takes the entire salable surplus, pays the necessary taxes, and in effect places the peasant in the position of a farm laborer. Not infrequently the peasant takes flight to escape the burden.

The moneylender computes the value of the rice he takes over at prices sometimes 20 percent or more below market quotations, which are lowest at the time of transfer, the start of the harvest period; he holds the rice off the market until later in the season when it can command higher prices.

The transfer of rice from grower to moneylender is in payment of the principal of the loan. The farmer is in addition obligated to pay high rates of interest. While usury is prohibited by law the lender (who wants as much interest as he can get) and the borrower (who needs the loan) agree on a fictitiously high figure to declare to the authorities as the value of the loan. Interest payments then look lower in percentage terms than they are in fact. Since the moneylenders are usually Chinese and Chinese are not allowed to own rice land, foreclosures are for the most part impossible.

Reforms

The interrelation of the problems of registration or formalization of land ownership, agricultural indebtedness, and the marketing of agricultural goods has resulted in simultaneous government action on these three fronts.

The program of land registration announced by the French in the late nineteenth century was expanded during the 1930's. The Board of Surveys, operating through land offices in each of the country's eighty-six districts, has been primarily responsible for land registration and certification of ownership. By 1950 between two and three hundred thousand land titles had been registered.

During the same period the government began to supply more adequate agricultural credit facilities. In 1933 the Office of Popular Credit (Office du Crédit Populaire) for all of Indochina was established (see chap. 14) in the hope that government credit would allow the Cambodian peasant to escape from the hold of the Chinese moneylenders. Interest rates were set at 12 percent and a number of rural banks (provincial agricultural credit banks) were established to deal directly with the borrowers.

The slow progress of land registration—resulting in a widespread inability to put up adequate collateral—and increasing red tape did much to limit the effectiveness of this program, as did the lack of sufficient working capital and the degree of over-organization involved. The peasant soon became resentful and suspicious about the large number of officials who descended upon the village to collect loans. The existence of a large class of "headquarters" officials is said to have done much to dampen any spirit of local participation.

The Office du Crédit Populaire de l'Indochine was dissolved in 1950, and in July of that year the Cambodian government established an Office du Crédit Populaire (OCP) of its own. The purpose of the new OCP was to encourage development in agriculture, handicrafts, and small industries by providing loan financing at low rates of interest.

The government sought to encourage the growth of agricultural cooperatives as mediums through which the farmer might obtain a better return for his crop and as sources of financial assistance. Money for the promotion of cooperatives was provided through the operations of the OCP. Of the 56,293,000 riels of loans and credit made available by the OCP in 1954, about 23 million riels, or 41 percent, went to the agricultural cooperatives. About 30,300,000 riels went to the provincial branch banks, and it is possible that some of this may have reached the cooperatives.

OCP financing earmarked specifically for the cooperatives was actually channeled through the local branch banks of the OCP at a rate of interest of 4 or 5 percent. The OCP also exercised considerable control over cooperative operations. The chairman of its governing council was the Minister of Agriculture.

As of April 1955 there were only nine cooperatives in Cambodia: three rice cooperatives (in Prey Chhor, Banam, and Mongkol

Borey), two general agricultural cooperatives (in Kandal and Kompong Cham), a timber cooperative, and three handicraft cooperatives. Some of the agricultural cooperatives engage in the milling of crops in addition to the part they play in collecting the harvest and providing financial assistance. At least two cooperative rice mills have been established with help from the United States.

Cambodian farmers did not have much confidence in this cooperative movement, and there are reports that cooperatives in existence prior to 1952 worked against the interest of their members; numerous frauds and other scandals made them the object of suspicion.

The rural credit system administered by the OCP failed to meet the needs of the population and in 1956 its activities were absorbed into a new and much more comprehensive cooperative organization known as the Royal Office of Cooperation (ROC). Placed under the Department of National Economy, the ROC is divided into four separate Directorates—Credit, Consumption, Production, and Commercial and is directed by an administrative council composed of the Secretary of National Economy, the Secretary of Agriculture, the governor of the National bank and a representative from each of the four directorates. Its capital is subscribed in equal parts by the royal government and by the affiliated cooperatives. Other financing comes from National Bank loans and foreign aid.

The over-all mission of the ROC is to create and organize the specialized cooperatives, to supervise their activities, to provide them with all material and financial facilities necessary to their operation, to dispose of produce, and to supply consumer goods and equipment. In carrying out these functions the ROC also tries to educate the rural population in the use of credit, in saving, and in the importance of the cooperative movement in general.

The activities previously carried out by the OCP have been taken over specifically by the credit cooperatives, with certain modifications: the amounts of the loans have been increased; the processing of loans has been decentralized from provincial to district level; and certain categories of land which were formerly unacceptable as collateral have now been made acceptable. Loans are made either to cooperatives or to individual members, with terms of one, five, and fifteen years and interest rates running from 7 to 12 percent. One-year loans are made to cover the expenses of one season's harvest; five-year loans, for acquiring land, animals, machinery, and equipment; fifteen-year loans, for special agricultural projects.

The producer cooperatives provide technical advice, dispose of produce, and advance credit to their members against future production. The interest rates—a minimum of 36 percent per annum—seem high but are actually much lower than the rates charged by the local moneylenders. The consumer cooperatives do not make monetary loans. The Commercial Directorate was created to coordinate the exchange of goods between the producer and consumer cooperatives.

The new cooperative organization seems to be more successful than the earlier OCP (see Table 10). In November 1958 a delegation from Cambodia attended the second Far Eastern Conference on Agricultural Credit in Tokyo and presented a report on the history and activities of the ROC. In concluding they noted that agricultural credit in Cambodia was still insufficient for a country of 900,000 peasant families cultivating 1,433,000 hectares of land, and that some kind of additional financing was required. On the other hand, in spite of a lack of material and technical means for disposing of producers goods, the ROC had managed to sell agricultural products to a value of 3.9 million riels and 12.7 million riels during the first half of 1958.

Fishing

Fishing is second only to rice cultivation as a means of livelihood in Cambodia. Since the majority of the country's villages border on waterways or have ponds, practically all of the rural population engages in fishing either on a part- or full-time basis. In many cases farmers divide their time equally between fishing and agriculture.

Various methods of fishing are used. The most common is the *samra* or weir method practiced in the Tonle Sap lake and in the larger rivers. The weir, or fence, made of bamboo, provides various forms of stationary and mobile traps into which the fish are driven, or in which they are caught as the water level descends. There is trawling in the larger bays and along the coast of the Gulf of Siam, together with the use of tidal fish traps.

Cambodia produces approximately 130,000 metric tons of freshwater fish annually, of which almost half comes from the Tonle Sap. About 60 percent of the catch is used for the production of dried fish, most of it for export. The fisheries on the Gulf of Siam produce between 20,000 and 30,000 metric tons of fresh- and salt-water fish each year and will increase in importance as Cambodia receives new fishing equipment.

Although the majority of commercial fishermen are Vietnamese and Cambodians, the industry is largely controlled by the Chinese, who lease the fishing grounds from the government on the basis of competitive bids. The Chinese then hire full-time or seasonal fishermen, mostly Vietnamese, to work for them, or they sublet sections of the leased area to part-time Cambodian fishermen. In most cases these lessees depend upon the Chinese for funds with which to buy boats and equipment, and eventually find themselves in debt for life. The terms of the loans oblige them to turn over their catch to the Chinese at prices fixed by the Chinese at levels well below those ruling in the established markets.

The government has attempted to curb Chinese domination of the fishing industry. In 1941 it established a fresh-water fishing cooperative, the Coopérative des Pêcheries d'Eau Douce du Cambodge, whose purpose was to provide financial assistance to Cambodian fishermen and to market their catch. Lack of capital, however, made it necessary for the cooperative to rely on the Chinese moneylenders for funds, thus defeating its original purpose. The Chinese also outbid the cooperative. The fishing cooperative's export monopoly over the catch of Cambodian fishermen officially ceased at the end of 1955. By that time difficulties were encountered in moving fish to Vietnam, a major market, not only because of the blockades of the Mekong but also because Vietnam was taking steps to protect its own fishing industry.

Forestry

Cambodia's extensive forest resources—much of them inaccessible—cover more than half the country's total area. There is a high proportion of hardwood but little, if any, teak. The forests are owned for the most part by the national government or by villages, which grant concessions to enterprises that want to work them. The lessees include Cambodians as well as Chinese and Vietnamese. To conserve the forests both from the devastation caused by slash-and-burn methods of agriculture and from abusive exploitation, the government has established two classes of forest domain: the classified and the unclassified.

Cutting of timber in the classified areas is closely regulated and concessions to cut a certain amount in a certain sector are based on public bidding. Exploitation of the unclassified domain is granted on an area lease basis; the government collects a certain percentage of the value of what is logged. Despite government measures little progress has been made in reforestation and fire prevention. The greatest obstacle is the refusal of the people themselves to heed the advice and exhortations of the government's agents.

Cut timber is generally shipped to the river banks by elephant or in wooden carts drawn by ten to twenty pairs of oxen. The logs are then tied into rafts and floated or towed by sampan to Pnompenh or Saigon.

INDUSTRIAL DEVELOPMENT

THE MAJORITY OF CAMBODIA'S INDUSTRIAL ENTERPRISES are engaged in the processing of agricultural products for export. Other industrial activity is confined mainly to traditional handicrafting and to some textile manufacturing and wood processing.

For the most part industrial units are small, often on a family basis, although there are a number of medium-sized plants that process timber and agricultural produce (mainly rice and rubber) into semimanufactured products. Approximately 100,000 workers, or less than 2 percent of the population, are engaged in industrial activity of some sort, but fewer than 6,000 workers, many of them in fish- or rice-processing factories, could be identified as industrial workers in the accepted western sense. In general, this industrial labor force is composed not of Cambodians but of Chinese and Vietnamese and is concentrated in Pnompenh and other large urban areas.

The rudimentary state of industrial development in Cambodia can be attributed to three main factors: a dearth of industrial raw material; the fact that Cambodia, as part of the French Union, was relegated to the role of supplier of primary commodities; and a general distaste among Cambodians for supervised employment. When the Chinese and the French established industries and plantations they had to recruit most of their labor force from outside the Cambodian community. With the exception of handicrafts Cambodians have shown little interest in business investment; capital for most of the machine-operated installations was supplied by the French and Chinese. The few Cambodians, usually government officials, who have accumulated large sums of money have shown little propensity for industrial investment.

Processing rice, timber, and other primary products for export has until recently been the virtual monopoly of Chinese and French firms. These firms not only maintained their Indochina head offices in Saigon but also shipped much of what they bought in Cambodia to Saigon for further processing for overseas shipment. Economic nationalism, together with the occasional stoppage of shipments to Saigon in recent years as a result of strained relations with Vietnam, has stimulated an expansion of Cambodia's own processing capacity.

Table 11 shows the number of establishments in many of Cambodia's industries in 1951 and 1957. There seems little doubt that the data refer in many instances to relatively large installations, though the estimate of 9,000 cotton goods establishments obviously encompasses a large number of very small enterprises, including handicraft operations. Though Table 11 poses certain problems of interpretation, it affords a summary picture of most types of industrial activity in Cambodia and points to the considerable expansion that has taken place in some industries—especially rice milling—since 1951.

Further development of industry in Cambodia depends both on foreign economic and technical aid and on greater enterprise by the Cambodians themselves. France and the United States—and more recently Red China and the USSR—are supplying financial and technical assistance.

One of the major obstacles to industrial development is the Cambodian outlook on industrial and commercial activities. As long as the present general lack of enthusiasm for industrial employment and investment persists, it is unlikely that industry will play a major role in Cambodian life. The government has stressed the need for technically trained men, but there is little evidence of much success in recruiting them. Cambodians who have acquired such training abroad sometimes encounter difficulties in obtaining suitable positions when they return home because they are suspected of having acquired new political notions as well.

Before important strides can be made in the establishment of facilities for end-product manufactures for domestic and possibly export markets, industrial development in Cambodia needs to make much more progress in processing primary commodities such as food, rubber, and timber. The development of more extensive manufacturing industries will probably depend to some extent on government financial assistance and on special privileges under Cambodia's customs regulations to protect them from lower priced imports. The limitations of the local market and the high cost of power are among the factors that might place Cambodian manufactures in a poor competitive position.

Processing Agricultural Products

Converting paddy rice into polished rice is the main industry in Cambodia. Since rice is grown throughout the country, husking and other rice processing is carried on to some extent by almost every family. Most of the rice surpluses, however, are processed in the large rice-milling establishments of Pnompenh. Formerly, when most of Cambodia's surplus rice was exported through Saigon, much of it was husked at large husking plants in Kompong Cham, Soairieng, and Kandal provinces and then sent to Saigon for further processing and re-export.

Converting paddy rice into rice alcohol is another of Cambodia's major processing industries. There are some fourteen distilleries; the most important of them is located at Russey Keo near Pnompenh and is a branch of the Société des Distilleries de l'Indochine. The concentration of alcohol production had been encouraged under the French in order to facilitate government control of this important source of revenue.

Nine plants located on the rubber plantations of Kompong Cham transform rubber latex into smoked sheets and sole crepe, most of it for export. They also prepare concentrated latex for direct shipment to overseas markets. Available statistics show that none of the rubber sent to Singapore—a major center of rubber processing in Asia—is in the latex form requiring conversion.

Another product of the rubber plantations is oil derived from the leaves of the rubber trees. Oil-producing industries include a network of plants in Kandal and Kompong Speu provinces that convert most of Cambodia's peanut crop into oil, about a third of which is exported.

One of Cambodia's most recent industries is palm sugar refining. The largest sugar refinery employs well over five hundred workers, making it the largest single factory in Cambodia. Much of the industry's output is sold locally, the rest is exported to Vietnam.

By-products of the fishing industry are: *nuoc-mam* (fish sauce); *prahoc* (fish paste); fish meal, which is used mostly as animal feed or fertilizer; and fish oil, used variously as lamp fuel, in the manufacture of paint, soap, and medicines, and in the treatment of hides and skins. The two largest fish-processing plants are in Kandal and Kampot.

Though a number of sawmills are located near the forests, the major sawmills are located in Pnompenh. Here the timber is converted into firewood or construction lumber. In a country that produces no petroleum and virtually no coal the use of wood for fuel is particularly important, not only in the home but also for Cambodia's railroad and many of the factories and boats. Both firewood and construction lumber are exported but the variety of tree types and the lack of standardization have posed marketing problems. Frequently the timber merchant will offer fine samples but be unable to match them in quantity when an order is placed.

The majority of the sawmills are owned and operated by Chinese, and Chinese also control the marketing of much of the timber products, as well as such forest products as bamboo, resins, gutta-percha, and rattan.

Manufacturing

There are approximately three hundred small tile and brick factories in Cambodia, over half of them in Kompong Cham, the rest scattered throughout the country. With the exception of two Chinese-owned plants in Pnompenh, pottery making is a family enterprise. It has been estimated that about one thousand families are engaged in it, mainly supplying local needs; in general it has not advanced beyond the handicraft stage.

Making cloth, laces, embroideries, and fish nets are traditional industries. They also are largely in the handicraft state, using primitive equipment and local raw materials. Most important in the textile field is production of the *sampot*, the garment worn by both men and women. *Sampot* weaving is done exclusively by women and with painstaking care. Both cotton and silk are used, some of which has to be imported.

Cotton is spun throughout Cambodia, each area specializing in its own designs. During World War II, a large cotton gin and spinning factory was established in Pnompenh by the Société Cotonnière de Nam Dinh, and a second mill was established to manufacture cloth and clothing.

Cambodia's small amount of jute, ramie, hemp, Malacca cane, and kapok produce is converted variously into rope, bags, and nets. Kapok is used principally in the manufacture of the bags required for the shipment of rice.

Other industries (see Table 11) include basketmaking, which employs some sixteen hundred people on a part-time basis, woodworking, metalworking and jewelry making. Jewelry establishments, generally small and frequently owned by Chinese, employ several hundred workers full time and about two thousand part time. There is also production of decorative articles fashioned from the tortoise shell of the Gulf of Siam, work in which Vietnamese men and women are commonly found.

A Cambodian cigarette industry now absorbs nearly all of the tobacco that reaches the market. Prohibition of cigarette imports protects the enterprise from foreign competition.

Industries that depend on modern techniques are not extensive. The larger woodworking shops in Pnompenh produce furniture, wagons, boats, and farm implements, but much of the work is still handicraft. There are in Pnompenh (perhaps in other areas also) small-scale electrical repair and machine shops. Paramilitary industries are virtually nonexistent.

Mechanical knowledge was introduced initially in Cambodia by the French. At present, efforts are being made to build up mechanical skills both through vocational training schools and through an apprenticeship system. An application of the apprenticeship system is to be found in the trucking business: each truck is operated by a driver and a "driver's aide," and it is the responsibility of the driver to pass on his technical knowledge to his assistant. The vocational schools are still few in number, and therefore apprentice training is of the greatest importance in developing a labor force skilled in mechanical trades.

Power and Mineral Resources

Water is very little used as a source of power, although Cambodia's hydroelectric potential is believed to be of considerable magnitude. As explained, wood is used extensively to power the various factories and the country's transportation equipment.

Supplied by two French companies, the Compagnie des Eaux et de l'Electricité de l'Indochine and the Union d'Electricité de l'Indochine, electricity is limited for the most part to Pnompenh and the other large cities. Two-thirds of all electric power generated is used in the capital. There are seventeen electric power plants in all of Cambodia, using diesel oil or low-grade natural gas as their source of power. Certain enterprises—for example, the rubber plantations—generate their own electric power.

A few minerals have been found: iron ore and traces of copper, manganese, gold, and coal in Kompong Thom; jet and phosphates in Kampot and Battambang; and gold, corundum, and zircon in Stungtreng. Other resources include salt, limestone, and potter's clay. There has been very little prospecting for or exploitation of mineral resources.

Cambodia's phosphate deposits are perhaps its most important source of mineral wealth. They are located chiefly in the provinces of Battambang and Kampot, and a phosphate processing plant has been erected in Battambang city, providing small quantities of fertilizer for agriculture.

Some salt is produced by the evaporation process, but the quality reportedly is poor.

Of the many other minerals that have been found, only gold, a few precious stones, marble, and quartz are of any importance to the economy at present.

The iron ore deposits at Pnom Dek in the province of Kompong Thom at one time roused great hopes. To overcome the primary obstacle of inadequate transportation, plans were drawn before World War II to establish a processing plant at the mine. The plan envisaged mining sixty thousand metric tons of iron ore annually and producing approximately twenty-five thousand tons of cast iron; it was rejected. French development plans after World War II made no mention of such a project. Recently, however, interest in the deposits has revived and the plan is being reconsidered.

Role of Government

Under French rule the government played a relatively minor role in the development of industry. It concerned itself mainly with granting concessions and collecting fees and taxes from those who undertook the exploitation of natural resources, mainly fishing and timber. With independence, however, has come a more active government interest in industrial development. Official attempts are now being made both to encourage industrial development and to reduce the extent of foreign control of existing industries.

Priority is given to the development of the processing industries, but the government makes frequent mention of the need for more cigarette factories, canneries, tanneries, and paper mills. The handicraft trades also have come in for a share of attention.

The product of Cambodia's artisans were at one time of extremely high quality, but increasing commercialization brought a reduction in standards. This is particularly true for metal goods, which are now made largely for the tourist trade and designed to appeal to the most unsophisticated tastes. Many original designs have been abandoned. Earlier French efforts to revive the former quality of the skills resulted in the establishment of a fine arts school at Pnompenh—l'Ecole des Beaux Arts—and of three artisan cooperatives, operating as self-governing guilds, to promote both the manufacture and marketing of handicraft products.

In 1955 these cooperatives worked with a government commission, the Service des Arts Cambodgiens, and had a membership of about thirty-five hundred. They also provided financial assistance to their members using funds made available by the Office du Crédit Populaire. With the establishment of the Royal Office of Cooperation in 1956, the OCP's functions were taken over by Credit Directorate of the ROC and a separate Cooperative des Arts Khmers was set up under the Directorate of Production. In 1958 this cooperative had a membership of about nineteen hundred and some sixty-eight artisans and small industries received loans from the ROC (see chap. 15).

A recently enacted law provides for resumption of ownership by the state of all mineral concessions not currently exploited. The government has established a monopoly over gold resources; gold may still be exploited privately but it must be sold directly to the government.

To limit foreign control of Cambodian industry but at the same time not alienate foreign investors, the government is attempting to foster mixed corporations of foreign and local capital in which it enjoys majority rights. A recent amendment to Cambodian commercial regulations denies any foreign firm the right to use a Cambodian name or title. This seems to foreshadow an attack on foreign-owned enterprises operating through Cambodian "straw men." A law of January 1, 1956 permitting the establishment of labor unions may indicate another effort of the government to weaken the industrial and commercial stranglehold of foreign interests on the Cambodian economy.

In December 1955 the Two Year Plan (see chap. 14) was enacted looking toward expansion in all fields. Shortly thereafter the government created the National Development Bank (Caisse Nationale d'Equipment), under the department of the National Economy, to serve as a repository for all foreign aid funds and to advance loans to private enterprise. Loans for mining and manufacturing charged 5 percent interest and might run as long as forty years. In February 1958 the National Development Bank received a credit of 52 million riels in United States aid to permit medium- and long-term loans for either the installation or expansion of industrial enterprises.

It appears that private enterprise has readily availed itself of these loan facilities. By the middle of 1958 the government had spent about 257 million riels in loans to nonagricultural production, almost half of the total amount allocated under the Two Year Plan, and most of this figure represented credits advanced to private enterprise by the Royal Office of Cooperation and the National Development Bank.

The most immediate results of the development program appear to be emerging in instances where a foreign government either has made a direct contribution of industrial equipment or has sent in technicians to build plants under its own aid. In June 1958 the Cambodian government accepted a gift of a 1,500-kilowatt thermal unit from the Czechoslovakian government. Under the Chinese aid program 500 million riels was earmarked for the installation of four factories (spinning and weaving, paper, plywood, and cement) and Chinese technicians arrived in 1957 and 1958 to begin work on these factories.

Through recent legislation the government has attempted to make private foreign investment more attractive, but although several types of enterprises have been studied, involving both local and foreign capital, by mid-1957 none had been established.

DOMESTIC AND FOREIGN TRADE

THE MOST IMPORTANT FIRMS IN CAMBODIA are the exporting and importing companies, some of which also do wholesaling and retailing. The majority of these are owned by Chinese or Sino-Cambodians; some of the largest firms, however, are owned by French citizens and a few others are controlled by Vietnamese and Indians.

The Chinese export merchants in Pnompenh are in close touch with Chinese commercial houses in Saigon. Chinese also function as agents in the rural areas for Pnompenh firms. Large numbers of village shopkeepers are Chinese, most of whom usually have important connections in both Pnompenh and Saigon. The Chinese are in fact so strong organizationally and financially that (with the possible exception of the one Chinese bank in Pnompenh) Cambodia's commercial banks have an informal arrangement not to lend them money; the Chinese are expected to be able to take care of themselves.

Rural storage facilities as well as the country's river and road transportation facilities are also usually in Chinese hands, although a few trucking agencies are now owned by Sino-Cambodians and Cambodians. The men who drive the trucks are Cambodian, but not long ago this was the job of the Vietnamese.

There are Chinese, French, and Cambodian commercial associations—and there may soon be some Vietnamese associations—but little is known about them. The Chinese associations are strongest and best organized. Chinese firms also belong to non-Chinese groups such as the Association des Exportateurs de Céréales, a leading cereal export association, said to be a French organization.

Chinese merchants frequently employ Cambodians to make contacts for them and to supervise their Cambodian staff. A Chinese export-import house in Pnompenh may, for example, employ an educated young Cambodian who knows French and has many contacts to handle its business correspondence. (The Cambodian language has not been generally used in business correspondence.)

At least four factors contribute to the predominance of the Chinese in the economic life of the country: They are genuinely interested in business, they belong to a closely knit community, they have spare cash they want to invest, they are willing to work hard to become rich. None of these factors is characteristic of Cambodians. Most of them are not interested in business or on the whole in accumulating wealth, and they are not clannish. There is evidence, however, of change in Cambodian attitudes toward commercial activity, but having become interested in entering the commercial field the Cambodian often encounters obstacles of another kind—lack of capital, organizational know-how, and the requisite technical skills.

Regarding foreign trade, at the end of the first year of independence Cambodia showed an unusual deficit in its balance of trade. Normally there would have been a surplus of exports over imports. The drought of 1954-55, affecting rice and fish production —two of Cambodia's major exports—undoubtedly contributed to the deficits of that year, but since 1955 the trade deficit has continually increased—by the end of 1958 it stood at several times the 1955 deficit.

This shift in the balance of trade in two and a half years is largely due to the extensive development program on which Cambodia embarked in its Two Year Plan for 1956-57. Under this plan the volume of imports was increased tremendously while exports, though showing a steady gain, lagged further and further behind. In order to finance its imports Cambodia has had to rely heavily on foreign aid and since 1955 an outstanding feature of Cambodia's external economic relations has been a shift to direct dollar credit from the United States and the diversification of its foreign aid sources through a series of new commercial and economic aid agreements with Communist China and countries of the Soviet bloc. The aid agreements, involving large amounts of free credit, have permitted an increasingly higher volume of import. The new commercial agreements, on the other hand, have not resulted in any appreciable expansion of the export trade and an unfavorable balance of trade will probably remain for some time a major concern of the Cambodian government. Summing up the situation in April 1958, Prime Minister Sim Var said:

Our products destined for export cost too much. The communication system is still inadequate . . . Our finances languish because of the weakness of our exports and the necessity of importing products which are essential for repairing war damages and equipping basic industry.

The Government and the Market

In pushing toward economic independence the Cambodian government seeks to end not only dependence on foreign aid, but also Chinese control of Cambodia's domestic commercial life. Cambodian firms are favored by the government in both domestic commerce and in the administration of controls over external trade. To avoid situations in which foreign traders gain advantages by doing business under a Cambodian name, the government has ruled that only firms whose capital and 40 percent of whose personnel are Cambodian will be considered as Cambodian establishments and qualified to use a Cambodian name.

Through development of the cooperative movement, the government is endeavoring to build up a Khmer-controlled national system of internal trade which, it hopes, will bypass the system still largely in the hands of Chinese. Credit cooperatives for farmers have been operative since 1954 under the Office of Popular Credit (see chap. 15) but in June 1956 a much more comprehensive cooperative organization was launched with the establishment of the Royal Office of Cooperation under the Department of National Economy.

The functions of the ROC as outlined at the time of its creation were to (1) establish credit, consumer, and producer cooperatives, (2) supervise their activities, and (3) provide all of the material and financial facilities necessary for their proper functioning. The ultimate goals of the ROC are to help the poorest Khmer cultivators to raise their standard of living, to educate the Khmer people in commercial activities, and to eliminate speculators, usurers, and middle men of any sort—particularly foreigners—from the commercial life of the country.

As originally set up, the ROC was composed of three divisions —credit, consumption, and production—each responsible for organizing and managing its own set of cooperatives. These divisions were under an administrative council composed of the Minister of National Economy, the Minister of State for Agriculture, the governor of the National Bank, and a representative from each of the cooperative divisions. A commercial division has been added to coordinate the activities of the producer and consumer cooperatives. Any local cooperative can become an affiliate of the appropriate national cooperative by purchasing one share at 5,000 riels.

The primary function of the central producer cooperatives is to advance loans against future production, to buy up produce, to resell it under the most favorable conditions, and to return any net gain after charges to the producers. Most of the producer cooperative activity involves agricultural products, but there are some cooperatives that handle the products of artisans and craftsmen.

The primary function of the consumer cooperatives is to buy merchandise as cheaply as possible and to resell to members at cost plus shipping and storage charges. Local cooperatives sell to members and occasionally to nonmembers, with a small markup to cover their own operating costs and those of the central office.

The consumer cooperative organization has played an increasingly important role in Cambodian domestic trade. In May 1958 it was awarded a priority in the disposal of consumer goods imported under the aid agreement with Communist China. The number of local affiliates rose from 76 to 264 between July 1957 and July 1958, and these distributed such basic commodities as cotton and silk goods, sugar, cement, iron and steel, jute bags, and condensed milk. In July 1958 the consumer cooperative organization proposed to decentralize its activities to provincial offices and outlets, and to allow local affiliates to have control of their own affairs within a fixed credit limit. It also proposed to procure more varied and essential items by direct importation from abroad and by purchasing from local and national industries. The commercial division of the ROC was apparently established in response to this last proposal. Its function is to provide the consumer cooperatives with merchandise which it cannot otherwise find and to help the producer cooperatives dispose of their goods through the consumer cooperatives.

In every village and city of Cambodia there is an open-air market place, and each vendor who sets up a stand there pays the local government a tax for the privilege. Despite the firm and unchanging stand which characterizes the Cambodian approach to most issues, full-scale bargaining is the rule in the market places. When a Cambodian quotes a price at which he will sell or one at which he will buy he has every intention of negotiating and he expects his "adversary" to understand that neither side opens on a fixed position. Bargaining is generally conducted in Vietnamese, not Cambodian. Agricultural produce is sold mainly by the Cambodians who produce it, but for products that are one or more steps removed from the source of production—for example, textiles —the vendors are generally Chinese, Sino-Cambodians, Vietnamese, or Indians.

Price markups are high. Most products sold come under retail price control but the ceilings are difficult to enforce and are often evaded. The normal administrative problems that accompany any effort at retail price control are compounded in Cambodian by a shortage of honest enforcement personnel. Wholesale prices are controllable for imported goods, since the import price appears on the government's import license and such licenses are not approved unless the price is acceptable to the government. There are many evasions, however, partly because of poor administration, especially outside of Pnompenh.

When black-market prices involve an essential product such as rice there is wide public protest. There has been considerable price speculation in the marketing of rice and other food crops in city areas, and the government has taken steps to check it. In 1955 the short supply of rice in Pnompenh was due partly to speculation, partly to the 1954-55 drought, and partly to the operations of political agitators during the election campaign. In August or September of that year the government not only ordered rice merchants to sell their supplies at official prices, but warned rice mills to run their facilities at full capacity or face requisition.

Transportation and Communications

Although rail, highway, and air transport are steadily gaining in importance, Cambodia's inland waterways are still its main means of transportation. Most of the important transportation routes center on Pnompenh. Of Cambodia's several inland ports only Pnompenh can handle vessels of 8,000 tons, and those only in the rainy season. All of the rivers are most navigable during and shortly after the rainy season. The rise and fall of the Tonle Sap River make it a virtual lock regulating the volume of traffic between Pnompenh and the Great Lake.

River craft are chiefly sampans and pirogues, canoe-like boats operated by hand, but junks and barges increasingly are being used. Some of the barges are automotive (mostly those used by the Michelin rubber plantations and the Shell Oil Company), but the majority are towed by tugs. Motor- and steam-propelled boats ply primarily between Pnompenh and Saigon. Because of the extent of tidal changes on the rivers, loading facilities at many inland ports are built on floating wharfs, in contrast to the fixed facilities at ports on the Gulf of Siam.

The movement of goods between Pnompenh and the outlying provinces is mainly by river for products shipped to the capital for export and mainly by truck for goods (chiefly imports) distributed to local markets from Pnompenh. Recent highway construction has facilitated shipment of rice from Cambodia's "rice bowl," which formerly had to depend upon the seasonal navigability of the Tonle Sap network.

Telephone and telegraph connect Pnompenh with most of the provincial capitals, but radio is the only immediate link with other points in Cambodia and with foreign countries, except for the radio-telephone link with Saigon. All internal telephone, radio-telephone, and telegraph services are operated by the government; there are reported to be about twelve hundred telephone subscribers. Foreign communication by radio-telephone or telegraph is handled through a private firm—the Compagnie Générale de TSF—under government contract.

Railways and Roads

Cambodia has only one railroad line, a single track running the 385 kilometers between Pnompenh and Poipet on the Thailand border. Here goods must be transferred from one line to the next. The total rolling stock in 1957 amounted to 24 locomotives, 47 passenger cars, and 392 freight cars. Tonnage carried over the line is mainly goods shipped from Poipet and by far the largest proportion of this tonnage consists of rice and other agricultural products.

The Saigon-Pnompenh-Battambang road, connecting with the highway system of Thailand and through it with Singapore, is one of the three national highways that make up Cambodian's road system. The other two connect Cambodia with Laos and Vietnam. Traffic on Cambodia's roads moves mainly by bicycle, pedicab (a three-wheeled taxicab), and oxen- or buffalo-drawn carts; motor traffic is only a small portion of the whole.

Cambodia's road network, as of December 1957, included a total of approximately 3,580 kilometers of national and provincial highways, of which about 1,620 kilometers were asphalt-surfaced, 1,090 stone-surfaced, and 870 earth-surfaced—the last, of course, usable only during the dry season. The destruction of bridges during the

Indochina hostilities greatly impeded road communications, particularly in the Pnompenh-Takeo-Kampot area. With American aid, a new four-lane highway is being built between Pnompenh and the new seaport of Sihanoukville, a distance of almost 200 kilometers. Bridges along the new highway will be able to support loads up to one hundred tons. The many rivers and swamps of Cambodia cause the road network to be dotted with an unusually large number of bridges which are subject to sabotage in the event of disorder.

Ports

Since the importance of Pnompenh as a port is directly related to freedom of access to Saigon by way of the Mekong, Vietnam's blockade of the Cambodian border in 1956 emphasized a serious Cambodian economic vulnerability. Cambodia has a right to freedom of navigation on the Mekong and therefore has proceeded with the development of Pnompenh as a port for ocean liners and with the negotiation of arrangements with steamship lines for direct shipments between Pnompenh and foreign markets without rehandling at Saigon. Since the use of this route is completely dependent upon friendly relations with Vietnam—and Cambodia and Vietnam are not always on friendly terms (see chap. 11)—the Cambodian government has developed an alternative route through the new port on the Gulf of Siam, Sihanoukville. This port will be equipped to handle ocean-going vessels of all tonnages and in all weather. It is scheduled to be open for use sometime in 1959. A new line of communication has been drawn in the network of Cambodia's domestic commerce—a road connecting Pnompenh with Sihanoukville (see Plate, Transportation Network). There are three other Cambodian ports on the Gulf of Siam—Ream, Kep, and Kampot—but none offers the possibilities of Sihanoukville.

The development of direct contact between Cambodian and overseas ports without the necessity for rehandling at Saigon will do more than foster Cambodia's economic independence of Vietnam; it will also weaken the hold that Chinese business houses have over the Cambodian economy. Chinese firms have usually done business through the Chinese commercial community in Saigon-Cholon— the ocean port through which most of Cambodia's external trade has formerly passed; thus any opportunity for Cambodians to do business with the outside world without having to ship through Saigon agents lessens the monopolistic control of Cambodia's Chinese merchants over the country's internal trade.

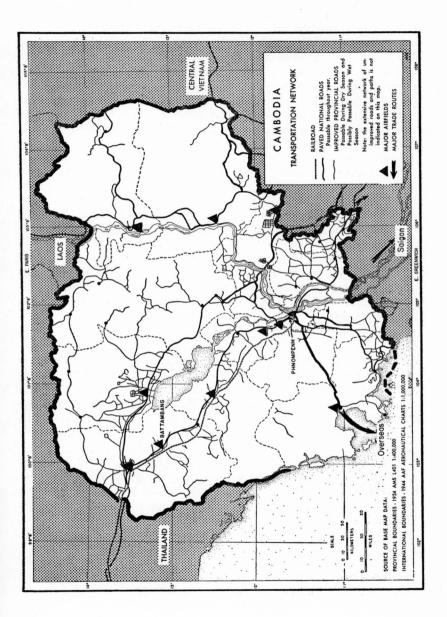

A shift of this kind is believed to have already taken place in Cambodia's timber trade. While the production of timber is mainly the province of Cambodian businessmen, the marketing of the product was in the hands of a Chinese cartel, which divided Cambodia into spheres of control. When foreign ships began to reach Cambodian ports directly, Cambodian businessmen began to sell part of their output directly to foreign firms. The development of the Gulf ports and the rail connection between Cambodia and Thailand may be expected to produce similar results (for the effect of these developments on the processing of Cambodia's primary commodities, see chap. 16). It is possible, however, that many Chinese firms in Pnompenh will themselves welcome an opportunity to deal directly with Chinese houses in Singapore and Hong Kong.

Although transportation by road is more expensive than by water and the only routes to the Gulf ports are by land, the final cost of moving goods to the ports may not be much, if any, greater than the cost of shipping them down the much longer route of the Mekong to Saigon (shipments to Saigon are sometimes taken part of the way by truck). Even if the cost of shipment to the Gulf ports were greater than the cost to Saigon, bypassing Saigon will enable Cambodia to earn a larger share of the total foreign exchange involved.

Air

Air service connecting Pnompenh with the rest of Indochina is provided primarily by Air Viet-Nam and Air France. Other companies servicing Indochina include Air Laos. C.O.S.A.R.A., Aigle Azur, and Société Indochinoise de Ravitaillement. Thai Airways connects Pnompenh with Bangkok. Civil Air Transport, an American company, also operates in Cambodia. Direct connections with Europe and Japan are provided by KLM and Air France.

A Franco-Cambodian air transport corporation, Royal Air Cambodge, with predominantly Cambodian government capital, has been created. It will first establish air liaison between Pnompenh and Siemreap, later extending its operations to include flights to Thailand and Vietnam.

Patterns of Foreign Trade

Cambodia's major exports are rice, rubber, and corn. Despite a temporary setback in export volume in 1955-56, the total value of exports of rice and rice derivatives has risen steadily and rice is today Cambodia's leading export product. Exports of rubber dropped off somewhat in 1956 but have begun to gain slowly in recent years. Together rice and rubber have supported a gradual and continuing rise in Cambodia's over-all export trade while other important products, including corn, have declined (see Table 12).

Since independence there has been a noticeable shift in the direction of rice and rubber exports. In 1954 France and her overseas territories consumed the largest share of Cambodia's rice crop, followed by Indonesia, South Vietnam, Malaya, Macao, and Hong Kong in that order. Today the rice sales to French Union countries have decreased and Malaya consumes almost as much Cambodian rice as France and the French Union together. Hong Kong has become the third best customer and Malaya and Hong Kong together account for over half of Cambodia's rice exports. By the end of September 1958 no rice exports were reported separately for Indonesia, South Vietnam, or Macao, while exports to the Philippines had increased and Japan was now an important customer. Prior to the breakup of the Indochinese customs union, France consumed almost all of Cambodia's rubber crop; by 1954, however, the United States was Cambodia's best customer for this product and by the end of 1958 it was buying more than three times the amount bought by France.

In terms of over-all export trade, Cambodia's principal markets, in order of importance, are France and the French Union, Malaya, the United States, Hong Kong, South Vietnam, the Philippines, and Japan. South Vietnam appears in this list because of its importance as a consumer of Cambodian corn, fish, meat, beans, and timber. Among the Soviet bloc countries, only Czechoslovakia has begun to buy Cambodian products and as of the end of September 1958 there was no sign of any appreciable export trade with the Chinese People's Republic. In August of 1958 Sihanouk visited Peking and expressed concern over the fact that the two-year-old commercial agreement had not resulted in any appreciable export to China in spite of increasing Cambodian imports from that country. Prime Minister Chou En-lai apparently agreed to increase purchases of timber, pepper, livestock, and Citröen cars assembled in Pnompenh.

As an agricultural country, Cambodia's major imports are automobiles and parts, machinery and mechanical equipment, cotton goods and other textiles, iron and steel, cement, electrical equipment, pharmaceuticals, and chemical products. The effort to raise the standard of living and speed industrialization in recent years has caused a sharp upswing in the import of these commodities (see Table 13).

A shift in the geographic pattern of imports, even more marked than that for exports, has accompanied this increase in import volume. In 1955 the principal suppliers of imports were, in order of importance, France and her overseas territories, Hong Kong, Japan, Malaya, the United States, Indonesia, India, West Germany, and South Vietnam. France was way ahead of any of the other suppliers. With the establishment of direct dollar credits under the United States foreign aid program (as against dollar aid previously made available only in equivalent French francs) Cambodia became less dependent on high-priced French products and began to shift the weight on its sources of essential commodities. As import volume increased, purchases from France remained at about the same level, those from the United States and Japan doubled, those from West Germany tripled. At the same time imports from the other former suppliers dropped off. Commercial agreements were signed with Communist China and the Soviet bloc countries and by the end of September 1958 Cambodia was importing from China, North Vietnam, the USSR, Czechoslovakia, and Rumania. At present Cambodia's principal suppliers in order of importance are France and the French Union, Japan, Hong Kong, the United States, West Germany, Malaya, and the Chinese People's Republic.

The over-all external trade picture at the end of September 1958 revealed that Cambodia's unfavorable balance of trade lies primarily in the direction of countries outside the dollar and sterling zones, particularly France and Japan (see Table 14). In spite of shifts in the geographic pattern of trade since independence, France alone remains both Cambodia's largest supplier and its best customer. During the last year however, exports to France dropped by about 14 percent while imports doubled. At the same time exports to Japan were cut in half; imports from Japan, almost tripled. The scales have been further tipped to the deficit side by mounting imports from West Germany and the Chinese People's Republic with almost no exports to balance them.

Cambodia's trade with South Vietnam has in the past been difficult to measure since use of Saigon as a transit point for goods has tended to inflate both the export and import figures for that country. It has been estimated that in 1954 and the first half of 1955 less than 5 percent of the value of imports recorded as having come from Vietnam really were of Vietnamese origin, the remainder being merchandise in transit. The differential is less in the case of Cambodian exports to Vietnam since Vietnam is an important market for Cambodian corn, fish, timber, meat, palm sugar, and beans. As Cambodia proceeds with development of the river port of Pnompenh and of the ports on the Gulf of Siam, its statistics on trade with Vietnam will reflect more accurately the volume of Vietnamese goods imported and of Cambodian goods sent to Vietnam for consumption there. The sharp decline in exports to South Vietnam since 1954 and the even more drastic decline in imports may in part be the result of shifting to new facilities; yet the accompanying drop in over-all exports of those Cambodian products which South Vietnam buys would seem to indicate that South Vietnam is losing its importance as a market for Cambodian goods.

Control of Foreign Exchange

The Cambodian government's primary concerns in controlling foreign exchange are to conserve export earnings in foreign currency and to assure an adequate supply of those commodities deemed essential to the welfare and economic development of the country. All exports must be approved and licensed and are further subject to controls requiring the repatriation of a large portion of the foreign earnings. The government sets minimum prices for all commodities licensed for export and normally requires the repatriation of foreign earnings in amounts at least equivalent to these prices.

Probably aware that some exporters were not surrendering the required amounts of foreign earnings, and certainly interested in stimulating exports, particularly to the dollar areas, the government has allowed exporters to retain part of their export earnings in foreign currencies—13 percent for shipments to dollar areas and 10 percent for shipments to other monetary areas. Since May 1957 exporters who are also important producers in Cambodia—e.g. rubber planters—have been permitted to retain an additional 10 percent for the importation of commodities essential to their operations.

Import controls consist of the allocation of certain amounts of exchange for particular commodities and the reallocation of these amounts to applicant importers on the basis of competitive bids. Imports to be paid for out of the foreign balances of Cambodian nationals are not exempt from government control.

Exchange authorization is also required for goods imported

under "barter" arrangements involving two-way shipments of equal value. Arrangements of this kind are stimulated by foreign exchange difficulties of the negotiating countries and are designed to secure the procurement of essential goods that would otherwise be difficult to pay for.

Foreign exchange controls are administered by a number of government agencies. The initial allocation of funds is made by the National Commission for Exchange Allocation under the Department of National Economy. These allocated funds are then administered by the National Exchange Office of the National Bank of Cambodia (see chap. 14). Minimum export prices are set by the Director of Foreign Commerce. The Bureau of Foreign Trade of the Department of National Economy receives bids from importers and makes a provisional allocation, but this is subject to the final approval of the National Exchange Office, which may reject requests for foreign exchange even if a bid has been approved and an import license granted.

The government has used its import control machinery as a means of fostering the growth of Cambodian importers to positions of greater prominence in the country's trading community. It has given preference to Cambodian firms over Chinese houses in the granting of import licenses and exchange permits. In March 1956 there were over 800 licensed importers in Cambodia compared with only 78 at the beginning of 1955. There can be little doubt that a large number of these were Cambodian firms. It is of some significance that in 1955 when a five-man government committee was set up to make out a list of products on which all export earnings would have to be converted into riels and to establish periodically price ranges for such exports, neither of the two members who were to represent the exporters was Chinese—one was a Frenchman, the other a Cambodian.

International Commercial Arrangements

Cambodia is party to a variety of commercial agreements with other countries. After the breakup of the former Associated States of Indochina the tariff preferences that Cambodia had accorded imports from France, Laos, and Vietnam were replaced by preferential arrangements on a bilateral basis. Cambodia has a clearing arrangement with Vietnam under which a payments balance between the two countries is struck every six months, to be settled in whatever currency the two parties find mutually acceptable.

Settlement has to be immediate for the amount which at any time exceeds U. S. $4 million (the accounts are kept in U. S. dollars). Cambodia also has a payments agreement with Laos.

Economic relations between Cambodia and Vietnam are subject to considerable fluctuation. There were disputes under the former joint customs arrangement when Vietnam delayed paying Cambodia its share of the customs revenue of the Associated States. More recently, political friction between the two countries resulted in border blockades and reported military adventures. There has also been friction between Cambodia and Thailand, but on less serious a scale (see chap. 11). In April 1956 Thailand made an undefined offer of close economic cooperation with Cambodia. Both Vietnam and Thailand oppose Cambodia's advocacy of the internationalization of the Mekong.

In June 1956 Cambodia took an important step by completing commercial and payments agreements with the Chinese People's Republic. The commercial agreement established an exchange of up to 5 million pounds sterling of specified products each way for one year. The payments agreement provided for direct payments between the central banks of each country. Both agreements have been reinstated each year by a simple exchange of notes. Shipments of cement, iron, silk, cotton goods, and hardware began to arrive from China in April 1957.

On the heels of this agreement came a series of agreements with other Communist countries. By the end of 1956 Cambodia had signed agreements of a similar kind with Czechoslovakia, and by the end of 1957 with the USSR and Poland. In November 1958 a commercial agreement was signed with North Vietnam.

Cambodia has also been negotiating for commercial agreements with Japan and India. Cambodia already had signed in December 1955 a Treaty of Amity with Japan which included economic, technical, and cultural cooperation.

Foreign Aid

Since independence Cambodia has accepted various kinds of economic assistance from a variety of sources, including the United States, France, Japan, the Chinese People's Republic, the USSR, Poland, countries of the Colombo Plan, and UNESCO and other specialized agencies of the United Nations. Fully aware of the political implications of economic aid, Cambodia under the leadership of Sihanouk has continually reaffirmed its policy of independence and neutrality in striving toward the goal of economic independence.

A speech in February 1956 by Sihanouk, then prime minister, to the National Assembly provides some idea of how these various sources of economic aid are ranked by the Cambodian government. Listing five nations from which substantial assistance could be expected, he ranked France as the most desirable—France "whose present policy with respect to Cambodia is the best." Second was the United States, "which possesses powerful means, but which only wants to help the countries which accept its supervision." Third was Japan. Fourth was Red China, "which is competing with the United States for economic aid to Cambodia. Although it requires no conditions, it is possible that it aims at a certain objective which I cannot yet see." The USSR ranked fifth. Later, in April, he outlined this policy again and reduced it to its central point: Cambodia would accept any and all foreign aid as long as it did not threaten Cambodia's sovereignty. Since then the largest amounts of aid have come from the United States and Communist China and the central issue in the negotiations for this aid has been the nature of the conditions under which it was, or would, be given.

American Aid

The Cambodian government has been critical of the fact that aid from the United States has not been an outright grant without such features as the "counterpart" fund. In fact, the government has displayed great sensitivity in general in its consideration of assistance from the United States. Speaking at a public meeting in April 1956, Sihanouk asked, "Must we refuse American aid?" and answered:

> No, for this aid is precious to us. We accept aid from the United States insofar as it does not interfere with our policy. The American aid must be given to us without conditions; we do not want to share the fate of Thailand, South Viet-Nam, the Philippines, and even France, who are forced to cede bases to the Americans on their territory. On the other hand, Yugoslavia has benefited from American aid without incurring any obligations.

The economic aid the United States has given Cambodia since 1950 is designed to accelerate economic development and raise standards of living. This aid has taken various forms: direct grants of equipment, including dredges for development of Cambodia's rivers into better channels of transportation, machinery for new rice-husking mills, equipment for irrigation systems and road construction (also the financing of the road connecting Pnompenh to the new Gulf of Siam port, Sihanoukville), and equipment for a medical school and a police academy; direct grants of health supplies; technical assistance in agriculture, education, health, industry, communications, and community developments; and dollars to pay for essential imports, not necessarily from the United States. The Cambodian government sells the dollars to importers in exchange for riels and deposits this local currency into a special fund—called a "counterpart" fund—to be used partly by the United States government in defraying its expenses in Cambodia and partly by the Cambodian government upon approval by the United States.

In 1955—the year of a bad rice crop in Cambodia—the United States sent 10,000 tons of rice plus 2,500 tons of paddy as seed for the next season. Rice was also sent by other countries.

In the first half of 1955 Cambodia received more than three times as much aid from the United States as from France and by the middle of 1956 the United States had become Cambodia's chief source of foreign aid. By November 1957, with the Communist Chinese aid agreement now over a year old, a special session of the Superior Planning Council was called at the request of the American ambassador to discuss the United States aid program for 1958. In this meeting the ambassador officially announced that aid for 1958 would amount to 33 million dollars (or 1,555 million riels) thus almost doubling the Chinese offer and bringing the total United States aid since 1955 to 5,500 million riels. In view of similar assurances given by the Chinese, the ambassador stressed that this aid was "unconditional."

Chinese Communist Aid

With the signing of a commercial and payments agreement between Cambodia and the Chinese People's Republic on April 24, 1956 the door was opened to further economic relations between the two countries. Communist China was quick to respond to Cambodia's dual need of economic assistance and guarantees of political autonomy. On June 21, 1956 the two countries signed a separate economic aid agreement in which China established a credit of 800 million riels (or 8 million pounds sterling) to be applied toward construction materials, equipment, merchandise, and technical assistance under Cambodia's development plan for 1956-57. Both the basic agreement, and the implementing protocol which followed it, affirm that no intervention or control of any kind will be exercised by China in carrying out the program. The agreement also sets forth the uses to which the credits are to be put: development of water resources, light industry, communication and transport, electric power facilities, schools, hospitals and research centers.

By the end of 1956, mixed Sino-Cambodian commissions had been set up both in Pnompenh and Peking and were busy with the practical aspects of the aid program. Six months later 50 million riels of credit had been committed and in November 1957 the National Planning and Development office published an over-all allocation of the total amount of the credits which indicated that the lion's share—500 million riels—would be spent for construction of four factories. During 1958 groups of Chinese technicians arrived in Cambodia to direct the location and construction of these factories, but none of them appears to have been completed to date.

By the end of 1958 very little of the credit set up under the June 1956 agreement actually had been spent, yet the Chinese were ready to send more aid for new projects. On August 24, 1958 Sihanouk and Chou En-lai signed a joint declaration in Peking in which the Chinese, after expressing satisfaction with the progress of the aid program and concern over Cambodia's unfavorable trade balance, let it be known that they were willing to send more aid to establish small-scale iron works, explore for subsoil fuels, and study other matters deemed necessary. In spite of reservations about Communist China's aims, Cambodia recognized the government of the Chinese People's Republic as *de jure* on July 24, 1958.

Soviet Bloc Aid

Aid from the Chinese People's Republic was followed shortly by aid from the USSR, Poland, and Czechoslovakia. In the wake of Sihanouk's visits to these countries, diplomatic relations were established with them and later a series of commercial, payments, and technical cooperation agreements were signed. In addition, the USSR offered to construct a 500-bed hospital in Pnompenh at a cost of 400 million riels, and Poland offered to contribute a complete surgical unit. With the signing of these agreements delegations of technicians arrived from each of the countries concerned, the Soviet delegation alone including experts on planning, economic organization, foreign commerce, industry, agriculture, irrigation, public health, education and culture, and construction. By the end of 1958 delegations of Cambodian specialists had been sent to most of these countries for training.

Other Aid

French economic aid has included the provision of funds and technical assistance for construction of the port of Sihanoukville on the Gulf of Siam and expansion of the facilities at the Pochentong airport near Pnompenh. By the end of 1958 neither of these two projects had been completed. Small amounts of aid have been received from countries under the Colombo Plan, particularly Australia, Canada, New Zealand, and India. The Japanese Red Cross has donated medications.

In addition to direct aid, Cambodia has become involved in at least two international collaborative efforts, one dealing with rural credit and the other with development of the Mekong basin. In June 1956 Cambodia joined with seven other Asian countries in arranging to set up a research and training center to help small farmers and in drafting a regional program for more effective and more soundly based rural credit. In November 1958 a Cambodian delegation attended the second Far Eastern Conference on Agricultural Credit in Tokyo. On May 26, 1958 Cambodia, Thailand, and Vietnam signed an agreement with the United States International Cooperation Administration for a program to study the Mekong River. Starting early in 1959 the program was undertaken by an American firm, to be completed in three years.

PUBLIC HEALTH AND WELFARE

GOVERNMENT OFFICIALS, westernized educators, and welfare workers have found it difficult to stir the Cambodian villager to sustained interest in methods that will produce better health, more income, and more material comfort. Some progress, however, has been made; when a new method can be proved of value to the peasant he usually is willing to give it a trial.

Efforts to introduce modern techniques of farming have met with some success among younger Cambodians, but the older farmers are still slow to see why one should overly assist a sufficiently bountiful Nature.

Many generations of Cambodians have accepted as effective the ancient methods of combating illness offered by bonzes, diviners, and sorcerers. In some instances these methods have proved sound by modern medical standards—for example, chaulmoogra oil used in the treatment of leprosy, herb teas for intestinal ailments, frequent bathing as a basic hygienic measure. In general, however, the traditional treatments consist merely of protective magic designed to propitiate the good spirits and to drive out the evil ones.

The good spirits, though mainly beneficent, are known to be touchy about their rights; being powerful they may cause illness in persons who do not show the proper respect or propitiate them at the right times. Evil spirits are always malevolent; by entering the body they cause illness and can only be driven out by a specialist.

Various preventive or curative measures are used, combining magic, prayer, and specific "medicines." Amulets worn somewhere on the body are popular means of warding off the spirits or hastening a cure (see chap. 5). The amulet may be a cylinder engraved with a Pali inscription; a piece of bark bearing cabalistic signs; a coin consecrated by a sorcerer (*kru*) or blessed by contact with a bonze's robe; a claw or tooth of a tiger or tooth of dog or crocodile; bones of a pregnant woman; the body of a fetus.

Diagnoses are often made by a diviner (*achar*). When evil spirits are suspected to be the cause of an illness, the *kru* is summoned. One of his treatments involves the making of a small raft or basket that is freighted with a small crude doll and an egg that has been rubbed over the sick person. Bonze doctors use prayer and medicines in their healing work. The remedies include special plants, oils, and potions made from excrement, and may combine symbolic, magical, and medicinal properties. Pumpkin seeds, for instance, which are used against fever, are symbolic of freshness.

The Cambodian government is striving to introduce the practices of modern medicine, continuing the efforts that the French initiated about a hundred years ago and carried on over the years since. The people accept western medical techniques but usually as a supplement to rather than as a substitute for their traditional measures. Reports indicate that confidence in folk medicine and magical practice persists, side by side with the partial acceptance of such innovations as DDT spraying, prenatal and postnatal care, quarantining, boiling of drinking water, vaccination, anti-venom injections. Because many Cambodians do not understand the theory of disease they also fail to understand the relationship between disease and scientific technique, so they call their native practitioners first, resorting to the western doctor only when no cure is forthcoming—at which time it is often too late to save the patient.

Standard of Living

No studies are available on the standard of living in Cambodia, but it seems clear that the average peasant at least does not live a life of hardship and despair. His diet of fish and rice is abundant and easily come by; his house is easy to build and maintain; he has solace and entertainment through his local pagoda, and if he wishes to range farther afield for festivals, there is the moneylender to make it possible. The average household is characterized by simplicity—in furnishings, food, and clothing—in keeping with the Buddhist attitude toward material possessions.

The staples of diet are plentiful in Cambodia and malnutrition is not a major social problem; but western-educated health experts believe that the old nutritional patterns need revision if disease is to be successfully combated. The World Health Organization, the United States, and France are cooperating with the Cambodian government in a health-education program for maternal and child care which includes dietary information. The Cambodian government is introducing scientific home economics into secondary schools.

Living standards for the workers on rubber plantations are comparatively high because they live in "model" villages built by the plantation owners. From 500 to 800 people live in each village; facilities include pagodas or churches, food markets, other shops, baths, theaters, public nurseries, playing fields, first-aid stations, restaurants, power plants, hospitals, and dispensaries. The dietary and sanitary standards here are high compared to those of the average Cambodian village.

A Cambodian government study of the cost of living for non-agricultural workers in Pnompenh in 1955 as compared with 1949 indicated not only a rise in costs but also a change in living standards as reflected in the expenditure pattern.

1. The cost of living rose by 100 percent from 1949 to 1955.
2. The major expenditure items within categories are rice and dried fish; lodging; black calico cloth; cigarettes and medicines.
3. The proportion spent for food is 60 percent of all expenditure; for housing and utilities, 20 percent; for clothing, 8 percent; for miscellaneous, 12 percent.
4. The greatest cost increase is seen in the miscellaneous items (258 over the 1949 base of 100, with bus fare increasing the most, then hair care, and cigarettes). Food is next with 205 (bananas the most, fresh fish and eggplant second, then dried fish and palm sugar). Housing and utilities are third with 178 (wood for fuel the most, then water, and lodging). Clothing increased least (128, with wooden shoes showing the greatest increase). Some of the cost increase in food, wood, and water probably reflects the 1954 drought.

Newspaper and magazine articles, photographs, and films suggest that the demand for western consumer commodities is developing in the cities. There has been an increase in the number of restaurants and places of amusement and certain westernized articles of clothing are gaining in popularity.

Welfare Efforts

Government concern for the public welfare has a long tradition in Cambodia. In the twelfth century King Jayavarman VII built hospitals and monasteries, open to all castes throughout the Khmer empire—from Laos to lower Cochin China. He built rest houses for travelers along the roads, distributed rice to the needy and the sick after it had been used as an offering to the gods, banned tax collectors from places where the sick were cared for. He considered doctors "warriors versed in the science of medicine rather than arms, who destroyed the enemies of the kingdom—sicknesses—by means of their own weapons—remedies." His words, carved in stone at Angkor Wat, are quoted by Cambodian leaders today: "May the kings of Cambodia—concerned with the welfare of the people that my foundation protects—attain the day of deliverance with their descendants, their wives, their mandarins, their friends, when sickness will be no more!"

Today the Cambodian government, with improved organization and techniques derived from the French, is continuing the tradition. Public hospitals are maintained as well as public rest houses (*salas*), along the principal roads. Modern utilities and sanitary facilities, developed under the French, have recently been further improved and extended more widely through the technical assistance programs of foreign nations, particularly the United States.

The purification of drinking water has been an important part of the health program for Cambodia and all Indochina since 1931. Under the French protectorate most provincial cities learned how to purify their water supply by means of alum, sand filtering, and chlorination. Some smaller towns (under 1,000 population) had pumping stations and purifying plants, and sometimes distribution systems. Villages (100 to 1,000 population) also had purifying plants and reservoirs of treated water but no distribution systems.

In general, however, the supply and distribution of purified water were extremely inadequate. Most of the farm families continued to drink from the polluted waters of rivers, irrigation canals, and surface water.

At present the World Health Organization, the United States, France, and the Cambodian government are cooperating to increase the sanitary facilities and the water-supply measures initiated many years ago by the French. Some two thousand pit privies have been dug with United States aid; tank reservoirs and pumps have been set up in most rural areas, and distribution facilities in the larger communities. With equipment supplied by the United States, many villages have dug wells as self-help projects. The city water systems of Battambang and Pnompenh are being modernized, also largely with United States aid.

There are few electric power installations outside of the larger cities (except for the rubber plantations, which have their own generating systems). Even in the cities electricity is expensive, of low voltage, of limited distribution, and constantly failing when all consumers use it at once. Oil lamps and candles, even in the capital, are common for house lighting. Present plans call for the building of larger generators and for a general step-up of facilities in cities; rural areas may have small generators for specific use.

Some attention has been given to public welfare both in the national budget allocations to the Department of Social Activity and in the recent Two Year Plan. The Department of Social Activity's share of the budget—3,210,000 riels in 1958—is, however, exceedingly small and ranks next to last among all of the departmental allocations. Under the Two Year Plan, community development projects received a total of 142 million riels.

The welfare standard set by the rubber plantation owners for their 10,000 workers is respected by the present government as one to be followed. Sihanouk, in a speech on current social problems facing Cambodia, said:

> I am going to submit to the Government a bill encouraging big capitalists and directors of major enterprises to improve the welfare of their personnel [as have] the owners of the rubber plantations who have created dispensaries, hospitals, and social services for their employees. Certain merchants have sent me gifts dedicated to social welfare. Directors of enterprises can pool their efforts for the construction of schools, dispensaries, and hospitals.
>
> We will follow the middle course between the Communists who deprive the rich of their property and the capitalists who live in opulent affluence.

Some social legislation (modeled on French patterns) affecting hours of work, wages, and workmen's compensation has been in existence since 1936. Originally only foreign workers were covered but Cambodians were later included.

In 1955 a system of family allotments was instituted under which employers were required to contribute a monthly sum for the welfare of the worker's family. A pension system for government personnel (including members of the armed forces and the National

Police) provides for old-age retirement and disability; the monthly pension is based on the average pay of the last three years' service, and takes account of the number of years worked.

The retirement age for government workers is fifty-five years. Magistrates retire at sixty. If a man dies either in office or in retirement, his widow receives half of his pension. Pensions are also provided for minor orphan children up to twenty-one years of age. The retirement fund is presently administered by a council composed of the Director of Finance, a representative of the Ministry of Interior, a judge designated by the Ministry of Justice, a civil servant of high rank, and a retired civil servant already under the pension system.

There are few welfare organizations, but the number is increasing. The pagoda, of course, has been for centuries a type of welfare organization devoted to the care of the body, mind, and spirit of Cambodians. In the present Cambodian government the premier is also Minister of Planning and Social Welfare. Although this may be a temporary measure, it indicates the importance the government attaches to social problems.

Private welfare organizations are relatively new. One of the most interesting of the existing organizations is the Comité Féminin d'Entr'aide, which was established in 1953 as a result of the efforts of a group of women, most of them American, to demonstrate the use of powdered milk. Encouraged by the Queen, it has developed into an influential organization attached to the hospital at Pnompenh and is concerned with prenatal and postnatal care and general maternal and child care. A benefit ball given by the organization a few years ago brought over 600,000 riels for its work.

There are Boy Scout and Girl Scout groups (two Cambodian Boy Scouts attended the World Jamboree at Niagara Falls in 1955), and school alumni and parent-teacher associations. Other welfare associations include the Society for the Assistance of Children, the Association of Cambodian Women, the Association of the Friends of the Secondary and Technical National Education, and the Medical Assistance Society for the Religious. The Oeuvre Nationale d'Entr'aide (the National Mutual Help Association) was created in 1949 to provide those in need with cash, food, and clothing. There are various ethnic welfare organizations: for example, the Association of Vietnamese in Cambodia operates a dispensary in Pnompenh open to all, and the Chinese take care of the physical and monetary needs of their compatriots.

Nutrition

For the Cambodian, meals are rituals that must not be interrupted. There is no talking. "Even the thunder respects the man who is eating."

Food is usually served in common dishes placed on floor mats around which the family sits. It is the custom for the food bowls to be covered with straw and a cloth. If any heavy work has been done prior to eating, Cambodians wash their whole bodies before the meal. Hands are washed again after eating. Whether these practices arise from sanitary considerations or are pure ceremonial tradition is not clear.

Dietary habits appear to be basically the same throughout the country, whether among Khmer, Chinese, or Vietnamese, in villages or in provincial capitals. Rice, fish, and water are basic. Rice is not as thoroughly milled in Cambodia as in many other rice countries, and less so in the rural areas than in the cities, as a result it retains many vitamins in the bran. The average per person consumption of rice in 1955 was almost one pound a day. *Nuoc-mam* sauce (Vietnamese in origin), made of fermented, highly spiced fish oil, is a diet staple for people at all social levels. *Prahoc* (of Cambodian origin), a spiced paste made of salted, dried fish allowed to ferment in jars, is also an important part of the diet.

Tea is drunk generally between meals. It is the first offering to a visitor, and refusal would be considered a rude and unfriendly act. Since tea is boiled, it is safe for drinking and can be accepted without hesitation. Water is drunk after meals, generally from a large water jug and a common bowl.

Supplements to the basic diet, depending on season, status, and wealth, are vegetables, meat (beef and pork), poultry, eggs, and fruits, particularly bananas.

The typical meal of a farmer consists of a ball of rice (which the Khmer eat with their fingers, the Chinese and Vietnamese with chopsticks), three dried fish, and a bit of *prahoc*. In the country two meals a day are usual—at 10:00 A.M. and at 5:00 P.M. In the cities the western habit of three meals a day prevails. The diet in the cities, particularly in Pnompenh, has recently been affected by such western items as soft drinks and ice cream; the elite favor French cooking, and there are French, Chinese, Vietnamese, and Indian restaurants. But rice, dried fish, and *nuoc-mam* sauce are still staples.

The following daily food ration of about 3,200 calories is standard for Vietnamese laborers on the rubber plantations of Cambodia and of all Indochina.

Rice	28	oz.	Fresh or canned meat	7	oz.
Nuoc-mam	.5	oz.	Dried fish	7	oz.
Tea	.2	oz.	or		
Salt	.7	oz.	Fresh fish	14	oz.
Grease	.7	oz.	Green vegetables	10.5	oz.
			or		
			Dried vegetables	5	oz.

Recent estimates by official Cambodian sources indicate, however, that about 20 percent of other Cambodians are either underfed or undernourished, owing not so much to lack of food as to the ignorance of the rural population about the principles of nutrition and about sanitation in food processing. The government hopes that education along these lines may become part of the school and community health programs. Cambodian officials point to the system of diet and sanitation on the French rubber plantations as one they would emulate for their own people.

Incidence of Disease

In spite of Cambodia's bountiful agricultural and water resources and the low population pressure, life expectancy is barely thirty years and 50 percent of the children die before they are a year old.

Practically every Cambodian is afflicted at some time with dysentery, malaria, tuberculosis, or all three. Dysentery is one of the major causes of infant mortality and of general debilitation of the population. Malaria is almost an occupational disease; in the wooded areas and plateaus where farmers cut wood and grow rice 2 of the 53 species of mosquitoes that carry malaria are found in above-average concentration. The high incidence of malaria may also be blamed on the Cambodian houses on stilts above muddy ground, often with animals who may be mosquito hosts quartered below.

Yaws is widespread, although not usually fatal. Trachoma, with its resultant blindness, is quite common. Cholera occurs, but not in epidemic proportions. Scrub typhus, caused by animal-borne ticks and mites, dengue fever, and hookworm occur throughout Cambodia. A few cases of leprosy and plague have appeared in Pnom-penh. Syphilis, scarlet fever, and measles, largely importations from the western world, occur now and then.

Medical Programs and Personnel

The first medical service in Indochina was created by the French in the 1860's to meet the needs of French troops; its services were soon extended to the native population. In 1890 at Pasteur's own request the Pasteur Institute was established in Saigon, and three other branches were set up in Vietnam to serve all of Indochina. The people of Indochina had the benefits of the world-famous work done at the Institute: the invention of anti-venom serum, the BCG test for tuberculosis, the discovery of the plague bacillus and of the role of fleas in its transmission.

The Public Health and Medical Services of Indochina organized in 1914 covered both the civil and military populations. A local health officer was attached to each province, responsible respectively to the health director of each of the five Indochinese territories. An inspector-general in Saigon was administrative head of the Services; in 1931 he was relieved of his military duties so that he might concentrate on civilian health. Up to World War II the Public Health Service supervised frontier health control, seaport and airport health services, vaccination, health inspections, general sanitation work, and hospitals. It also reviewed local state plans and budgets and cooperated with the Pasteur Institutes on research.

During this period hospitals were established in Pnompenh and the provincial capitals; infirmaries, maternity centers, dispensaries, and first-aid stations were set up in rural areas. There was some training of personnel—nurses, midwives, public health officers, etc. The available personnel, however, was limited, visits by provincial and territorial health officers to rural areas were infrequent, money and supplies were low, and there was no permanent machinery charged with the continued education of Cambodians in hygiene and health practices. Nevertheless, positive health gains resulted from the French efforts. In 1936, 600,000 Cambodians were vaccinated against cholera; in later 1936 and 1937, although there was a severe cholera epidemic in Thailand, no cases of cholera occurred in Cambodia. Smallpox vaccination had also been effective. In 1924 there were 5,000 cases, but by 1928 only 1,300. The regulation of health and sanitation in Cambodia today is patterned upon the French system. The Cambodian Sanitary Code (*Règlement Sanitaire*), adopted on November 7, 1930 and modified in later years, continues to be the basic sanitary law.

When Cambodia became independent the Ministry of Health came under the control and guidance of the Cambodian government. The Ministry operates, as it did under the French, on a basis both of private regulation, affecting only individuals, and of public regulation, affecting all people of a particular category. Its authority extends over the entire country; it sets standards for entrance into nursing and technical schools, initiates curricula, gives examinations for licenses, makes staff appointments of doctors and other medical personnel, authorizes transfers of individual doctor's or dentist's offices from one area or one province to another, issues licenses for the sale of certain drugs, and promulgates municipal ordinances on sanitary measures.

The problems and responsibilities of the Ministry of Health remain basically the same as they were during the French protectorate. The Ministry is seriously understaffed. The posts are political and the chief is constantly being replaced. (In 1955 there were five different Ministers of Health.)

In the field of public health the most acute problems are water supply and sewage disposal. Even in the cities, water supply is inadequate. Recently a contract has been made with the Japanese government for improving the water system in Pnompenh. Of fourteen provincial hospitals, six have water only part of the day and seven no water at all. The rural population mainly depends on open shallow wells and ponds for all water needs—drinking, bathing, watering stock, etc. Some regions have practically no water in the dry season. Sewage disposal is nonexistent in rural and suburban areas. Sanitary wells and pit privies are a present objective of health aid, largely given by the United States. Insect and animal control, inspection of meat and vegetables, health education, and control of various types of poisonous plants and snakes are still pressing problems.

In the medical field inadequacy of supplies, facilities, and personnel is the urgent problem. In 1957 Cambodia had fifteen hospitals with a total of 2,751 beds, four dispensaries, one hundred twenty-three infirmaries, one leprosy center, and one insane asylum. Since then the government of the USSR has contributed a 500-bed hospital capable of handling 500 out-patients per day, which is under construction in Pnompenh. In addition the Czechoslovakian government has contributed a complete surgical unit for one of the provincial hospitals. The country's medical and health staff in 1957 consisted of:

Public		Private	
Medical doctors	14	Medical doctors	19
Health officers	86	Doctors	6
Pharmacists	4	Dental surgeons	3
Dentists	4	Midwives	18
Nurses	632		
Midwives	60		
Other	162		

Source: *Statistical Yearbook of Cambodia* (1937-1957), June 1958.

The government's activities, aided by considerable foreign assistance, include malaria and dysentery control, sanitation, nursing training, health education, improvement of medical facilities, training of doctors in Cambodia, and scholarship programs for study abroad.

The first medical school in Cambodia was opened in 1956, staffed by French doctors and equipped by the United States. It should graduate its first doctor in about four years. Construction of a nursing school to be attached to the medical school is under way.

At the present time hospital facilities are being expanded with aid from the United States, France, the USSR, and Czechoslovakia. The enlarged Preah Ket Mealea Hospital in Pnompenh is in effect a national hospital center. It has 800 beds for a city population of 400,000 to 500,000 plus patients from the provinces. Its facilities include general medicine, tuberculosis wards, contagious disease wards, surgery, pediatrics, maternity service, clinical training, pharmacy, etc. Construction of two hospital centers for tuberculosis and contagious diseases is planned.

A bonze hospital for all sects was opened in 1956 to serve the 60,000 to 70,000 ordained bonzes. At its official opening the Secretary of State for Public Health stated that the King and Queen had brought life to the famous maxim of King Jayavarman VII engraved at Angkor: "The pain of their subjects, and not their own pain, is the sadness of kings."

France recently contributed a 60-bed hospital ship equipped

for surgery. It is to circulate on the Tonle Sap and the Mekong, giving medical assistance to Cambodians living along the lake and rivers. Dispensaries and first-aid stations are being set up all over Cambodia, and first-aid manuals and all drug labels are to be written in Cambodian. A model rural health center for training personnel is under construction outside Pnompenh. Some nurses and midwives are being sent to Bangkok for an intensive training period of a few weeks.

Malaria control demonstration centers and spraying areas have been highly effective. Children in the experimental area at Snuol were found to be free of malaria; but 80 percent of the children in an adjacent area had the disease. No mosquitoes of the malarial variety were found in any of the treated areas. The people have been shown how they can cooperate in preparing houses for spraying and in improving sanitation.

World Health Organization teams demonstrate practical working methods of malaria control adapted to local needs and give on-the-spot training to natives. WHO is cooperating also in the control of yaws and trachoma; Cambodians are becoming aware of the relationship of trachoma to prevalence of flies. It is not unusual to see a Cambodian sleeping or resting with a cloth over his eyes; babies' eyes are usually carefully covered.

Two thousand pit privies have recently been constructed throughout the provinces as a result of the work of health educators. Well-digging by villages as a self-help project has been encouraged by the Ministry of Health; the United States is to furnish the pumps. Much of the foreign aid is directed toward control of dysentery through sanitary measures: water systems and wells, drainage, sewage disposal systems, and pit privies. There is extensive health education in the schools and in the rural communities. Numerous chlorination projects are under way, and the water systems of Pnompenh and some provincial capitals are to be improved and expanded. Training of sanitary engineers and public health administrators has also progressed with foreign help.

Since public health projects are generally fostered by the government, approved by the king, and in some instances even financially supported by the royal family, they carry a sponsorship the Cambodian respects. Furthermore, care of the sick is an important part of the Buddhist concept of the individual's responsibility to serve society, so that support of public projects of this nature has a strongly religious and moral basis.

Social Problems

Cambodia has few of the more violent social problems that plague most industrialized nations today. Murder and sexual crimes are at a minimum. Petty thievery is common (in spite of the Buddhist prohibition), in part because the Cambodian's concept of private property is not a strict one. Habitual drunkenness and alcoholism are almost unknown, though a large amount of wine is consumed, mostly during festivals and other social occasions.

Drug addiction is rare in rural areas, but is widespread among the Chinese and Vietnamese in the cities. Opium has long been a government monopoly and the source of considerable revenue: in 1938 it represented about 15 percent of total revenue for Indochina as a whole, though smuggling was common. Cambodian government control of opium is now stringent. Import, export, selling, stocking, buying, or any other transaction involving the drug or poppies and poppy seed are all punishable, even as first offenses. Selling or giving opium to a minor is punishable by imprisonment of one to five years and a fine of 10,000 to 50,000 riels; if a minor is involved in an offense the punishment of the adults involved is doubled. Production of opium pipes is forbidden. Search without warrant on suspicion regarding drug violations is permitted any time of day or night. These measures suggest that there has been some threat of spreading drug addiction and that the government is determined to stamp it out.

Juvenile delinquency has been virtually nonexistent in Cambodia. During a recent meeting in Rangoon (sponsored by the United Nations) on crime in the Far East, however, Cambodian representatives were among those who attended the session on juvenile delinquency; it was apparently felt that, though new to the Far East, the problem could become one to be reckoned with as a result of the dislocations of war and the rapid industrialization now taking place in many areas.

FORMAL EDUCATION

ONE ASPECT OF THE NEW CAMBODIAN NATIONALISM is a changing emphasis in the goals of education. Traditionally the purpose of education was to master and practice the Buddhist doctrine, thus gaining "merit." Today the student may also seek an education both as a means of personal advancement and as a patriotic duty. The educational goal of the French administration was to create a body of civil servants. Today an avowed aim of the Cambodian government is to train administrative and technical experts for a society that is becoming aware of the need for accelerated economic and social advancement.

Sihanouk declared quite early the importance of training workers to operate the local industries Cambodia needed. He stressed the social and economic importance of agriculture and urged the Ministry of National Education to bring about better relations between civil servants and peasants.

The government also educates that it may govern more easily. "My objective in life is to educate my people to be good citizens," declared Chet Chhem, National Inspector of Primary Education, virtual overlord of the educational system.

As the official attitude has changed, so has the attitude of the student. Education used to be an adjunct of religion; today it provides an opportunity for social and economic betterment. In contrast with the years before World War II young people now flock to school in numbers greater than can be accommodated. The prime objective of most peasants, however, still is to train their sons in rice farming, in the ancient pattern.

Before the French educational reform measures of 1918, few people learned to read and write Cambodian. The pagoda schools taught the boys to copy and read the sacred texts in Pali (see chap. 4), but this was of no practical value since Pali is not generally used. Girls were not taught at all. In 1920 a reliable observer reported that French administrators were frequently unable to find in municipalities of several thousand people even one person who could read and write Cambodian.

Under French tutelage more and more Cambodians learned to read and write, but this ability often was wasted, since the villagers have little opportunity and no great desire to read. Most of the children who attend school do not go beyond the third year; such training, if not reinforced by practice, is lost in the course of later years.

Literacy in Cambodia in 1956 was officially estimated at about 60 percent, but no indication was given as to the degree of effective literacy, or as to how this literacy was apportioned among the various languages of the country. Those Cambodians who have progressed through the secondary schools are fluent in French, but these are a small proportion of the population. Cambodian is being promoted extensively.

UNESCO is attempting to inculcate elementary ideas of hygiene and "cooperative action," bypassing literacy goals for the time being.

The Educational System

All public education, both liberal and technical, is under the jurisdiction of the Ministry of Education, except for a few specialized schools connected with other national ministries. The Ministry of Education ranks first in the allocation of government funds and in 1956-57 it received 70 million riels of United States aid. It exercises very detailed control: it sets forth the syllabuses, hires and pays the teachers, inspects the schools, and is responsible for supplies and other expenditures. An inspector of primary education under the National Inspector is assigned to each province. An Education Advisory Board studies questions which the Ministry submits to it. A Cultural Committee is responsible for enriching the Cambodian language, which is deficient in modern technical terms. There is a Commission for the Preparation of Textbooks, and a National Commission for UNESCO. In June 1957 a Superior Council for National Education was created at the cabinet level.

Primary Education

Primary education is conducted both in official schools and in pagoda schools, or "renovated temples." In 1956-57, there were 1,478 official primary schools with an enrollment of about 220,570 boys and 85,920 girls. Since 1951 this represents almost tripling of the schools and more than tripling of the enrollment. The ratio of girls has increased from 11 percent in 1931 to 38 percent in 1957.

Primary education is divided into two "cycles" of three years each. At the end of the three years pupils may take the state examination for the *Certificat d'études primaires élémentaires*. Those who complete the six-year course receive the *Certificat d'études primaires complémentaires*. A large percent of the pupils drop out after the first cycle. In 1956-57, there were 12,032 graduates of the first cycle, and 3,862 of the second.

The pagodas have in the past been central in Cambodian education. For centuries the bonzes have taught boys in the pagodas, and young men traditionally spend some months at a pagoda as part of their religious training. The French utilized this ancient educational institution by fitting it into their over-all system at the primary level. Bonzes were trained in French teaching methods and were sent back to establish "modernized pagoda schools"; these had the same curriculum as the primary state schools except that French was not taught. The essence of the bonzes' training was the acquisition of an organized body of knowledge to replace the extremely fragmentary and amorphous bits of information they formerly passed on to their students. In fact, before the "modernized pagoda schools" were established the students were little more than servants of the bonzes, learning only religious precepts and, perhaps, a little carpentry.

Although the government has stated that it intends to replace the pagoda schools by secular schools, the number of such schools in operation in 1957-58 was the same as in 1951-52 and the enrollment has actually increased somewhat. As of the end of 1958, there was a total of 1,472 pagoda schools open with a total of 90,987 pupils of whom all were boys. A few girls had attended up until 1944.

The curriculum in the primary schools is composed of ethics, civics, history, arithmetic, geography, science and hygiene, Cambodian language, French language, manual work and draftsmanship, and physical training. The aim of Cambodian primary education is to reinforce rather than to disturb national patterns of thought. It professes to "take the child from the rice field and take it back to the rice field."

In the official schools, lessons are given in Cambodian the first year but the teaching of French is begun in the second year;

during the second three-year cycle all instruction except in Cambodian ethics is in French. Instruction in pagoda schools is entirely in Cambodian.

Secondary Education

Secondary education is given in 15 schools, with a total enrollment in 1956-57 of 8,990. This represents a considerable expansion since 1950-51 when there were only 5 schools with an enrollment of 1,640. Secondary schooling is also divided into two three-year cycles, the first leading to the *Diplôme d'études secondaires du premier cycle* and the second to the *Baccalauréat,* which is given in two parts. Until recently only one secondary school—the Lycée Descartes (formerly Lycée Sisowath)—provided the entire two cycles. In 1956-57, the secondary schools graduated 457 people from the first cycle and 70 from the second cycle.

Besides the Lycée Descartes in Pnompenh, the other secondary schools include the Teacher Training College and the Girls' College in Pnompenh, the Preah Sihanouk, Suong, and Chihè Colleges in Kompong Cham, Battambang College, and four new schools at Siemreap, Soairieng, Takeo, and Kampot.

The Teacher Training College, established in 1942, is the only separate normal school, although a teacher training section has operated at the Lycée Descartes since 1935. An American educational mission is undertaking to lay the groundwork for another normal school. In March 1958 a Center for Pedagogical Preparation was opened at Kompong-Kanthuot. Student-teachers are given instruction in both general and specialized teaching and in lesson planning. Practical exercises in teaching are followed by critical comment.

The seondary school curriculum is similar to that found in France, and the *Baccalauréat* is said to be the equivalent of the French *Baccalauréat.* Teaching is in French, and most of the staff are French, owing to the lack of qualified Cambodians. In 1956-57 out of a total secondary school staff of 183 only 2 were Cambodians.

Technical schooling has not been very popular in Cambodia but its popularity is increasing. Only 242 students were enrolled in such schools in 1952, while 633 were enrolled in 1957. Completion of the second primary cycle is a prerequisite to technical schooling, and possibly those who achieve this stage feel that greater opportunities lie in continued liberal arts study rather than in technical fields. There are five technical schools of which the Pnompenh

Technical College is the largest. Others include an apprenticeship school for tailors and shoemakers, workshop schools which offer a two-year course preparatory to entrance into the Technical College, a school of Cambodian arts, and a Practical School for Industry.

Higher Education

The National Institute of Legal, Political, and Economic Studies, which trains civil servants, is the only higher education establishment in Cambodia. Its students, numbering about 250, are selected by competitive examination. Classes are held in the evening. The diploma, awarded after two years' work, is the equivalent of the university law *Baccalauréat* of the law faculties in the French Union.

Other facilities for higher education are provided through government assistance for overseas study. A certain number of government scholarships are available and recently thirty Cambodian students have been assisted in this regard by cooperation between the Cambodian and United States governments. Formerly Cambodian students went primarily to Paris but more of them are now going to the United States, Canada, Communist China, and the USSR for specialized training. Delegations of Khmer educators left Cambodia in May 1958 for study in the United States, Canada, and the USSR.

Specialized Schools

Specialized schools outside the system controlled by the Ministry of Education include the Public Health Officers' School; the National Schools of Agriculture and Stockbreeding and of Forestry; the School of Public Works; and the Royal Medical School. A National School of Commerce has also been proposed. The newly organized National Institute of Khmer Civilization emphasizes the study of literature in Pali and Sanskrit. The School of Instruction in Buddhist Precepts was recently opened in the capital. Some three hundred Pali schools, located in pagodas, are open to bonzes. The Higher School of Pali, established in Pnompenh in 1914, gives instruction, in close association with the Buddhist Institute, in history, geography, mathematics, sciences, and classical (Pali, Sanskrit, and Cambodian) and modern languages (choice of English or French). (The Association of Friends of the Pali Schools encourages the development and revaluation of Pali and Cambodian.) The School of Fine Arts, founded in 1917, trains craftsmen in such arts as the traditional goldsmithery, lacquer work, wrought-iron work, weaving, leather work, sculpture, and painting; a woodcarving school at Pursat and a music school in Pnompenh are affiliated with it. The Prek Leap Agricultural School, which includes an experimental farm, trains agricultural agents. Other training institutions are the Training School for Public Works Surveyors and Draughtsmen and the Officers' Reserve College.

Public French Education

In addition to the public education administered by the Cambodian Ministry of National Education, a small French-administered public school system is provided through cultural agreements between the French and Cambodian governments. This establishment includes only one primary school with an enrollment of about 700 and one secondary school with an enrollment of about 480. The primary purpose of these schools is to permit children of French nationals in Cambodia to receive the same education that they would in France, but they are also open to Cambodian students.

Private Schools

Private schools must be licensed by the Ministry of Education. Instruction in the Cambodian language must be given for at least three hours a week. Of the 221 private schools in 1957, 174 were Chinese and 2 were French, with 1,778 pupils. As of 1958, no figures were available for the enrollment in the Chinese private schools, and the remaining 45 schools, with a total enrollment of 5,899, were not broken down as to ethnic composition. It is known, however, that in 1952, there were about 15,000 pupils attending the Chinese schools, and that there were 20 Vietnamese schools with 2,400 pupils and 9 Cambodian schools with 455 pupils.

Many of the Chinese schools in sizable Chinese communities are maintained on a trade-group basis. In rural areas, Chinese schools are understood to be in dialect groups (such as Cantonese, Hakka, Hainanese, Hokkienese, Tiechieu). Instruction is in Mandarin. The best Chinese schools are the Tiechieu and Cantonese in Pnompenh. The Chinese circumvented a French limitation of Chinese schools to the primary level by extension programs; and for higher education they go to Vietnam, China, France, or Hong Kong. Chinese Communist cells are said to be active, especially in the Hokkien schools, but their influence has not been great enough to allow Communist textbooks to be issued.

Teachers, Methods, and Standards

Cambodia has long had an acute teacher shortage. The shortage has resulted in low qualifying standards: only about 5 percent are "diploma teachers," those who have satisfactorily completed thirteen years of elementary and secondary schooling plus one year of normal school. Most of the others have earned only the primary school certificate.

In 1957 there were 7,627 primary school teachers, 183 secondary school teachers, and 38 technical school teachers. No recent data are available for the number of teachers in the National Institute of Legal, Political, and Economic Studies or the specialized schools. Of the total teaching staff 211 persons were French or of some other foreign nationality. The composition of the Cambodian teaching staff is shown in Table 15. Work shop, physical education, language and art teachers form part of the complement of the primary and secondary schools.

Teaching has not been attractive as a career because the pay has not been good and because the prestige of teachers is lower than that of civil servants. Today, however, higher pay and fewer civil service openings are causing more graduates to turn to teaching.

Bonzes, after a nine-month training course, are qualified to teach in the pagoda schools, but one of the problems here is the rapid turnover of personnel: for example, 514 bonze teachers left the religious life in 1945-46, and the exodus has not abated. New bonzes are trained every year; 818 were attending courses in 1951-52.

Cambodian teaching relies on memorization. Discipline is emphasized. Textbooks and other equipment are almost nonexistent. Teachers use a monthly professional journal for material.

According to a UNESCO report, within a limited scope and despite shortages of facilities and personnel, Cambodian teaching standards are on the whole good. A major problem is the lack of opportunity for a majority of children to receive more than three years of schooling. In 1958 only two-thirds of the children between the ages seven and twelve were enrolled in the primary schools.

The present system is in most respects based on the educational reform carried out by the French throughout Indochina in 1918. The consequent forty-year lag deprived Cambodia of later methods and organization which could have taken into account the full implications of its national independence and of the progress made in education in other parts of the world. Current proposals to tailor the system more closely to Cambodian needs, as opposed to French administrative needs, have not yet matured. Shortages of many essential things—money, trained personnel, buildings, and textbooks—are serious handicaps.

In recent years there has been a spate of secondary school construction in the provinces, but without adequate attention paid to the salaries of the teachers. In a meeting of the cabinet in September 1958, Sihanouk said that the administration could no longer support such building projects, they were becoming too much of a burden on the national budget. Secondary school teachers of adequate training are still in short supply and the government has considered ways of recruiting more foreign teachers to maintain the standards of the basic curriculum.

ART AND INTELLECTUAL EXPRESSION

DERIVED IN LARGE PART FROM INDIAN CULTURE, Cambodia's artistic and intellectual tradition has passed through several phases that parallel the main periods of Cambodian history (see chap. 2). During the early Fu-Nan period (from early in the first century A.D. to 535 A.D.), and especially during the later Angkor periods (802-1432), Cambodia reached peaks of intellectual and artistic achievement. Very little remains of the earlier period, but the later period is perpetuated by the great stone monuments of the Angkor region dating from the ninth to the thirteenth centuries.

The temples of Angkor are by no means the only remains of that great period. Angkor was the capital of an empire that included most of modern Laos and Thailand and part of Malaya. All over this area stone monuments, steles, temples, and statuary bear witness to the spread of Cambodian civilization. Unfortunately most of the literature of the time was written on materials easily destroyed by the tropical climate and insects. But from the inscriptions carved on the stone monuments the quality of what has been lost may be judged. There one can find—in poetry and prose—royal edicts, laws, records of victorious battles, hymns to the gods, records of donations to monasteries and hospitals.

These inscriptions, as well as the architectural remains, leave no doubt of Cambodia's cultural debt to India. But there are also many signs of both other foreign influences and true native inspiration. Neither in art nor literature were the Indian patterns slavishly copied. There is nothing in India quite comparable to the classic simplicity and unity of the Cambodian Angkor Wat or the Bayon. Most Indian temples are dominated by multitudes of sculptured forms of writhing human and animal figures, some of them fantastic. Similar figures may be found in the Cambodian structures, but they are limited to a decorative role, subordinate to the over-all structure. The Naga (a seven-headed snake), which is the mythical ancestress of the Khmer people and a constantly recurring theme, is frequently reduced to a functional, decorative position: it may, for example, serve as a banister on a bridge or a staircase.

Similarly, the literature surviving from the period displays a distinct Cambodian character, especially the poetry. The dominant literary themes are derived from the Hindu epics, but many others are adapted from Khmer history and mythology. Especially important is the cult of the devarajas, the god-kings, who were worshiped as reincarnations of Vishnu, Siva, Buddha, or other Indian deities.

When the Thai conquered a large part of the Cambodian empire and established themselves within their present national boundaries, they absorbed much of the culture of the conquered population. This Cambodian influence was further fortified when Thai raiders carried off tens of thousands of the best Cambodian scholars, artists, and craftsmen as slaves during the dark days of the recurrent Thai-Cambodian wars. In one devastating blow, for example, the Thai carried away almost the entire population of Angkor, the Cambodian capital. Cambodian culture never quite recovered from this setback. Even today Cambodians are inclined to look to the Thai for cultural and spiritual guidance.

The artistic and intellectual life of modern Cambodia, then, is overshadowed by the greatness of its past. That past glory seems irretrievably lost. The spirit that built the magnificent stone temples of Angkor no longer exists. Now there appears little or no desire to perpetuate genius imperishably in stone. Craftsmanship is limited largely to creating tourist items which endlessly repeat the ancient themes. The learning of the Brahmans, whose poetry and prose were inscribed on walls and steles all over ancient Kambuja, is all but forgotten. At the Cambodian court a bare half dozen descendants of the Brahmans still carry on by rote—without understanding, though with remarkable accuracy—some few practical applications of the ancient astronomy and mathematics in preparing the annual calendar of Cambodia.

The state of Cambodia's artistic life appears to be of little concern to educated laymen. Their attention, so far as it is focused on public matters, is now devoted chiefly to local political problems and the pressing problems of establishing proper relationships with the great powers and with Cambodia's neighbors.

There is evidence, however, of a new intellectual stirring. Since World War II a new sense of dedication seems to have taken hold of many young men and women, and a few have expressed their feelings in a literature dealing with contemporary social and political problems. But this spirit has not thus far spilled over into the visual arts, which continue uninspired and have only been saved from total extinction by the intervention of the French.

Intellectual Expression

Although a conservative and religious people, the Cambodians have a very practical bent. There is little tendency toward intellectual theorizing of the type that creates schools of thought. Cambodians spend little time questioning the whys and wherefores of the world about them. What is, is. The explanations for things may be found in the authority of the Theravada Buddhist texts and from the bonzes who are the true intellectual leaders of the country. These authorities are not questioned or challenged on most matters.

The Cambodian approach is nonintellectual rather than anti-intellectual. The Cambodian is not doctrinaire; he is convinced—and his conviction is sustained by a deeply satisfying religious faith.

Learning is not a thing desired for its own sake. Religious learning is sought because through it one learns the "way" or the "path" to nirvana—release from the endless and painful cycle of existence. In the pagoda schools, reading and writing until recently were taught chiefly for religious purposes. Worldly learning, the rational type taught in western schools, is now desired more and more because it opens the door to government employment, to prestige, and to the material comforts of life.

The Cambodian also seeks the emotionally satisfying intuitive learning that comes from meditation. This spiritual enlightenment is what he considers true learning—far more important than rational and worldly enlightenment. All male Cambodians are expected to spend time in the pagodas in contemplation. In the monasteries and libraries, many bonzes may be seen poring over old manuscripts and religious books, but the objective is religious merit rather than intellectual or worldly knowledge.

Cambodian intellectual life has been impeded by a lack of schools of higher learning. Under French rule there was no university or school beyond the *lycée* level, and such schools as existed were too few and small. It was, moreover, extremely difficult to obtain permission to go to France to study.

New intellectual currents unquestionably are stirring. The bonzes are beginning to study English and eagerly receive American publications printed in Cambodian. The political problems of the postwar years have evoked lively interest and discussion. Theories, however, are seldom discussed, but rather the purely practical aspects of things, or at least what appears practical to the Cambodians. Political doctrines excite little interest as such. This was evidenced in the framing of independent Cambodia's constitution: the framers were satisfied with merely adapting the French constitution.

Art

Music

The form of artistic expression most common in Cambodia is singing to traditional music improvised lyrics about the familiar, contemporary scene. This is done everywhere in the nation. The little boy tending the water buffalo, children playing together, young men and women courting, members of the wealthy and educated classes at social functions—all find pleasure and release in this pastime. While the words may be improvised, the number of tunes is surprisingly limited. About 1938 a scholar estimated that only three hundred melodies were used, some of which were importations from Thailand and Laos. Some of these songs undoubtedly are very old, carried orally from one generation to another since there is no Cambodian musical notation system.

An allied and perhaps equally common form of popular amusement is the playing of musical instruments. Both the making and playing of musical instruments may be considered traditional arts in Cambodia. Western visitors are surprised at the rapidity with which Cambodians learn to play unfamiliar instruments without formal instruction. Most Cambodians play some instrument, and many make their own, ornamenting them with elaborate inlay work. There is likely to be music at almost every social and festive gathering. One person at a social gathering may spontaneously improvise songs about the persons present, and if instruments are available others will accompany him; at least there will be rhythmic hand clapping and group singing of traditional refrains.

Although some western musical instruments—such as the saxophone, which ex-King Sihanouk himself plays—have been introduced, native Cambodian instruments are still highly popular. A full orchestra seen, for example, at the Royal Ballet, would consist of three xylophones, two with wooden bars and one with metal bars; a *komthom,* a large horseshoe on which there are sixteen flat gongs beaten with mallets by a player sitting in the center of the horseshoe; some one- and two-stringed violins; several wind instruments, including flutes, flageolets, and bagpipes; and a series of long drums of different sizes. The music played by these orchestras is sometimes described as "water-drop" music. The pantomime theater, seen in the villages, may use the saxophone during sad sequences.

Music accompanies all celebrations and festivals. Any procession will be preceded by tom-toms and violins. Amateur village orchestras are common, and families may perform impromptu private concerts after dinner.

Cambodian music is often not appreciated by those accustomed to western music, and western music usually is unpleasant to Cambodians, although Latin American music seems to be very popular. The Cambodian scale has five tones, compared with seven in the western scale. Orchestral music has no harmony, in the technical musical sense; the melodies are usually simple, composed of scarcely modulated notes and resembling the medieval church chants of Europe. The players do not use a score but follow the lead of one instrument, usually a xylophone, improvising much as they choose. The rhythm usually is two-beat, easily maintained by hand clapping when there is no instrument.

Singers use head and throat tones rather than the deeper chest tones. War songs are never heard—only songs of love or of the joy of living, and songs celebrating good cheer and drinking. Most of the oldest songs are love lyrics or laments.

Legends, Drama, and Dance

Also popular among most Cambodians is the recounting of old stories and legends, usually in poetry form. These are generally taken from such ancient Hindu epics as the Ramayana, from their Cambodian counterparts, or from the events of mythical and legendary Cambodian history.

The stories abound with princesses in distress, princes in disguise, miraculous creatures, giants, magic, and omens. They present humans living in a world they cannot control. The life they live now, whether good or bad, is the reward for their conduct in past reincarnations; what they do determines their life in future reincarnations. This theme of the fruits of karma (the principle of causality) runs through all Cambodian literature, ancient and modern, and is also frequently alluded to in ordinary conversation. Life is something to be accepted with placidity and resignation.

Ancient legends and stories provide themes for nearly all Cambodian dramatic presentations, of which there are three main forms. Ranked in order of cultural importance, these are the Royal Cambodian Ballet, the shadow plays, and the popular or folk theater. There is no tradition of realistic acting, although some students have presented a few adaptations of French plays—especially of Molière, who particularly appeals to the Cambodians' love of humorous irony and caricature. Traditional Cambodian drama (except in the shadow play) combines pantomime and singing and dancing. Roles are danced in pantomime with traditional steps, postures, and hand movements, while a chorus sings the story accompanied by an orchestra.

The "Chinese" shadow play (Nang Sbek), usually presented at pagodas during festivals, is a form of puppet show. Shadow pictures, made by holding a series of perforated panels between a light and a white screen, depict scenes of the drama, while the legend is recited from behind the screen. Some of these panels, traditionally made from leather, are complicated and often jewel-like. All designs are strictly traditional.

The Royal Cambodian Ballet maintained by the Court is not a truly popular entertainment. The dancers, wearing masks or white make-up and dressed in elaborate costumes, execute difficult but stylized steps, which are repeated in varying sequences for the different dramas. The repertoire of the Royal Ballet is limited to about thirty dramas in the Royal Library; no new ones have been written for many years.

Actually the Cambodian ballet is a Thai adaptation of the ballet of ancient Angkor, which died out around the fifteenth century and was revived about a century later in Cambodia as an importation. For centuries thereafter it was called the Siamese ballet. The dancers were mainly Thai, and the lyrics were sung in Thai; not until the twentieth century was the use of Cambodian revived. Today Cambodian ballet is an important tourist attraction, exciting apparently little interest among the Cambodians themselves except in palace circles.

More appreciated by Cambodians are the "folk dramas" performed by wandering troupes. These include farces and popularized versions of the classical ballet—making use of the national talent for improvising songs and for caricaturing persons in the contemporary scene, especially Chinese, Vietnamese, French, and other foreigners.

Outside the theater, dancers also are employed in certain ceremonies such as weddings. One rustic ceremonial dance, the Leng Trot, performed occasionally by small troupes in the Siemreap region, appears to be a survival of an ancient magic hunting rite. The two chief figures, the "hunters," are armed with imitation rifles, and the "prey" is represented by a man riding a sort of hobbyhorse with a stag's head on one end and a tail and bell at the other. While hunters and prey portray the hunt by various comic antics, a fourth figure executes dance steps resembling those of the Cambodian ballet. A chorus accompanies the dance, keeping the beat with long poles at the top of which are belled crosspieces. Whatever its original purpose, the Leng Trot is still danced as a magic rite to encourage the monsoon rains when they are late.

Popular dancing, which declined after the great days of Angkor, has been enjoying a revival in the form of a dance imported from Thailand: the Lamthom, danced both by couples and groups, combines features of western social dancing with the classical ballet. Couples dance together, simulating courtship, but do not touch. Footwork is less important than the graceful posturing with the hands in motions typical of the Cambodian ballet or Indian dancing. The Lamthom now is popular among all classes; it is the only form of "folk" dancing to be seen.

Recent Literature

Postwar Cambodian literature is only beginning to reflect the new currents and foreign influence. The new sense of dedication noted in some young Cambodians may be seen in a few new novels. Some writers still cling to ancient legendary plots or use an ancient historical setting, while introducing new social messages. Rim Kin in his *Kla Han*, for example, used ancient Angkor for his setting, but he attempts to show that wealth and prestige may be gained by one's efforts and conduct in this life and need not be dependent only upon one's conduct in past reincarnations. One should, he argues, achieve merit not only for a reward in a future life, but in this life as well.

Other novelists with a social message use the contemporary scene to attack contemporary problems. The tendency of too many young Cambodians to seek employment in the government is dealt with in two recent novels: the hero of *Vanna*, by Chay Choun, goes into the army as the best way to serve his country; the heroine of *La Destinée de Mademoiselle NaKri,* by Miss Souy Hyeng, urges her fiancé to go into business to help save the country from the economic control of the Chinese and the Vietnamese.

Such novels are the early outpouring of a force likely to become stronger in the near future—yet they do not receive wide attention in Cambodia. Very few books are published, and periodicals are not plentiful. Cambodians in general read little and buy even less since each book bought may be read by ten different people. A normal edition of a book is 500 copies, while 3,000 indicates a best seller. The opportunity for the young writer to obtain an audience is therefore highly limited. Outside of journalists there are scarcely any professional writers in the country.

Yet, while there are few opportunities for publication, there are unique opportunities for unfettered production by the artist. There are no dominating schools of thought or of writing one must follow; there are no literary critics or journals; and Cambodians need write only for Cambodians, since their language is read by few foreigners and there is no fear of foreign criticism.

Visual Arts

The visual arts reveal the essential conservatism of the Cambodians. Little that is spontaneous or extemporaneous is to be seen. Ancient themes are preferred, and they are constantly and unimaginatively repeated. There rarely is any effort to improve or adapt.

Probably the nearest approach to an emotionally charged art is found in the pagodas. While pagoda art is itself very limited, it is practically the only form of visual art receiving any amount of popular attention.

After the French brought peace and prosperity in the last half of the nineteenth century, the Cambodians replaced their decaying pagodas with new wooden structures produced in the old style with much loving care. The pediments were lavishly painted or carved with traditional motifs drawn from legends and epic poems, while the points of the eaves swooped upward in graceful Naga tails. The results were true works of art that have been greatly admired by western observers. In recent decades, as these structures succumbed to humidity and insects, they frequently have been replaced with concrete structures, more lasting and easier to build. Instead of individual carvings that lend a special character to each pagoda, concrete molds are used repeatedly, creating a uniform pagoda decoration. Designs, which in wood could be deeply and intricately carved, had to be smooth, shallow, and round to conform to the exigencies of the concrete molds. Formerly the villagers would donate labor and use free materials from the forests, saving money to pay for decorating the finished structure; today all the money may go for the basic structure, leaving little for decoration.

Crafts

In the nineteenth century and earlier, many Cambodian artisans were employed to provide artistic luxuries for the wealthy classes and the numerous royalty. Silver and gold work was of high quality, especially in making jewelry and the little boxes which hold the ingredients for betel-chewing, at that time an important social ritual among all classes. In the twentieth century, however, the making of both jewelry and the little boxes has languished, for the wealthy classes have abandoned the chewing of betel and have turned to European-type luxury manufactures. By 1917 Cambodian craftsmanship was fast dying, and some special crafts, such as the making of niello ware, were already forgotten. Many craftsmen turned to rice farming to win a livelihood. A survey showed that only 132 artisans were left in all Cambodia, and that most of them were no longer practicing their crafts.

Albert Sarraut, the French governor-general, with the approval of King Sisowath, attempted a revival of crafts. Craftsmen were assembled in Pnompenh in a school of fine arts operated in conjunction with a museum. They were employed as masters to train young craftsmen under the traditional apprenticeship system. The French avoided interfering, hoping to exclude European influence and prevent frustration of Cambodian initiative.

A new generation of Cambodian craftsmen has been trained, but the results are generally uninspiring. Ancient themes are meticulously repeated for appeal to the tourist trade. Cambodians who can afford the products show only polite interest and provide little patronage. While some of the craftsmen put small individual touches to their designs, more often standard designs by others are used. The craftsmen themselves enjoy little prestige, and rarely would a member of an educated or prosperous family think of engaging in any such work himself, for it would be considered degrading.

The principal crafts now practiced are the working of silver and gold, the making of jewelry, and the sculpture of ebony, colored hardwood, and stone. The silver and gold work consists largely of cigarette boxes, sugar and cream sets, and similar tourist-trade items, with designs based on the figures and floral patterns seen on the stone carvings of Angkor. The wood sculpture, similarly based on ancient models, consists of sculptured heads and Buddhas. Probably the best jewelry is that made by local Chinese craftsmen, but a few Cambodians are also skilled in this craft. Stone sculpture and ivory carving are local household industries in some parts of Cambodia, catering especially to local demands for Buddhas. There is also some tortoise-shell work, but it is done chiefly by Vietnamese.

Household implements are practical and unadorned and often are either of Chinese manufacture or formed after Chinese patterns. Pottery making, a local Cambodian industry in several areas, shows little sign of artistic orientation, although the bowls and pots are attractive in form. When a nicer dish is desired for use at the table, a decorated Chinese bowl is usually purchased. If wall decorations are desired in the more properous homes, Vietnamese lacquered pictures or European prints may be used.

Some common objects, however, are often decorated—among them the oxcart, the pirogue (dugout canoe), and the rice-harvesting knife—and made according to designs pictured on the bas-reliefs of the ancient temples. These objects reflect pride in workmanship, but the amount of actual carving and decoration is usually scanty. Here, too, as in nearly all forms of Cambodian art, designs are traditional. Dragons and Nagas' heads are the most common themes, with perhaps some floral patterns.

One of the few folk arts in which all Cambodians take special pride is the making of *sampots*, the sarong-like national costume. *Sampot* weaving is a widely scattered local industry. At court different colors are worn for different days of the week. The rectangular pieces of material that are used for the *sampot* may be given any one of an infinite number of designs. For the most common workaday use, the Cambodians use cheap materials, imported usually from Japan, but for any sort of special occasion, they prefer native hand-woven materials.

Each Cambodian *sampot* is woven separately by hand. Frequently, native vegetable dyes, which are available only in certain months, are especially mixed for each *sampot,* so that no two garments are quite the same. The simplest are made in linear or in plaid patterns. One popular variety uses heavy silk threads of one color for the woof and another color for the warp to produce a shimmering effect in solid colors. The most complicated and original *sampot* is the *hol,* in which the design is produced by pre-dying the threads with different colors along their length, a process requiring three months.

Less complicated but more lavish are the *sampots* woven with gold or silver thread. Sometimes the metallic thread is used to produce only shimmering strips, but royal *sampots* or those of the ballet dancers have silver throughout the woof.

The Pace of Change

Although France ruled Cambodia for some ninety years, French culture made a remarkably small impact upon the intellectual life of Cambodia. Sheltered by the deep convictions of their religion and by their conservatism, Cambodians remained essentially Cambodian. There was no great intellectual life at the time the French came; there is none today. Cambodian leaders have received a French education, but it has been tempered by their training in the pagoda.

In the homes of both the educated and the uneducated, and in the government offices of Cambodia today, the astrologer and the bonze (who may sometimes be the same person) play an important part in guiding the policies of Cambodia and the private lives of Cambodians. King and peasant heed their warnings and consult them on every important decision. Few care to make decisions unless the omens are right. Since all things are predestined by the events of past life, one need only read the signs to know what is to happen in the present. If a discrepancy occurs between the prediction and the actual event, the error is in the failure of the astrologer, not in the system. One must seek the best possible astrologer or bonze.

Modern Cambodian intellectual life—a curious mixture of the old and the new—is passing through a transitional period. Cambodia has formally adopted a modern democratic government and is in the process of adopting a modern educational system. These innovations, together with increased contacts with the outside world, have lessened the dominance of old ideas. With independence achieved, new influences are at work and the pace of cultural change is bound to be much more rapid. Cambodia is unlikely to remain a museum piece.

Under French colonial control, resistance to western culture was often a matter of national pride. Today that resistance is no longer fashionable. Cambodians now feel freer to admit western ideas and techniques, although they still have some suspicion that anyone bringing these gifts might have ulterior motives. French culture is likely to permeate Cambodia more successfully than it did when France ruled the country, but it will be tempered by cultural influences from the United States and other lands.

VALUES AND PATTERNS
OF LIVING

THE VALUES AND PATTERNS DISCUSSED HERE are those of the Cambodians proper—between 85 and 90 percent of the total population; no attempt is made to describe the values of the foreign elements or of the native tribes.

The value system of the Cambodians derives from several different cultural traditions—Khmer, Indian, and French—and shows the influence of at least two distinct formal religious doctrines—Brahmanism and Theravada Buddhism. It is therefore not a homogeneous, unicultural system. The entire complex of values is not shared equally by all segments of the population, some tend to be more influenced by certain elements than others.

Influences

One set of values derives from a combination of ancient Khmer culture with Indian Hinduism, oriented toward a system of fixed classes with ascribed status and important rank distinctions. Each person is supposed to have a definite place in the social order and a clearly prescribed role to go with it. There is also a strong identification of the people with their local pagodas, with their nation, and with a divine sovereign who symbolizes the unity of people, land, religion, and government. This tradition still affects all parts of the society to some extent. There are formal patterns of respect and deference between people of superior and inferior rank. Status consciousness, supported by ancient Hindu rituals at birth, marriage, and death, is most to be found among the lay nobility and upper-class commoners in the urban areas, but the rural peasantry are also affected by it and pay proper respect to officials.

A second set of values derives from Theravada Buddhism. The basic concepts here are the unity of all life and the ultimate spiritual perfectibility and equality of all mankind. Specific doctrines include acceptance of the secular social order, religious detachment from worldly affairs, the individual's responsibility for his own status in life, and the possibility of altering one's status through a combination of individual merit and reincarnation. The achievement of merit is possible through service to community, pagoda, and nation, and by adhering to various prescriptions for personal conduct. Among the latter, emphasis is on the avoidance of suffering and of causing suffering, on self-discipline and improvement, humility, passivity, temperance, nonaccumulation of wealth, harmonious relations with others. Informal observation of these principles is considered highly meritorious and commands a certain prestige. The greatest value, however, is attached to service in a pagoda as a bonze, whether for a temporary or permanent term. It is a primary honor for parents when a son takes these vows and dons the garb of a bonze.

Where ancient Khmer-Hindu tradition places a high value on fixed status and rank consciousness, the Buddhist tradition places a high value on individual achievement and, in principle, the ultimate equality of all men. The Buddhist tradition is focused in the permanent religious institution but, since nearly all Cambodian men, of whatever station, serve terms as bonzes, it also has strongly influenced all other aspects of Cambodian society. The strongest popular focus of the tradition is probably in the rural areas among the peasantry, for whom the doctrines serve as a rationale for their lower status in the total rank and class system of the society.

A third set of values derives from the cultural tradition of the Catholic French middle class; it has penetrated Cambodian society through government and education. This tradition places a high value on the individual's ability to raise his status in life by the direct and practical means of secular education and economic advancement. It stresses active rather than passive aspects of achievement and the accumulation of material wealth as a means of achieving both personal and social ends.

This tradition is most influential among Cambodia's civil servants and upper classes, who have been directly exposed to French education and who served in the previous French administration of Cambodia. Little of it has penetrated to the rural areas. Today the widest divergence in values and general outlook is between the secular-minded, French-educated governing classes of the urban centers and the more religious-minded, conservative peasantry. This gap is to some extent bridged by the widely diffused Buddhist doctrines and ethics, which serve as a common reference point for all ranks and classes and permit the existing social order to be consistently rationalized from any politics.

Social Relationships

Cambodians prefer to have their social relationships clearly defined so that each person involved has a distinct status and a prescribed role to play. There is security in thus knowing precisely where an individual stands, what is expected of him and others, what he and others can and cannot do. The rules of etiquette between people of different status and rank are carefully spelled out, and every status and rank has its appropriate and circumscribed roles for every situation. Once the situation has been recognized and the appropriate formal courtesies exchanged. Cambodians are willing to shift to a more informal kind of interchange, but the basic definition of the situation and the limits of behavior must still be adhered to. The Cambodian cannot comfortably develop his social relationships from an initially informal, personal basis, defining the situation and the roles as he goes along.

Conversely, if a Cambodian wants to assume a role which his current status does not permit him in particular situations, he cannot simply extend his role informally, as Americans for instance do. He must first formally shift his status, then assume the appropriate role. This shift must be clear and abrupt—"black or white"—and must be publicly announced. When Sihanouk, for example, felt that his status as king did not permit him to play the kind of role he wanted in Cambodian politics, he abruptly switched to another status—prime minister—that allowed him more latitude in dealing directly with the people. Cambodians do not view such expedient changes in status as evidence of irresponsibility, as some westerners viewed the abdication of King Edward VIII. Shifting of governmental status or political affiliation requires finality and abruptness, but no rationalization in terms of principles.

Once a person has made such a shift, he does not wish to be held to the obligations and responsibilities of his former roles or to be considered liable for the policies or actions which he then advocated. There are many examples of this in Cambodian life. For example, when a man becomes a bonze he severs his connections with his family and his future relationship with his parents is that of any younger person to older people rather than that of parent and child. In political life, rebel leaders have surrendered and formally renounced their previous role, thus becoming eligible for high posts in the government. A criminal, once he has served his prison term, may reassume his status as a free citizen without prejudice.

The Cambodian's greatest anxiety is that he will be unable to perceive the nature of the situation in which he is involved at the moment, and hence not know how to act or what to expect of others. He is therefore particularly sensitive to cues which will tell him what kind of a situation he is in and what he must and must not do. If other people do not act quite the way he expects them to, he is immediately on his guard, anxious to understand what is happening. If he feels that the situation is different from what he had thought, he begins to probe to determine what the actual situation is so that he can adjust his role accordingly. He does this cautiously because he is afraid of causing embarrassment to himself and others; he does not want to give the impression that he is trying to overassert himself or change the situation to suit himself.

A Cambodian to whom an assignment has been given will ask very detailed questions; usually he is gifted at finding a "blind spot" in the explanation given him. He will not execute an order until he is sure that he knows precisely what he is to do.

Once a situation has been clearly defined and is recognized, the Cambodian is anxious lest he himself step out of line or provoke someone else to do so. He is worried about incompatible personalities, especially in family situations, because they may cause tempers to flare and the proper limits of behavior to be exceeded. For the same reason he is suspicious of frivolity and disturbed when children begin asserting a maturity beyond their years. In his daily social life he is particularly careful to show proper respect and courtesy, lest he cause others to be resentful. When talking with superiors he is affable but discreet.

If Cambodians are unable to understand the nature of a situation or are placed in two conflicting situations at the same time, their tendency is to withdraw completely. One of the ways in which a Cambodian handles irresolvable family situations, for example, is to retreat to the pagoda as a bonze. If he does not understand political situations, he becomes passive, uncooperative, unreachable.

If the Cambodian feels that a situation is clear but that someone is stepping out of line, he will "freeze" as a warning that the person has gone too far. If someone above him exceeds proper authority he may simply fail to carry out the order. When abuses of authority cannot be repelled in this way he may show a more active resentment by complaining. Popular grievances are brought to official attention in various ways: bonzes act as channels for complaints that the peasant is unable to express directly; the king traditionally holds regular audiences where complaints may be registered.

In dealing with a Cambodian, therefore, it is essential to explain a new situation clearly to him, then to make sure that he knows precisely what is expected of him and that there is common agreement as to the proper limits of behavior and authority. Otherwise he may suddenly become suspicious and uncooperative.

An interesting example of this type of behavior was reported by an American visitor who had told his Cambodian driver to have his car repaired. When the chauffeur failed to do so, the American reprimanded him. In a day or two the chauffeur resigned for a stated reason that was obviously false. He took another job in the same city and continued to act in a friendly manner toward the American whenever he met him. The American learned later that he should have given the chauffeur a written and signed order to be handed to the garage mechanic. The chauffeur felt that he himself could not order the mechanic to do the work, but at the same time that he could not refuse to obey the American. With no way to reconcile these conflicting demands, he quit. Telling the "white lie" was his means of preventing embarrassment for the American, for it was the American who had not realized where the lines were drawn.

A principal role of any leader in Cambodian society is to explain. In government and politics during the fast moving postwar years many new situations arose in which the people could not perceive their proper role. In such cases, the leader is expected to deal with the people in an informal, personal manner, patiently instructing and answering all questions. He is not seeking personal support in the sense that American political candidates seek to justify their policies or affirm their personal integrity. He is trying, rather, to re-establish on a new basis the formal lines of authority and responsibility between the government and the governed, so that the people will cooperate. If the leader fails to explain the new situation adequately he faces the possibility that they will simply withdraw from it completely to avoid doing something improper.

The follower is expected to respond by exerting himself to

understand clearly the nature and limits of the new situation and
the prescription for his role in it. For this reason he questions,
probes, and searches to make sure that he knows all possible ramifications and implications of what is being explained to him. Cambodians are famous for looking for hidden meanings in speeches;
the intent is not to criticize or trip up the speaker—which would
be extremely embarrassing to both parties—but rather to make sure
that all is fully understood.

It has been said that Cambodians never really negotiate, that
they enter into parleys with goals they do not intend to modify or
with basic principles they do not intend to relinquish (see chap. 11).
Actually Cambodians do not have the western concept of "negotiation," on which the above objections are based.

If there are persistent disagreements between Cambodians
themselves, it is because each of the parties involved feels that the
other does not clearly understand the situation. Resolution can come
only through mutual probing and explanation that enables both
parties to reach a common definition of the situation. If this is impossible, both sides react by withdrawing, leaving the matter unresolved but with the hope that time and circumstances will remove
the issue altogether or that one side will ultimately see the light.
Some disagreements between Cambodians are known to have lasted
for thirty years, with no recourse to threat or coercion or political
maneuver.

Cambodians, then, are not inclined to argue about principles—
an agreement on principles is initially assumed—or to seek a compromise solution. Action can only take place after the total situation
has been defined and mutually agreed upon. Intermediaries are
sometimes called in, but they are supposed only to give advice and
clarification and to help maintain the essential surface smoothness
of the negotiation rather than to press for a solution at all costs.

Independence and Individuality

Cambodians place high value on personal independence, but do
not conceive of it quite as Americans do. To a Cambodian, independence connotes freedom from any obligation or commitment
beyond the prescribed role of his immediate status and the particular situations he is in. The individual is expected to fulfill the
requirements of his present status or statuses in particular situations
as they come along, but the ability and freedom to shift status, with-

in certain limits, at will and to make a clean break with the past is highly prized.

At the same time, Cambodians rarely confuse their formal roles in society with their informal, personal roles. When they are in situations which demand that they play a formal role they respond properly, but when such situations end they can shift immediately to personal roles. The only requirement is that the individual make it absolutely clear when he is acting a formal role and when he is acting as an individual; he must not inject personal overtones into formal situations.

With these two aspects kept distinct, there is a high tolerance for variations in personal behavior, subject only to the admonitions of the Buddhist code of personal ethics. Sihanouk, for example, is quite aware of the kind of role he can and cannot fill as king or prime minister. But his personal life is completely detached from this and he may enjoy his own forms of relaxation and pleasure without fear of appearing undecorous as a public official. This may seem peculiar to Americans, who feel that a public official should lead an unimpeachable private life, but it does not seem peculiar to Cambodians. If a Cambodian official is censured for his private life, it is because he fails to observe the required behavior in respect to private life situations and not because he might disgrace the particular public office which he holds. Public and private roles are judged on different bases.

Personal Conduct

Cambodians feel that the individual should be continually attuned to the Buddhist code of personal conduct. A high value is placed on proper standards of sexual behavior and on premarital chastity and marital fidelity. Nonviolence is another important precept, and crimes of violence such as assault, murder, and rape actually are rare in Cambodia. Temperance, diligence, thrift, and self-discipline are stressed. Children are taught to despise lying as being incompatible with their natural pride and Buddhist precepts, but "social lying" as a means to avoid embarrassment to oneself or to others is considered a different matter. Adults will bear false witness only when completely terrorized, and even hardened criminals will seldom persist in a lie if called on to take an oath involving their eternal life and their family before the holy images of the pagoda.

The more a Cambodian can pattern his conduct along these

ethical lines, the greater will be his achievement of religious merit and the better will be his life in his next incarnation. He also hopes that his good conduct and his giving of service and material support to the pagoda will be publicly noticed and approved and that he will gain increasing respect from his fellows in this life—perhaps with positive recognition in terms of a higher post in the religious hierarchy, a better job in government, or a more prominent position in village affairs.

In the past Cambodians have felt little compulsion to "succeed" in a material sense or to gain more power as individuals. Acquisitiveness is not a dominant characteristic; adequacy is the objective in life. If a rice farmer, for instance, finds he has more than enough money for himself and his family, he gives the surplus to the pagoda.

At present, however, some Cambodians are beginning to examine their values in the light of the modern world. The place of wealth in their value system is one of the basic concepts they are pondering. The accumulation of wealth has not been considered as a way to win merit or as a source of economic or political power. Wealth has existed outside the "respect pattern" of Cambodian life, but today it is attaining a value in terms of the promotion of the national interest. Sihanouk recently equated money and independence thus: "Without financial independence (independence from foreigners both externally and internally) there is no political independence." The national interest is of great importance in the Cambodian scale of values, and to amass wealth may become patriotic and religiously acceptable.

The Rhythm of Life

Cambodia is a predominantly agricultural country and, as in most agricultural areas of the world, sowing time and harvesting time are highly important in the life cycle. Festivities and marriages can be postponed, but no one can afford to court disaster by sowing his rice late or by transplanting the tender shoots when the soil already has hardened, or by bringing in the harvest late, not leaving enough time before the approaching rainy season for the crop to dry sufficiently to keep it from mildewing in storage.

These iron laws affect other activities. Idle farm labor becomes available for other tasks, such as building roads, after the harvest is in. The Cambodian farmer will use the fall season to repair his house, or to build a boat which he may sell to a Chinese to supplement his cash income, or to tap some wild resin trees. He may decide to go into the city to work a while or to visit relatives; he has disposed of his crop, made payments on his debts, and has some spare cash on hand (or will borrow some) to spend on the Water Festival. His mind is at ease.

Fall, therefore, is the period of big doings in Cambodia. It is the time the Cambodian government generally chooses for major political events such as elections. The average Cambodian, unworried by major material problems, is now receptive to all matters that may provide a break in the routine of his everyday life.

The formal Cambodian calendar is a combination lunar-and-solar calendar, that is, the months are based upon the movement of the moon, but the yearly cycle of months is corrected so as to bring them into accord with the movement of the sun.

The lunar months are also the basic units for the Cambodian religious calendar. There are alternately months with 29 and 30 days; the former are known as "female" (*ko bei*) months, the latter as "male" (*ko buon*). The "sex" of the months is of great importance in Cambodian life; marriages cannot be celebrated during the "male" months.

Several major religious landmarks serve as departure points for the Cambodian calendar. The one currently used the most is 543 B.C., the year in which Buddha entered nirvana. According to the calculations of the Buddhist clergy, the exact date of the new year changes every year, but the civil calendar begins on either the 12th or 13th of April.

A "Little Era," which follows the solar calendar, begins each year on the 12th or 13th of April but takes 638 A.D. as its point of departure. A "Great Era," used in the inscriptions on the monuments at Angkor Wat, began in 78 A.D. The significance of these base years is not clearly understood.

The Cambodians also use a twelve-year-cycle calendar of Chinese origin, which is also used in neighboring Vietnam. It carries the names of animals, followed by a numeral from 0 to 9. Each year is designated by a combination of the name of the proper animal of the year and of the proper numeral, as shown in Table 16. It takes sixty years for all number and animal combinations to repeat themselves.

The more westernized Cambodians and the Cambodian government in its official transactions use the western calendar. Only rarely will one find the Buddhist day, month, and year indicated alongside the western identifications in an official government communication.

The months are divided into two fortnights: one from the new to the full moon (*khnot*), the other from the full moon to the end of the lunar cycle (*ronoc*). The days are numbered from one to fifteen (or fourteen) with the addition of the word *kot* ("who grows") for the first fortnight, and the term *noc* ("who destroys himself") for the fortnight of the declining moon.

The eighth and the fifteenth days of the first fortnight and the eighth and the last day of the second fortnight are holidays (*thngai sel*). During the holidays of the first fortnight the faithful go to the pagodas where Buddhist texts are explained to them by the bonzes. During the other two holidays the bonzes must publicly confess their shortcomings; the laity engage in merrymaking.

Weekdays in Cambodia correspond exactly to our own, with the same stars and planets representing the days of the week. For each day a special color is supposed to be predominant, but this custom is tending to disappear. The colors and planets of the Cambodian week are as follows:

Cambodian Name of Day	Planet	Color	Western Equivalent
Thngai atit	Sun	red	Sunday
Thngai can	Moon	orange	Monday
Thngai angkar	Mars	violet	Tuesday
Thngai put	Mercury	green	Wednesday
Thngai prahos	Jupiter	cloud-grey	Thursday
Thngai sok	Venus	blue	Friday
Thngai sau	Saturn	black	Saturday

Certain days of the week are considered to have special significance. For example, some villagers will refuse to lend money on Monday but will gladly make purchases on that day because "everything that shall be brought into the house shall prosper." Saturday is considered a "bad" day throughout most of Cambodia because it is liked by demons and spirits; it is, however, a "good" day to appeal to these inhabitants of the spirit world.

Before one engages in operations of any type in a particular area of Cambodia it is important to know whether the day chosen is considered propitious; any mishap connected even remotely with the operation will be attributed to the fact that it was undertaken on an inauspicious day.

An American economic aid specialist who had come to Cambodia in the middle of April for a one-month inspection tour of the country found himself faced successively with: the celebrations of the Cambodian New Year (three days around April 2); the European-style weekend—Saturday afternoons and Sundays during which no one works; the Cambodian monthly holidays (see Plate, Yearly Cycle of Cambodian Holidays); Constitution Day celebrations (May 5-6); the Plowing of the Holy Furrow (about May 10); Saint Joan of Arc (a holiday by courtesy to the French and to Cambodia's Catholics, on May 12); and the Entering of Buddha into Nirvana (May 14). The American specialist had to return home, his mission unaccomplished, muttering to himself "those Cambodians never work."

The impression that Cambodians seek to evade their work obligations through the celebration of many holidays is easy to gain. However, the Cambodian calendar does include several months of the year when there are few holidays outside each week's day of rest. Besides the official holidays, there are many family events the Cambodian celebrates, following a tradition that has not altered over many centuries. Celebrations in proper style of marriages, births, and deaths may often last as long as six days, and a Cambodian will travel long distances to attend such family events.

Thus the average work year of a Cambodian would include, in addition to the approximately seventy Sundays and regular Buddhist rest days, fifty to sixty religious or other holidays. In actual practice, western organizations operating in Cambodia consider a 220-day work year a good average for a Cambodian worker.

Holidays of all sorts are treasured by the Cambodians. With their keen sense for theatrics they insist that celebrations must be well-staged affairs, with fireworks, costumes, floats, and parades. Men in public office are often judged according to their performance in organizing such exhibitions. Sihanouk's popularity is in some part due to his personal sense of the dramatic; he introduced into Cambodian politics the sort of "sideshow" elements that are familiar to Americans during a political campaign. Many Cambodians will travel hundreds of miles, particularly during the idle, dry months, to see a well-staged parade or ceremony.

These same characteristics make Cambodians great fans of spectator sports. Soccer, though a French import, has become a national sport, and there are soccer fields near most schools even in the rural areas. Schools also usually have outdoor basketball courts. Bicycle races are another popular western import, and European-style automobile races under the auspices of the Royal Cambodian Automobile Club, in which French, Chinese, and Cambodians

YEARLY CYCLE OF CAMBODIAN HOLIDAYS

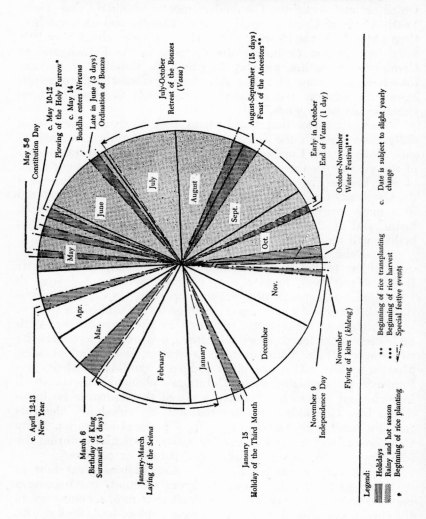

May 5-6 Constitution Day

c. May 10-12 Plowing of the Holy Furrow*

c. May 14 Buddha enters Nirvana

Late in June (3 days) Ordination of Bonzes

July-October Retreat of the Bonzes (Vassa)

August-September (15 days) Feast of the Ancestors**

Early in October End of Vassa (1 day)

October-November Water Festival***

November Flying of kites (khleng)

November 9 Independence Day

January 15 Holiday of the Third Month

December

February

January

Mar.

Apr.

May

June

July

August

Sept.

Oct.

Nov.

January-March Laying of the Seima

March 6 Birthday of King Suramarit (5 days)

c. April 12-13 New Year

c. Date is subject to slight yearly change

Legend:

Holidays

Rainy and hot season

Beginning of rice planting

* Beginning of rice transplanting

** Beginning of rice harvest

*** Special festive events

participate, have been a regular feature of postwar social life in Pnompenh.

Boat races, with longboats (hewn out of a single tree trunk) that often are manned by a crew of more than forty, are an old tradition throughout Cambodia and the main feature of the Water Festival at Pnompenh. The best crews of the country vie for the honor of showing their prowess in front of the king and his court, who watch the proceedings from a floating reviewing stand. Hundreds of thousands of Cambodians from all over the country come to Pnompenh for this spectacle.

Kite flying is a pastime that enjoys popularity; the kites are artistically made, often representing birds and dragons. Other recreations include motion pictures, when available, and dances held in the communal hall of the village or at the pagoda.

NATIONAL ATTITUDES

The Land and the Nation

DURING THE RECENT WAR, danger from Vietminh bands caused the Cambodian government to resettle some of its citizens. But Cambodians, very much attached to the particular pagodas they attend, were reluctant to leave their lands. Rather than take arbitrary action, the government sought to persuade them. Significantly, the Minister of Cults, who was sent to the villages, first spoke with the religious leaders; only when he succeeded in convincing the bonzes of the seriousness of the military situation did the people agree to leave.

A Cambodian believes that permanent separation from his homeland may affect his reincarnation; he may never find his way back to his country. Banishment is a worse fate than death; so the Constitution prohibits exile. The king, the religion, and the people are bound together with the land—thus they form the nation.

The common past also is a binding cord. Educated Cambodians are proud of the glorious episodes of their history, ashamed of the present backward conditions, and alert to what they feel is a challenge to lead their country into adjustment with modern ways and western techniques of living. This is, in their view, a question of survival. Either they solve their economic, social, and political problems, or Cambodia will be swallowed up by other nations. Some of the younger intellectuals, educated in France or the United States, are deeply dissatisfied with the existing system and constitute a source of latent rebellion.

The peasant sees the nation and his religion personified in his king, before whom he bows deeply or prostrates himself. Royal commands are faithfully and unquestioningly followed provided they fall within the area of the king's recognized authority, and provided that the people believe that their king is dedicated to the welfare of the nation.

The Royal Palace is an extremely important symbol in Cambodia, signifying the center of the world and the pivot of the universe in religious terms. The city of Pnompenh is considered a microcosm, and the king makes a "cosmic procession" at his coronation by going in turn toward the "four cardinal points," wearing the costume and crown of each particular point as he does so.

The seven-storied parasol over his throne also symbolizes the power of the king, and represents the stages of the world around the central pivot. According to Cambodian legend, the parasol is inhabited by a powerful spirit who counsels the king wisely. The throne room of the palace, where the parasol and other royal appurtenances are kept, is called the "room where the deva counsels." The headgear of the king includes a wide-brimmed hat, supposedly recalling the legend of the Old Man and the Sweet Cucumbers—the gardener who became king.

A most important symbol is the Sacred Sword, which is revered as the safeguard of the kingdom. It is cleaned regularly, since a spot of rust on it would presage grave consequences. The Sacred Sword was formerly handed the king at his coronation, with the ancient Indian phrasing, "Take, for thou art the Lightning of Indra" (in Hindu legend Indra was the great national god of the Indo-Aryans).

Modern national symbols include the flag and an anthem. Specifications for the Cambodian flag were set forth in a royal decree in 1948. Its width is equal to two-thirds of its length, and it is made up of a large middle horizontal band of red with narrower bands of blue at top and bottom, a white image of Angkor Wat being imposed on the red band. The national anthem is titled *Nokareach* (a combination from two words that mean "country" and "reign").

May Heaven protect our King
And give him happiness and glory;
May he reign over our hearts and our destinies.
He who—heir to the builder Monarchs—
Governs the proud and old Kingdom.

The temples sleep in the forest
Recalling the grandeur of the Moha Nokar.
The Khmer race is as eternal as the rocks.
Let us have confidence in the faith of Kampuchea
The Empire which defies the years.

Songs rise in the pagodas
To the glory of the holy Buddhist faith.
Let us be faithful to the creed of our ancestors
So that Heaven may reward us
Of the old Khmer country of the Moha Nokar.

For the most part, the religious leaders of Cambodia, the bonzes, see their country as the repository of Buddhist values that must be protected and preserved. They also are foremost in defending Cambodian traditions and customs. French efforts to romanize the Khmer script, for example, failed because of the opposition of the bonzes. Change, however, increasingly challenges the position of the bonzes. They are attempting to accommodate modern nationalism, industrialization, scientific inquiry, and western "progress" within the philosophy of Buddhism. At the same time they are coming under criticism from some intellectuals who feel that sixty to seventy thousand "unproductive" bonzes are far too many, in purely economic terms, for the rest of the population to support.

Cambodia's foreign ethnic minorities look upon the country as a land of economic or political opportunity rather than as a nation. Vietnamese and Chinese inhabitants do not for the most part consider themselves Cambodian. Their loyalties are either nonexistent or directed toward their native lands. They tend to scorn the Cambodians for their lack of commercial aptitude.

Other Nations

Most Cambodians have an extremely vague idea both about other countries, except those that are neighboring, and about the world in general. Many, among those who have given the matter any thought at all, accept as a fact that the world is flat. An American official questioned a number of Cambodians about their idea of the location of the United States and received quite remarkable and entirely fanciful answers.

The Cambodian attitude toward world politics was expressed by Sihanouk when he recommended that Cambodian policy toward the Big Power conflict be that of an ant standing aside while elephants fight. The ant, of course, has his own goals, and his own anthill to run—unless it is trampled in the conflict.

Cambodians respect those nations which have most influenced their culture: India and France. India is revered as the "father" of

Cambodian customs, the homeland of Buddhism (although India is not Buddhist), and therefore a holy place. Both Brahmanism and Buddhism came from India, and both have affected Cambodia over the centuries. India epitomizes the kind of modern adaptation Cambodia would like to make. In recent years Sihanouk has been influenced by Nehru's example of neutralism. Cambodians look to India for help, but, significantly, they tend to reserve recourse to Indian aid for a situation of almost desperate need, perhaps because India is not notably able to give much help immediately. Individual Indians who live in Cambodia, however, are often disliked because of their usurious practices.

Despite a nationalist effort to engender hatred toward the French during the struggle for independence, Cambodians generally did not dislike them. An American observer declares, "The French won the Cambodians, body and soul." Cambodian intellectuals realize that French intervention saved Cambodia from being swallowed up by Vietnam or Thailand. They recognize that the French took the first important steps toward bringing Cambodia abreast of contemporary thought and action. Some of the King's closest advisers have been and are French. The conspicuous jobs in government have now gone to Cambodians; but Frenchmen are in trusted advisory positions. Educated Cambodians are aware of some of the French excesses even while they value their cultural contributions.

Vietnamese are most profoundly disliked. They have encroached on Cambodian lands, and the government of Vietnam has exerted or sought to exert control over the government of Cambodia for some centuries. At the annual graduation of the military academy, a mock Vietnamese village is set up on the palace grounds and the "Vietnamese" are routed. Cambodians are reported "not to bother reading Vietnamese propaganda tracts because they know they are lies."

The Thai are called "brothers" by the Cambodians. Alike in religion and in Indian influence, Thai and Khmer get along relatively well together, despite ancient wars and more recent Thai domination and current territorial disputes.

Cambodians seem to have a rather passive attitude toward Laos. Laotians are part of the same "family" group, sharing a common religious and cultural heritage. No great problems of any nature have arisen.

China is looked on as part of the same family, but more distantly related. "After all, the peninsula is Indochinese," a Cambodian points out. China itself is not feared and the numerous Chinese in Cambodia are respected as good businessmen. Non-naturalized Chinese are not treated as equals, but they are not hated as the Vietnamese are.

Americans are not well known in Cambodia. Until the recent spate of government missions, very few Americans had been there. A peasant is apt to assume that anyone of western origin is French. In general, marvel about the United States among educated Cambodians is combined with a feeling of skepticism generated by American government policies that affect Cambodia. Interestingly, Filipinos are regarded as more American than Asian.

TABLES

Table 1. ESTIMATE OF POPULATION AND PERCENT DISTRIBUTION OF ETHNIC GROUPS BETWEEN PROVINCES, 1950

Province	Khmer Number	Khmer Per-cent	Vietnamese Number	Vietnamese Per-cent	Chinese Number	Chinese Per-cent	Europeans Number	Europeans Per-cent	Total Population Number	Total Percent
Battambang	339,354	9.6	15,923	5.1	15,626	7.2	97	2.2	371,000	9.1
Kampot	222,617(a)	6.3	8,659	2.7	21,673	9.9	19	0.4	252,968	6.2
Kandal(b)	460,128	13.0	52,318	16.5	15,542	7.1	5	......	527,993	13.0
Kompong Cham	522,880	14.8	31,564	10.0	16,010	7.3	257	5.8	570,711	14.0
Kompong Chhnang	175,111	4.9	16,773	5.3	4,113	1.9	3	......	196,000	4.8
Kompong Speu	171,861	4.9	252	0.1	4,341	2.0	15	0.4	176,469	4.3
Kompong Thom	203,717(c)	5.8	5,310	1.7	2,471	1.1	2	......	211,500	5.2
Kratie	72,585(d)	2.1	4,403	1.4	2,431	1.1	20	0.5	79,439	2.0
Preyveng	307,668	8.7	45,958	14.5	7,403	3.4	......	......	361,029	8.9
Pursat	115,253(e)	3.3	9,649	3.1	4,732	2.2	20	0.5	129,653	3.2
Siemreap	211,108	6.0	2,278	0.7	1,672	0.8	2	......	215,060	5.3
Stungtreng	42,000	1.2	2,636	0.8	2,360	1.1	4	......	47,000	1.1
Soairieng	193,983	5.5	8,993	2.9	3,954	1.8	120	2.7	207,050	5.1
Takeo	343,714	9.7	14,880	3.8	5,601	2.6	100	2.4	364,295	8.9
City of Pnompenh	150,000	4.2	100,000	31.4	110,000	50.5	3,800	85.1	363,800	8.9
Total	3,531,979	100.0	319,596(f)	100.0	217,929	100.0	4,464	100.0	4,073,967	100.0

(a) Includes Cham and Saoch.
(b) Excludes Pnompenh.
(c) Includes 6,000 Kuoy.
(d) Includes Cham and Phnong.
(e) Includes Pear and Cham.
(f) Probably includes other minorities not elsewhere tabulated (including Cham-Malays, etc.).
Estimates of Vietnamese population for the same year have been given as 291,596, or 7.1 percent of total population.

Source: Adapted from working papers prepared under contract with the Human Relations Area Files at the University of Chicago under the direction of Norton S. Ginsburg and Fred Eggan, citing from *Annuaire Statistique du Cambodge*, 1952, p. 12.

Table 2. **ESTIMATE OF DISTRIBUTION OF ETHNIC GROUPS WITHIN EACH PROVINCE, 1950**

(percentage of province total)

Province	Khmer	Viet-namese	Chinese	Euro-peans	Total
Battambang	91.5	4.3	4.2	....	100.0
Kampot	88.0[a]	3.4	8.6	....	100.0
Kandal[b]	87.2	9.9	2.9	....	100.0
Kompong Cham	91.6	5.5	2.8	0.1	100.0
Kompong Chhnang	89.3	8.6	2.1	....	100.0
Kompong Speu	97.4	0.1	2.5	....	100.0
Kompong Thom	96.3[c]	2.5	1.2	....	100.0
Kratie	91.4[d]	5.5	3.1	....	100.0
Preyveng	85.2	12.7	2.1	....	100.0
Pursat	88.9[e]	7.4	3.7	....	100.0
Siemreap	98.2	1.1	0.7	....	100.0
Stungtreng	89.4	5.6	5.0	....	100.0
Soairieng	93.7	4.3	1.9	0.1	100.0
Takeo	94.3	4.1	1.5	0.1	100.0
City of Pnompenh	41.2	27.5	30.2	1.1	100.0
Total Population	86.7	7.9[f]	5.3	0.1	100.0

(a) Includes Cham and Saoch.
(b) Excludes Pnompenh.
(c) Includes 6,000 Kuoy.
(d) Includes Cham and Phnong.
(e) Includes Pear and Cham.
(f) Probably includes other minorities not elsewhere tabulated (including Cham-Malays, etc.). Estimate of Vietnamese population for the same year has been given as 291,596, or 7.1 percent of total population.

Source: Adapted from working papers prepared under contract with the Human Relations Area Files at the University of Chicago under the direction of Norton S. Ginsburg and Fred Eggan, citing from *Annuaire Statistique du Cambodge, 1952,* p. 12.

Table 3. POPULATION IN SIX SELECTED PROVINCES AND THEIR CAPITALS, 1955

Name	Province	Capital
Battambang	500,000	100,000
Kandal	648,000[a]	500,000[b]
Kompong Cham	594,000	100,000
Kompong Thom	200,000	5,000
Kampot	200,000	4,000
Kratie	180,000	7,000
Total	2,322,000	716,000

(a) Estimate taken from working papers prepared under contract with the Human Relations Area Files at the University of Chicago under the direction of Norton S. Ginsburg and Fred Eggan.

(b) Pnompenh, capital of Cambodia. The names of other capitals are the same as the provinces.

Source: National Tourist Office of Cambodia, *Tourist Notes, Cambodia*, I, No. 2 (1955), 24-26.

Table 4. **NEWSPAPERS OF CAMBODIA, MAY 1956**[a]

Name	Political Coloration	Issues Weekly
Rampuchea	Semiofficial government	Daily, except Sunday
Sangkum Reastr Niyum	Popular Socialist Community (of Sihanouk)	1
Pracheathipatay	Democratic party	2
Meatophum	Independent	3
Pracheachon	Pro-Communist	1
Pracheaserey	Popular Socialist Community sympathizer	1
Wat Phnom	Left-wing neutral	1
Cong Thuong Pao	Pro-Nationalist Chinese	3
Mekong Yat Pao	Pro-Red Chinese	2
Journal Yat Pao	Pro-Nationalist Chinese	2
Journal de Phnom Penh	Pro-Nationalist Chinese	1
Jen Minh Jeh Pau	Pro-Red Chinese	2
French:		
La Liberté	French-inspired	Daily, except Sunday
La Depêche du Cambodge	Unknown	Daily, except Sunday
Realités Cambodgiennes	Government-inspired	1
Agence Khmère de Presse **(Bulletin)**	Cambodian press service	Daily

(a) The newspaper *La Cambodge* discontinued publication in the spring of 1956; a similar paper, *Angkor*, is now being printed on the same presses.

Table 5. THE TWO-YEAR PLAN (1956-58)

A. *Expenditures*

	(millions of riels)	
	Planned	*Spent*
General	175	90
Production		
Agriculture	113	26
Agricultural water control	337	87
Livestock breeding	81	21
Forests	92	9
Fisheries	88	....
Mines, industries, and crafts	49	5
Aid to small private enterprise	570	257
Basic Construction		
Electrification and water supply	132	33
Railroads	90	26
Roads and bridges	574	1,058
Ports	231	272
Navigable channels	13	....
Aeronautics	162	99
Communications	128	33
Social Development		
Education	275	170
Public health	230	81
Town planning and community development	160	142
	3,500	2,455

B. *Sources of Funds*

American aid	1,531
French aid	404
People's Republic of China	62
USSR	22
Colombo Plan	29
National Budget	132
Municipal Budget	35
Diverse contributions (Royal Office of Cooperation and National Development Bank)	238
Other aid	2
	2,455

Source: National Bank of Cambodia, *Monthly Bulletin,* October 1958.

Table 6. BUDGET OF THE CAMBODIAN GOVERNMENT
(1958 Provisional)

A. *Expenditures by Department*

	Thousand riels
National Assembly	12,203.1
Council of the Kingdom	3,919.0
Presidency of the Council of Ministers	21,271.1
Social Activity	3,210.0
Labor	2,115.2
State Investments	4,914.4
Planning	9,033.1
Foreign Affairs	91,746.2
Interior	102,024.0
National Security	304,271.3
Information	10,468.3
National Education	597,960.1
National Economy	12,327.3
Agriculture	131,124.5
Justice	35,304.3
Cults	11,069.1
Health	202,501.7
Public Works and Telecommunications	406,760.7
Finance	335,545.0
National Defense	352,231.0
	2,650,000.0

B. *Receipts*

Direct taxes	96,700
Indirect taxes (including monopoly excises)	649,400
Customs and excises	1,200,000
Income from state properties	81,340
Other sources	622,560
	2,650,000

Source: National Bank of Cambodia, *Monthly Bulletin*, April 1958.

Table 7. SUMMARY OF OCP OPERATIONS IN 1954
(thousand riels)

Advances to affiliated provincial credit institutions	30,330
Loans for livestock	750
Advances to agricultural cooperatives	23,006
Advances to handicraft cooperatives	552
Advances to small industries	1,655
Total	56,293

Source: National Bank of Cambodia, *Monthly Bulletin*, April 1955.

Table 8. RICE ACREAGE AND PRODUCTION IN CAMBODIA'S PROVINCES, 1956-57

Provinces	Area Harvested (hectares)	Production (metric tons)
Battambang	141,000	161,000
Pursat	37,000	52,000
Kompong Chhnang	47,000	61,000
Kompong Cham	128,000	197,000
Kompong Thom	79,000	79,000
Kandal	82,000	117,000
Kompong Speu	84,000	116,000
Takeo	145,000	161,000
Kampot	91,000	82,000
Preyveng	207,000	171,000
Soairieng	132,000	113,000
Kratie	9,000	17,000
Siemreap	44,000	45,000
Stungtreng	8,000	7,000

Source: *Statistical Yearbook of Cambodia (1937-1957)*, June 1958.

Table 9. PERCENTAGE OF FARM UNITS OF VARIOUS SIZES
(by province)

Province	Up to 12 acres	12 - 15 acres	25 - 125 acres	Over 125 acres
Battambang(a)	76.3	18.3	5.3	0.1
Kandal	99.0	0.9	0.1	.02
Kompong Cham	96.8	2.8	0.4	
Preyveng	87.0	10.5	2.4	0.1
Soairieng	80.3	16.5	3.0	0.2
Kandal(b)	99.2	0.7	0.1	
Kompong Cham(b)	99.8	0.2	0.01	

(a) Data for the first five provinces listed relate to rice farms.
(b) Data relate to farms producing other crops and located on the banks of rivers.

Source: *Bulletin Economique de l'Indochine*, April-June 1952.

Table 10. STATUS OF RURAL CREDIT COOPERATIVES (1958)

Cooperatives	Number	Membership	Loans made by them (thousand riels)
Credit (province)	13	92,489	121,050(a)
Consumer (rural)	272	83,485	105,578(b)
Corn producers	11	3,717	3,391
Rice producers	1	461	54
Rice mills	2	799	1,256
Tobacco	1	10,838	716
Salt	1	70	30,000

(a) This figure represents only loans made to individual members; advances to other cooperatives are included in the amounts which they granted.
(b) Loans of merchandise.

Source: National Bank of Cambodia, *Monthly Bulletin*, October 1958.

Table 11. **INDUSTRIAL ESTABLISHMENTS IN CAMBODIA**

Type	1951	1957
Rice mills	47	765
Distilleries	12	12
Palm sugar refineries	22	72
Cigarette factories	0	3
Power sawmills	8	29
Hand sawmills	170	234
Coking coal plants	335	140
Lime kilns	60	16
Electric power plants	17	17
Brick and tile plants	208	170
Match factories	0	1
Tanneries	5	8
Soap factories	14	14
Fish sauce production	19	27
Soya sauce production	5	16
Printing plants	11	15
Silk weaving	2	45
Foundries	3	
Mechanical repair	16	
Electrical repair	5	
Nickel plating	3	
Button manufacturing	1	
Potteries	11	no data
Candlemaking	10	
Shoe manufacturing	16	
Dyeing plants	6	
Stone cutting	7	
Jewelry making	116	
Woodworking factories	20	
Smithies	4	58
Hardware manufacturing	17	
Blanket manufacturing	(est.) 1,000	
Cotton cloth manufacturing	(est.) 9,000	no data
Marble sculpturing	25	
Ice making	6	
Carbonated drinks	0	14

Source: *Statistical Yearbook of Cambodia (1937-1957),* June 1958.

Table 12. PRINCIPAL EXPORTS
(millions of riels)

Product	First nine months of: 1957	1958
Rice and derivatives	573.5	703.6
Rubber	400.1	411.3
Corn	125.0	112.8
Fish and products	25.7	27.4
Pepper	48.9	25.4
Soya	35.3	23.7
Kapok	29.1	22.5
Livestock, leather and hides	45.8	19.8
Beans	30.8	11.6
Timber	12.9	3.8

Source: National Bank of Cambodia, *Monthly Bulletin,* December 1958.

Table 13. PRINCIPAL IMPORTS
(millions of riels)

Products	First nine months of: 1957	1958
Cotton textiles and yarn	130.1	181.8
Machinery and equipment	66.3	168.1
Automobiles and parts	47.6	166.5
Other textiles	46.9	128.6
Iron and steel	87.7	126.7
Electrical equipment	51.0	107.7
Pharmaceutical products	71.3	94.7
Metal products	65.1	91.9
Cement	44.4	67.4
Chemical products	29.7	65.4
Vegetables and fruits	51.8	50.6
Jute bags and fabric	32.6	49.3
Milk products	34.6	39.8
Bicycles and parts	22.2	39.0
Beer	23.9	31.2
Paper and paper products	47.7	25.4

Source: National Bank of Cambodia, *Monthly Bulletin,* December 1958.

Table 14. BALANCE OF TRADE
(millions of riels)

Monetary Zone	1955	1957	1958
Dollar zone	+ 260.2	+ 255.2	+ 137.1
Sterling zone	— 172.1	— 108.0	+ 60.1
Organization for European Economic Cooperation	— 97.2	+ 73.7	— 280.3
Other zones	— 252.8	— 571.4	— 569.1
	— 261.9	— 350.5	— 652.2

Source: *Statistical Yearbook of Cambodia (1937-1957)*, June 1958; and National Bank of Cambodia, *Monthly Bulletin*, December 1958.

Table 15. CAMBODIAN TEACHING STAFF IN PUBLIC EDUCATION (1957-58)

Type	Men	Women
Primary school teachers	3,171	502
Secondary school teachers	2	......
Workshop teachers	3	......
Workshop assistants	20	......
Physical education teachers	3	......
Khmer language teachers	4,079	475
Art teachers	6	2

Table 16. PRESENT SIXTY-YEAR CYCLE WITH CORRESPONDING BUDDHIST AND WESTERN DATES*

Names of Animals					
Cut RAT	*Cut-Chasak* 6th YEAR 2467 1924	*Cut-Adthasak* 8th YEAR 2479 1936	*Cut-Samritthisak* 0 YEAR 2491 1948	*Cut-Tosak* 2nd YEAR 2503 1960	*Cut-Catvasak* 4th YEAR 2515 1972
Chlov OX	*Chlov-Saptasak* 7th YEAR 2468 1925	*Chlov-Nopposak* 9th YEAR 2480 1937	*Chlov-Eksak* 1st YEAR 2492 1949	*Chlov-Treisak* 3rd YEAR 2504 1961	*Chloo-Panhcasak* 5th YEAR 2516 1973
Khal TIGER	*Khal-Adthasak* 8th YEAR 2469 1926	*Khal-Samritthisak* 0 YEAR 2481 1938	*Khal-Tosak* 2nd YEAR 2493 1950	*Khal-Catvasak* 4th YEAR 2505 1962	*Khal-Chasak* 6th YEAR 2517 1974
Thas HARE	*Thas-Nopposak* 9th YEAR 2470 1927	*Thas-Eksak* 1st YEAR 2482 1939	*Thas-Treisak* 3rd YEAR 2494 1951	*Thas-Panhcasak* 5th YEAR 2506 1963	*Thas-Saptasak* 7th YEAR 2518 1975
Rong DRAGON	*Rong-Samritthisak* 0 YEAR 2471 1928	*Rong-Tosak* 2nd YEAR 2483 1940	*Rong-Catvasak* 4th YEAR 2495 1952	*Rong-Chasak* 6th YEAR 2507 1964	*Rong-Adthasak* 8th YEAR 2519 1976
Mosanh SNAKE	*Mosanh-Eksak* 1st YEAR 2472 1929	*Mosanh-Tresak* 3rd YEAR 2484 1941	*Mosanh-Panhcasak* 5th YEAR 2496 1953	*Mosanh-Saptasak* 7th YEAR 2508 1965	*Mosanh-Nopposak* 9th YEAR 2520 1977

Momi HORSE	*Momi-Tosak* 2nd YEAR 2473 1930	*Momi-Catvasak* 4th YEAR 2485 1942	*Momi-Chasak* 6th YEAR 2497 1954	*Momi-Adthasak* 8th YEAR 2509 1966	*Momi-Samritthisak* 0 YEAR 2521 1978
Mome GOAT	*Mome-Tretsak* 3rd YEAR 2474 1931	*Mome-Panhcasak* 5th YEAR 2486 1943	*Mome-Saptasak* 7th YEAR 2498 1955	*Mome-Nopposak* 9th YEAR 2510 1967	*Mome-Eksak* 1st YEAR 2522 1979
Vok MONKEY	*Vok-Catvasak* 4th YEAR 2475 1932	*Vok-Chasak* 6th YEAR 2487 1944	*Vok-Adthasak* 8th YEAR 2499 1956	*Vok-Samritthisak* 0 YEAR 2511 1968	*Vok-Tosak* 2nd YEAR 2523 1980
Roka ROOSTER	*Roka-Panhcasak* 5th YEAR 2476 1933	*Roka-Saptasak* 7th YEAR 2488 1945	*Roka-Nopposak* 9th YEAR 2500 1957	*Roka-Eksak* 1st YEAR 2512 1969	*Roka-Tretsak* 3rd YEAR 2524 1981
Ca DOG	*Ca-Chasak* 6th YEAR 2477 1934	*Ca-Adthasak* 8th YEAR 2489 1946	*Ca-Samritthisak* 0 YEAR 2501 1958	*Ca-Tosak* 2nd YEAR 2513 1970	*Ca-Catvasak* 4th YEAR 2525 1982
Kor PIG	*Kor-Saptasak* 7th YEAR 2478 1935	*Kor-Nopposak* 9th YEAR 2490 1947	*Kor-Eksak* 1st YEAR 2502 1959	*Kor-Tretsak* 3rd YEAR 2514 1971	*Kor-Panhcasak* 5th YEAR 2526 1983

*Key (as in 1st box, 2nd column):
Cut-Chasak—Cambodian name for the year
6th YEAR—6th Year of the Rat in the 60-year cycle
2467—the Buddhist year
1924—the Julian year

Source: Adapted from Porée, Guy, and Eveline Maspéro, *Cérémonies des Douze Mois*, p. 85.

RECOMMENDED READING

RECOMMENDED READING

The following are recommended as additional reading on the basis of quality and general availability.

Annuaire des Etats Associés: Cambodge-Laos-Vietnam: 1953. Paris: Société Diloutremer, 1953.

Association of French Rubber Companies. *The Rubber Estates in Viet-Nam and Cambodia.* Paris: Société d'Editions Techniques Coloniales, 1952.

BILODEAU, CHARLES, et al. *Compulsory Education in Cambodia, Laos, and Viet-Nam.* Paris: UNESCO, 1955.

BRIGGS, LAWRENCE P. *Ancient Khmer Empire.* New York: American Philosophical Society, 1951.

————. "Sketch of Cambodian History," *Far Eastern Quarterly*, VI (1947), 345-363. (Human Relations Area Files: Indochina, Source No. 13.)

BRODRICK, ALAN H. *Little Vehicle: Cambodia and Laos.* London: Hutchinson, 1949. (Human Relations Area Files: Indochina, Source No. 25.)

BURTT, E. A. (ed.). *The Teachings of the Compassionate Buddha.* New York: New American Library, 1955.

Cambodia. Direction de la Statistique et des Etudes Economiques. *Bulletin Mensuel de Statistique.* Pnompenh, May-June 1955.

————. *Journal Officiel du Cambodge,* Decree No. 306-NS, June 6, 1955; Decree No. 2-NS, April 2, 1955.

"Cambodia," *Encyclopaedia Britannica* (1953 ed.), IV, 638 ff.

Canada, Department of Mines and Technical Surveys, Geographical Board. *Indochina: A Geographical Appreciation.* Ottawa, 1953.

CHATTERJI, B. R. *Indian Cultural Influences in Cambodia.* Calcutta: University of Calcutta, 1928.

CHRISTIAN, P. "Son Ngoc Thanh," *Indochine Sud-Est Asiatique* (Saigon), October 1952.

————. "Le Viet-Minh au Cambodge," *Indochine Sud-Est Asiatique*, February-March 1952 (Special Issue).

COLLARD, PAUL. *Cambodge et Cambodgiens*. Paris: Société d'Editions Geographiques, Maritimes et Coloniales, 1925.

DAVID, SAVILLE R. "West Sees Order and Stability Achieved by Cambodians"; "U. S. Faces Severe Buffeting in Unsettled Cambodia"; "U. S. Persuasion with Tactful Logic Termed Urgent in Cambodia," *Christian Science Monitor*, March 12-15, 1956.

France-Asie (Saigon), Special Issue. "Présence du Cambodge," RENE DE BERVAL (ed.), November-December 1955.

GOUDAL, JEAN. *Labour Conditions in Indochina*. Geneva: International Labour Office, 1938. (Human Relations Area Files: Indochina, Source No. 6.)

GOUROU, PIERRE. *Land Utilization in French Indochina*. Washington: Institute of Pacific Relations, 1945. (Human Relations Area Files: Indochina, Source No. 2.)

Gouvernement-Général Indochine. *Les Arts Indigènes au Cambodge, 1918-1936*. Hanoi: Imprimerie d'Extrême-Orient, 1937.

HAMMER, ELLEN J. *The Struggle for Indo-China*. Stanford: Stanford University Press, 1954.

HARRISON, BRIAN. *Southeast Asia*. London: Macmillan, 1954.

HAUMULLER, MARCEL. "Rapport Concernant l'Enseignement Distribué aux Minorités Ethniques du Cambodge," *Education* (Saigon), I (May 1948), 50.

Institut d'Emission des Etats du Cambodge, du Laos et du Viet-Nam, Service des Etudes Economiques et Financières. *Etudes et Documents*. Saigon: Imprimerie d'Outre-Mer, 1952-54.

League of Nations. *Public Health in French Indochina*. Washington, 1944.

————. "Report of French Indochina." In *Intergovernmental Conference of Far-Eastern Countries on Rural Hygiene*. Geneva, 1937.

LECLERE, ADHEMARD. "Le Théâtre Cambodgien," *Révue d'Ethnographie et de Sociologie* (Paris), No. 11-12 (1910), 257-282. (Human Relations Area Files: Indochina, Source No. 178.)

LE GALLEN, M. "La Famille." In G. MASPERO (ed.), *L'Indochine—Un Empire Colonial Français*, Vol. II. Paris: Van Oest, 1930.

LEMAY, REGINALD STUART. *The Culture of Southeast Asia*. London: Allen and Unwin, 1954.

MARCHAL, H. "Bonzes, Pagodes et Fêtes en Pays Khmer," *Indochine Sud-Est Asiatique* (Saigon), May 1951, 45-46.

————. "Considérations sur le Cambodgien," *Sud-Est Asiatique*, May 1950, 40-45.

————. "Jeux, divertissements et chants populaires au Cambodge," *Sud-Est Asiatique*, August 1950, 20-27.

MAY, JACQUES (ed.). *Atlas of World Diseases*. New York: American

Geographical Society, 1950 to 1956. (Series of plates issued at intervals; seventeen plates as of 1956.)

MIGOT, O. "Le Bouddhisme en Général," *Bulletin de la Société des Etudes Indochinoises* (Saigon), XXI (1946), 29-41.

————. "Le Bouddhisme en Indochine," *Bulletin de la Société des Etudes Indochinoises*, XXII (1947), 23-29.

MILLER, E. W. "Industrial Resources of Indochina," *Far Eastern Quarterly*, August 1947. (Human Relations Area Files: Indochina, Source No. 16.)

MONOD, G. H. *Le Cambodgien*. Paris: Larose, 1931.

MORIZON, RENE. *La Province Cambodgienne de Pursat*. Paris: Les Editions Internationales, 1936. (Human Relations Area Files: Indochina, Source No. 174.)

————. *Monographie du Cambodge*. Hanoi: Imprimerie d'Extrême-Orient, 1931.

National Tourist Office of Cambodia. *Tourist Notes: Cambodia*. Pnompenh, 1955.

OLIVIER, GEORGES, and HENRI CHAGNOUX. "Anthropologie Physique des Chams," *Bulletin de la Société des Etudes Indochinoises* (Saigon), XXVI (July-September 1951), 271-318.

POREE, GUY, and EVELINE MASPERO. *Cérémonies des Douze Mois*. Pnompenh: Commission des Moeurs et Coutumes du Cambodge, 1950. (Human Relations Area Files: Indochina, Source No. 138.)

————. *Moeurs et Coutumes des Khmèrs*. Paris: Payot, 1938. (Human Relations Area Files: Indochina, Source No. 83.)

Press Office of the Royal Palace (ed.). *Modern Cambodia*. Pnompenh, 1950.

ROBEQUAIN, CHARLES. *The Economic Development of French Indo-China*. London: Oxford University Press, 1944. (Human Relations Area Files: Indochina, Source No. 3.)

SAM, SARY. "L'Economie du Cambodge," *Cambodge*. (Pnompenh), April 1954.

————. *La Grande Figure de Norodom Sihanouk, telle qu'Elle Est Dépeinte par les Documents de Valeur Historique Découverts dans les Archives du Palais Royal*. Pnompenh: Imprimerie du Palais Royal, 1955.

SAM, SARY, and SAY MAU. *Bilan de l'Oeuvre Norodom Sihanouk Pendant le Mandat Royal de 1952 à 1955*. Pnompenh: Imprimerie Albert Portail, 1955.

SAURIN, E. "Les Ressources Minérales du Cambodge," *Bulletin Economique de l'Indochine* (Saigon), August 1952.

SEBEOK, THOMAS. "Studies in Linguistics," *Far Eastern Quarterly*, II (1943), 349 ff.

SIMMONS, J. S., T. F. WHAYNE, G. W. ANDERSON, and H. M. HORACK. *Global Epidemiology, Vol. I: Part 1, India and the Far East; Part 2, The Pacific Area*. Philadelphia: Lippincott, 1944.

310

STRICTLAND-ANDERSON, LILY. "The Cambodian Ballet," *Musical Quarterly*, XII (April 1926), 226-274.
SZAZ, ZOLTAN M. "Cambodia's Foreign Policy," *Far Eastern Survey*, October 1955.
THOMPSON, VIRGINIA. *French Indo-China*. New York: Macmillan, 1937. (Human Relations Area Files: Indochina, Source No. 7.)
THOMPSON, VIRGINIA, and RICHARD ADLOFF. *Minority Problems in Southeast Asia*. Stanford: Stanford University Press, 1955.
United Nations. "Economic Survey of Asia and the Far East, 1955," *Economic Bulletin for Asia and the Far East* (Bangkok), VI, No. 4 (February 1956).
————. *Report of the Ad Hoc Committee on Forced Labor*. New York, 1953.
United States Department of Commerce: World Trade Information Service. *Economic Reports*, "Basic Data on the Economy of Cambodia," Part I, No. 55-40 (April 1955).
United States Information Service. *Cambodia-American Relations*. Pnompenh, 1955.
University of Chicago, NORTON S. GINSBURG and FRED EGGAN (eds.). *Area Handbook on Cambodia*. HRAF Subcontractor's Monograph, 1955.
VERNEAU, R., and G. PANNETIER. "Contribution a l'Etude des Cambodgiens," *L'Anthropologie*, XXXI (1921), 279.

OTHER USEFUL SOURCES

Akademiya Nauk SSSR, Tikhookeanskiy Institut (Institute of the Pacific of Soviet Academy of Sciences). *Krizis Kolonial'noy Sistemy* (The Crisis of the Colonial System). Moscow, 1949.
ALBERT, J. B. *Indochine d'Autrefois et d'Aujourdhui*. Paris, 1934.
Annuaire Statistique du Cambodge, 1949-1951-1952. Pnompenh: Imprimerie Nouvelle, 1953.
BAZE, WILLIAM. "Les Cent Mille Eurasiens d'Indochine," *France-Asie*, VIII (August 1952), 489.
Der Befreiungskampf der Voelker von Vietnam, Khmer und Pathet Lao (The Liberation Struggle of the Peoples of Viet-Nam, Khmer, and Pathet Lao), author unknown. Berlin (Soviet Sector): Dietz Verlag, 1954.
BENEDICT, PAUL K. "Languages and Literatures of Indochina," *Far Eastern Quarterly*, VI (August 1947), 379-389.
BENEDICT, RUTH. *Thai Culture and Behavior* (Southeast Asia Program, Data Paper No. 4). Ithaca: Cornell University, February 1952. (Originally published 1943, mimeographed.)
BERNARD, S. "Quelques Aspects de la Chance dans les Contes Populaires du Cambodge," *Bulletin de la Société Etudes Indochinoises* (Saigon), XXVII, No. 3 (1952).

Other Useful Sources

"A Bibliography of the Physical Anthropology of Indo-China, 1938-47," *American Journal of Physical Anthropology,* VII (May 1949), 39-51.

Bilan de L'Oeuvre du Premier Gouvernement du Sangkum Reastr Niyum, Présidé par S.A.R. Samdech Préah Norodom Sihanouk Upayuvareach. Pnompenh, 1956.

BITARD, T. "Essai sur la Satire Sociale dans la Litterature du Cambodge," *Bulletin de la Société Etudes Indochinoises* (Saigon), XXVI, No. 2 (1951).

BODARD, LUCIEN, *et al.* "Les Etats Associés d'Indochine," *France-Illustration* (Paris), June 28, 1952 (Special Issue).

BOISSELIER, J. "Génie de l'Art Khmer," *Sud-Est Asiatique* (Saigon), December 1950.

BRUZON, ETIENNE. *Annales du Service Météorologique de l'Indochine.* Hanoi, 1936.

Bulletin Economique de l'Indochine, April-June 1952.

Bulletin Economique de l'Indochine (Saigon), "Le Traité Franco-Cambodgien du 8 Novembre," 1949.

Bulletin des Terres Rouges, (Saigon), Nos. 55 and 58, 1st and 4th trimestre, 1951.

CAMBEFORT, GASTON. *L'Introduction au Cambodgien.* Paris: G. P. Maisonneuve, 1950.

Cambodge (Pnompenh daily newspaper), 1943-1956, *passim.*

Cambodia. *Code Civil.* Pnompenh: Imprimerie Royale, 1951.

————. *Code Penal.* Pnompenh: Imprimerie Royale, 1950.

————. *Code de Procédure en Matière Civile.* Pnompenh, 1939.

————. *Code de Procédure en Matière Pénale.* Pnompenh: Imprimerie Royale, 1949.

————. *Déclaration de S.A.R. Samdech Preah Upayuvareach devant l'Assemblée Nationale pour Demander l'Investiture de Son Cabinet.* Pnompenh, 1955.

————. *Défense en Justice.* Pnompenh: Imprimerie Royale, 1951.

————. Direction de la Statistique et des Etudes Economiques. *Bulletin Economique,* 1955-56.

————. Direction de la Statistique et des Etudes Economiques. *Annuaire Statistique du Cambodge.* Pnompenh, 1952.

Cambodia. *National Bank of Cambodia Monthly Bulletin,* 1955 to 1958, *passim.*

————. *Notice de Renseignements sur l'Application au Cambodge des Lois Sociales.* Pnompenh: Imprimerie Albert Portail, 1938.

————. *Statistical Yearbook of Cambodia, 1937-1957.* Pnompenh, June 1958.

CHARPY, B. "Images de la Cérémonie du Sillon Sacré," *Indochine Sud-Est Asiatique* (Saigon), August 1951.

————. "La Pêche en Eau Douce au Cambodge," *Indochine Sud-Est Asiatique,* April 1951.

————. "La Pêche en Eau Douce au Cambodge," *Indochine Sud-Est Asiatique,* (April 1954), 31-40.

CHET CHHEM. *Elementary School Primer.* (Trans., Bernard B. Fall. 1956.) Pnompenh: Ministry of Education, n.d.

Commissariat de la République Française au Cambodge. *La Lettre et L'Esprit des Accords Franco-Khmers.* Pnompenh: Imprimerie Albert Portail, 1953.

DEUTSCHER, ISAAC. "How the Russians Bet a Little in Asia to Win a Lot in Europe," *The Reporter,* September 23, 1954.

DEWEY, THOMAS E. *Journey to the Far Pacific.* New York: Doubleday, 1953.

Documents Relating to the Discussion of Korea and Indo-China at the Geneva Conference, April 27–June 15, 1954; and Further Documents Relating to the Discussion of Indo-China at the Geneva Conference, June 16–July 21, 1954. London: Her Majesty's Stationery Office, 1954.

Dominion of Canada. *House of Commons Debates.* Ottawa, May 3, 1955.

DOUGLAS, WILLIAM O. *North of Malaya.* New York: Doubleday, 1953.

DURDIN, TILLMAN. "Cambodia Finds More Security Under Increased Independence," *New York Times,* March 9, 1954.

DUTT, VIDYA PRAKASH. "The Impasse in Indochina," *India Quarterly* (New Delhi), January-March 1952.

Editor and Publisher: 1958 International Yearbook Number. New York: Editor and Publisher, February 1958.

Embassy of India in the United States. *Indiagram* (Washington), 1950, *passim.*

EMBREE, JOHN F. "Thailand, a Loosely Structured Social System," *American Anthropologist,* LII (April 1950), 181-193.

EMBREE, JOHN F., and LILLIAN DOTSON. *Bibliography of the Peoples and Cultures of Mainland Southeast Asia.* (Yale University, Southeast Asia Studies.) New Haven, 1950.

ESNAMBUC, B. "L'Orfèvrerie Khmère," *Indochine Sud-Est Asiatique,* April 1954.

FALL, BERNARD B. "The Cease-Fire in Indochina—An Appraisal," *Far Eastern Survey,* September and October 1954.

————. "Indochina Since Geneva," *Pacific Affairs,* March 1955.

————. "Rückblick auf Französisch-Indochina" (Looking Back Upon French Indochina), *Atlantis* (Zurich), June 1955.

————. *The Viet-Minh Regime.* (1st and 2d eds.) (Cornell University, Southeast Asia Program.) Ithaca and New York: Cornell University and Institute of Pacific Relations, 1954, 1956.

France. Direction de la Documentation. Notes, Documentaires et Etudes: *Conférence Inter-Etats.* (No. 1447.) Paris, March 9, 1951.

Documents Relatifs aux Problèmes Indochinois. (No. 555.) Paris, February 24, 1947.

Rapport de la Commission de Conciliation Franco-Siamoise. (No. 811.) Paris, January 23, 1948.

Traité entre la France et la Cambodge. (No. 1241.) Paris, December 7, 1949.

————. Haut Commissariat de France en Indochine, Centre d'Information Economique. "Notes sur la Situation de la Main d'Oeuvre au Cambodge," *Bulletin de l'Economie Indochinoise,* April-June 1952.

FRANCK, HARRY A. *East of Siam: Ramblings in the Five Divisions of French Indochina.* New York: Century, 1926. (Human Relations Area Files: Indochina, Source No. 23.)

French Embassy in the United States, Cultural Division. "Science: Anthropology." Parts I and II in *French Bibliographical Digest,* No. 15, Series II. New York, January, February 1956.

French Embassy in the United States, Press and Information Division. "Full Texts of Agreements on the Cessation of Hostilities in Viet-Nam, Laos, and Cambodia," *Information Bulletin, Issue No. 7, Indochinese Affairs,* September 1954.

French Ministry for Overseas Affairs. *Chroniques d'Outre-Mer* (Paris monthly), 1952, *passim.*

GAUTHIER, J. *L'Indochine au Travail dans la Paix Française.* Paris: Eyrolles, 1949.

Gouvernement-Général Indochine, Direction des Affaires Politiques et de la Sûreté Générale. *Contribution a l'Histoire des Mouvements Politiques de l'Indochine Française.* 5 vols. Hanoi, 1953.

GROSLIER, GEORGE. "Contemporary Art Studied in the Light of Its Past Forms," *Eastern Art,* II (1930), 127-141.

HAMMER, ELLEN J. *The Struggle for Indochina Continues* (Supplement to the *Pacific Spectator,* No. 3). Palo Alto, California, 1955.

Hansard. *Parliamentary Debates, House of Commons, November 8, 1954.* London: Her Majesty's Stationery Office, 1954.

HENDERSON, EUGENIE. "The Main Features of Cambodian Pronunciation," *Bulletin of the School of Oriental and African Studies,* XIV (1952), 149-174.

HUMPHREYS, CHRISTMAS. *Buddhism.* (2d ed., revised edition.) London: Penguin Books, 1955.

International Commission for Supervision and Control in Cambodia. *Interim Reports.* (1st *Report* covers August 11 to December 31, 1954; 2d *Report* covers January 1 to March 31, 1955.) London: Her Majesty's Stationery Office, 1955.

KAHIN, GEORGE MCTURAN. *The Asian-African Conference: Bandung, Indonesia, April 1955.* Ithaca: Cornell University Press, 1956.

LAFERT, R. "Pêche Miraculeuse au Cambodge," *Indochine Sud-Est Asiatique* (Saigon), June-July 1953.

La Liberté (Pnompenh daily newspaper), 1947, *passim.*

LASKER, B. *People of South East Asia.* New York: Knopf, 1945.

314

LECLERE, ADHEMARD. *Cambodige: Fêtes Civiles et Réligieuses.* Paris, 1916.

————. *Recherches sur le Droit Public des Cambodgiens.* Paris: Augustin Challamel, 1894. (Human Relations Area Files: Indochina, Source No. 179.)

LE GALLEN, M. "Moeurs et Coutumes." In G. MASPERO (ed.), *L'Indochine—Un Empire Colonial Français,* Vol. I. Paris: Van Oest, 1929.

LEMIRE, CHARLES. *Cochinchine Française et Royaume de Cambodge.* Paris: Challamel Aîné, 1889. (Human Relations Area Files: Indochina, Source No. 104.)

LEVI, SYLVAIN. *L'Indochine.* 2 vols. Paris: Société d'Editions Géographiques, Maritimes et Coloniales, 1931.

LEVY, ROGER. "Indochina: Keystone in Asia—a French View," *India Quarterly* (New Delhi), January-March 1952.

————. *L'Indochine et Ses Traités.* Paris: Centre d'Etudes de Politique Etrangère, 1947.

LINGAT, R. "L'Influence Juridique de l'Inde au Champa et au Cambodge," *Journal Asiatique* (Saigon), CCXXXVI-CCXXXVII (1948-1949), 273-290.

MAJUMDAR, R. C. *Hindu Colonies in the Far East.* Calcutta: General Printers and Publishers, 1944.

MARTIN, ROBERT P. "Uncensored Story of Indo-China," *U. S. News and World Report,* June 25, 1954.

MARTINI, F. "Aperçu Phonologique du Cambodgien," *Bulletin de la Société de Linguistique de Paris,* XLII (1942-45), 112-131.

————. "Le Bonze Cambodgien," *France-Asie* (Saigon), November-December 1955 (Special Issue).

————. "Organization du Clergé Bouddhique," *France-Asie,* November-December 1955 (Special Issue).

MAUREL, E. "A Scientific Mission to Cambodia," *Popular Science Monthly,* XXX (1887), 310-322. (Human Relations Area Files: Indochina, Source No. 114.)

MOUHOT, H. *Travels in the Central Parts of Indo-China (Siam), Cambodia and Laos during 1859-60.* 2 vols. London: J. Murray, 1864.

————. *Voyages dans les Royaumes de Siam, de Cambodge, de Laos et autres parties centrales de l'Indo-Chine.* Paris, 1868.

Münchener Illustrierte (Munich), ". . . und den Krieg Führen die Dummen" (. . . and the Fools Get Themselves Killed) a series, September and October 1953.

NAMARUPA (pseud.). "Perspectives d'une Communauté de Défense dans le Sud-Est Asiatique," *France-Indochine* (Paris), No. 105 (March 1954).

NEWMAN, BERNARD. *Report on Indo-China.* London: Robert Hale, 1953.

Newsweek, "The Crisis: After Black Friday," May 17, 1954.

————. "Indo-China: The Other Front in Asia," April 20, 1953.

NORODOM, H. R. H. KANTOL. "Comments on the Law and Practice in

Cambodia." In *Studies in the Law of the Far East and Southeast Asia.* Washington: George Washington University, 1956.

PAVIE, A. *Recherches sur la Littérature du Cambodge, du Laos, et du Siam.* Paris: Leroux, 1898.

RAJAN, B. "Le Train de la Contrebande," *Indochine Sud-Est Asiatique* (Saigon), No. 8 (July 1952).

Réalités Cambodgiennes (Pnompenh weekly newspaper published by the Cambodian government), 1956, *passim.*

SHEN-YU, DAI. *Peking, Moscow, and the Communist Parties of Colonial Asia.* Cambridge: Center for International Studies, Massachusetts Institute of Technology, 1954. (Mimeographed.)

SKINNER, G. WILLIAM. *Report on the Chinese in Southeast Asia, December 1950.* (Cornell University, Southeast Asia Program, Data Paper No. 1.) Ithaca, 1951.

SOUYRIS-ROLAND, A. "Contribution à l'Etude du Culte des Genies Tutélaires ou 'Neak Ta' chez les Cambodgiens du Sud," *Bulletin de la Société d'Etudes Indochinoises* (Saigon), XXVI (1951), 161-174.

Sud-Est Asiatique (Saigon), "L'Evolution du Mouvement Khmer-Issarak," No. 17, October-November 1950.

TESTON, EUGENE, and MAURICE PECHERON. *L'Indochine Moderne.* Paris: Librairie de France, 1932.

THOMPSON, V. and R. ADLOFF. "Cambodia Moves Toward Independence," *Far Eastern Survey,* XXII, No. 9 (August 1953).

THOMPSON, VIRGINIA. *Labor Problems in South East Asia.* New Haven: Yale University Press, 1947.

Time, "Indochina—War of Gallantry and Despair," April 5, 1954.

Time, "Royal Popularity," February 21, 1955.

Time (Pacific Edition), "Unorthodox King," June 22, 1953.

United Nations. *Demographic Yearbook.* New York, 1952.

————. Department of Social Affairs, Division of Social Welfare. "Asia and the Far East Seminar on the Prevention of Crimes and the Treatment of Offenders" (Rangoon, 1953). Part IV of *Comparative Survey on Juvenile Delinquency.* New York, February 1954.

————. Food and Agricultural Organization. *Yearbook of Food and Agricultural Statistics, 1953.* Rome, 1953.

————. International Labour Organization. *Year Book of Labour Statistics.* Geneva, 1955.

UNESCO. *Press—Film—Radio.* Vol. V. Paris, 1951.

————. *World Handbook of Educational Organization and Statistics.* (1st ed.) Paris, 1951.

United States. U. S. Army, European Command, Information and Education Division. "The Situation in Indochina." Special issue of *EUCOM Information Bulletin,* October 8, 1950.

————. Congressional committee reports as follows:

> *The Far East and South Asia,* report of Senator H. Alexander Smith, January 25, 1954.

The Foreign Operations Administration, report of Senator Mike Mansfield on a study mission to France, Italy, Nepal, and Indochina, November 1953.

Indochina, report of Senator Mike Mansfield, October 27, 1953.

Report on Indochina, report of Senator Mike Mansfield on a study mission to Viet-Nam, Cambodia, Laos, October 15, 1954.

Report of the Special Study Mission to Pakistan, India, Thailand, and Indochina, May 12, 1953.

Special Study Mission to Southeast Asia and the Pacific, January 29, 1954.

Viet-Nam, Cambodia, and Laos, report by Senator Mike Mansfield, October 6, 1955.

————. Department of Commerce, Bureau of the Census. *Statistical Abstract of the United States*. Washington, 1954.

————. Department of Commerce, Bureau of Foreign Commerce. *Basic Data on the Economy of Cambodia*. (World Trade Information Service, Economic Reports, Part I, No. 58-4.) Washington, January 1958.

————. Department of State. *Mutual Defense Assistance in Indochina*. (Treaties and Other International Acts Series: 2447.) Washington, 1950.

————. Department of State. *Mutual Security*. (Treaties and Other International Acts Series: 2603.) Washington, 1951.

————. Department of State, Office of Public Affairs. John M. Allison, "Our Far Eastern Policy." Reprint from the *Department of State Bulletin*, April 28, 1952.

————. Department of State, Office of Public Affairs. *Background: Indochina: The War in Viet-Nam, Cambodia, and Laos*. Washington, August 1953.

————. U. S. Information Service. *Free World* (Manila), IV, No. 7 (October 1955).

————. Library of Congress. *Indochina: A Bibliography of the Land and People*. Washington, December 1950.

————. Library of Congress, Division of Orientalia. *Southern Asia Publications in Western Languages*. (Quarterly Accessions List, Current.) Washington, 1955, etc.

————. Library of Congress, Division of Orientalia. *Southern Asia Publications in Western Languages*. (Quarterly Accessions List, since 1951.) Washington, 1953.

————. Office of Strategic Services, Research and Analysis Branch. *Indochina: Linguistic Groups*. (Provisional edition.) Washington, 1945.

U. S. News and World Report, "U. S. Inherits Another Headache," December 10, 1954.

————, "The War Nobody's Trying to Win," March 19, 1954.

UPASAKA, PURUSAKARA. "Le Peuple Cambodgien Est Plus Buddhique que Ses Bonzes," *Indochine Sud-Est Asiatique,* XXXI (July 1954), 25-31.

"Village Cham au Cambodge, Chrui Changva," *Indochine Sud-Est Asiatique* (Saigon), Special Issue, No. 21 (1951), 80-89.

World Culture (Peking fortnightly), Special Supplement, "A Chronicle of Principal Events Relating to the Indochina Question," April 1954.

World Health Organization. *WHO News Letter,* VII, No. 3 (March 1954).

World Radio Handbook, 1958. Hellerup (Denmark): O. Lund-Johansen, 1958. (Distributed by UNESCO.)

INDEX

324

Board of Surveys, 206f.
Boat races, 283
Boats, 216, 224, 283
Bokeo, city, 49
bong, form of address, 57
Bonzes, Buddhist monks, 2, 5, 19,
26, 36, 54, 56, 57, 58, 80, 90, 111,
130, 140, 143, 149, 248, 273f.,
275, 280; conduct of, 66f., 69f.;
dress of, 38, 66, 70; education of,
155, 255, 262; influence of, 142,
147f., 151, 261, 269, 284, 286;
as medical practitioners, 238f.;
organization and role of, 62, 64-
70; political activity of, 72f., 95,
101, 114, 115, 117; sects of, 68,
70ff., 89, 124; status of, 66f., 83,
88, 272; as teachers, 253, 257.
See also Gurus; Mohanikay sect;
Schools, pagoda; Thommayut sect
Books, 140, 146, 149, 266
Border disputes, with Thailand, 4,
14, 22, 103, 114, 153, 156, 201,
233; with Vietnam, 3, 4, 22, 114f.,
157f., 201, 226
Boroughs, in Pnompenh, 139
Boundaries. *See* Border disputes;
Geography
Boy Scouts, 243
Brahma, 74
Brahmanism, 2, 9, 10, 11, 73f., 75,
260, 271, 287
Brahmaputra River, 24
Bricks, manufacture of, 169, 215
Bridges, construction of, 28, 225f.
Brigade de Circulation Routière.
See Road Traffic Brigade
British Commonwealth, 154. *See also*
Great Britain
Brokers, rice, 206
Bronze Age, 7
Buddha, 55, 61f., 64, 65, 66, 67,
72, 74, 76, 260, 268, 279
Buddhism 2, 5, 11, 22, 33, 39, 59-
73, 75, 80, 93f., 95, 144, 147,
152, 159, 166, 239, 249, 261,
284, 287; calendar, 279ff.; doc-
trines, 60ff., 75, 76, 251; ethical
and moral code, 56, 61, 62f., 78,
87, 249, 250, 277; influence of,

54, 58, 64, 195; organization in
Cambodia, 68-73, 119f., 121; recent changes in, 5, 71ff.; relations with Brahmanism, 73f.; role
of clergy, 64-8; role in values
system, 271, 272, 277f.; scriptures,
36, 60ff., 70, 71, 73f., 261, 280.
See also Bonzes; Buddha; Church
and state; Clergy; Merit; Nirvana;
Reincarnation
Buddhist Congress of Rangoon,
1954-56, 166
Buddhist hierarchy. *See* Hierarchy
Buddhist Institute, 57, 71f., 128, 255
Budget, state, 4, 170, 171, 185ff.; of
1958, 242, 296 (table); expenditures, 171, 185, 186f., 191, 195,
242, 252, 258; revenues, 3, 185,
187, 214, 231, 233, 250. *See also*
Taxation; Taxes; Two Year Plan
Buffalo, breeding of, 201
Bureau of Foreign Trade, 232
Bureau of Psychological Warfare,
146
Bureau of Study and Investigation
for the Defense of the Interests
of the People, 134f.
Burma, 2, 24, 28, 30, 59, 143, 147,
155, 159, 164
Burmese, in Cambodia, 48, 49
Bus transport, 27f., 240
Business houses, Chinese, 187, 220,
226, 228. *See also* Export-import
firms

Cabinet, government. *See* Council
of Ministers
Cadre Committees, of the Vietminh,
106f.
Cafés, 142
CAI. Compagnies Autonomes d'In-
fanterie. *See* Independent Infan-
try Companies
cai, labor recruiter, 175
Caisse Nationale d'Equipment. *See*
National Development Bank
Calendar, Cambodian, 260, 279-82,
302f. (table)
Calendar, Chinese, 279, 302f. (table)